THE INDIAN IN AMERICA

the text of this book is printed
on 100% recycled paper

The

New American Nation Series

EDITED BY

HENRY STEELE COMMAGER

AND

RICHARD B. MORRIS

THE INDIAN IN AMERICA

By WILCOMB E. WASHBURN

ILLUSTRATED

HARPER COLOPHON BOOKS
Harper & Row, Publishers
New York, Evanston, San Francisco, London

First HARPER COLOPHON edition published 1975

STANDARD BOOK NUMBER: 06-090436-4

75 76 77 78 10 9 8 7 6 5 4 3 2 1

Contents

Illustrations

*These illustrations, grouped in a separate section,
will be found following page 106.*

1. "The Murder of Jane McCrea"
2. Silver Passport issued by authorities of the Colony of Virginia
3. Indians of the New World eating human flesh and pouring gold down a Spaniard's throat
4. Title page and frontispiece of typical Indian captivity narrative
5. "Escape of Israel Putnam from the Indians"
6. Silver Belt Medal bearing the Royal Mint mark, engraved with the arms of Great Britain
7. Silver gorget engraved with the royal arms of George III
8. Athapascan or Eskimo Mask
9. Double-barred silver cross from the Six Nations Reserve
10. Powder Horn commemorating the Indian Congress at Fort Picolata
11. Mammoth Tusk from northwest Alaska
12. Sioux catlinite pipe and stem
13. The Washington Covenant Belt
14. Brass tomahawk and peace pipe presented to Tecumseh
15. Iroquois "false face" wooden mask
16. Pottery, probably Zuñi

Maps

Editors' Introduction

THE tragic story of the Indian in America, from pre-Columbian times to our own day, is the grand theme of Dr. Washburn's book. From the initial landings of the Spanish discoverers in the Caribbean area to the surrender of Geronimo in 1886 and the final pacification of the Sioux in South Dakota five years later the Indian retreated under the relentless pressure of white European settlers and the expanding American frontier. Long before the end had come he had lost his mastery of the Western world.

Facile generalizations about the North American Indians will not be found in this volume. The Indians had no common language, operated on diverse and distinct cultural levels, and their families, tribes, and governments were structured very differently from each other. Some were nomads; others lived in settled farming communities. Some were traditionally warlike; others, peaceful. With notable exceptions they failed to unite or confederate even under threat of common danger. It is that failure, along with their initial backwardness in weapons, that the white man quickly exploited to his own ends.

In sum, to relate the experience of the first Americans and to describe their complicated relationships both to each other and to the encroaching European settlers one needs draw upon the disciplines not only of history but of archeology, anthropology, ethnography, demography, sociology, and social psychology. Legal concepts such as "property" must be comprehended through Indian eyes, and the conflicting life goals of white and Indian brought into focus.

What Dr. Washburn has given us in this book is interdisciplinary history in its truest sense. He has chosen to relate the Indian experience on three distinct chronological and psychological levels. In the first period he sees the Indian on a plane of relative equality with the white man. Then the European settlers were obliged to acquire Indian lands by purchase and to negotiate with them by treaties and other instruments. During this period the white man borrowed heavily from Indian culture, notably in the area of agriculture, while the Indian came to depend upon European trade goods. In the second period that equality between the races was successfully challenged by the white man. As a result, the Indians were uprooted—when not exterminated—and settled on reservations. One of the shabbiest stories in American history, coming to a climax in the years from the 1870s to the 1920s, this era marked perhaps the nadir of Indian well-being, shot through as it was by white man's callousness, corruption, greed, and indifference. Lastly, Dr. Washburn finds in the contemporary scene a new relationship emerging between the Indian and the rest of America.

Americans today have a greater awareness of past injustices perpetrated upon racial and ethnic minorities than in earlier times. The way Indians, along with blacks, Oriental Americans, and Mexican Americans, among others, have been treated, as President John F. Kennedy once observed, "still affects the national conscience." That national conscience toward the Indians was manifest in a long series of federal reforms, and through this thicket Dr. Washburn walks sure-footed. He exposes the reservation period as one of tragic neglect and broken promises, examines the movement toward individual allotments, considers the Indian reforms of the New Deal and their reversal in the 1950s, and then makes comprehensible the complex legal and political currents that characterize the present Indian scene.

Dr. Washburn has found that neither carrot nor stick, neither force nor persuasion succeeded in converting the Indian into a white man. The reservation policy failed, as he sees it, because it sought to create a hybrid personality—a red white man and a Christian heathen. These various and often futile reform efforts and the Indian reaction thereto are incisively described, and the plight of the Indian treated with sympathy and compassion.

Despite this long record of past injustices, mistakes, and mutual misunderstandings Dr. Washburn ends on a hopeful note. He sees the federal government's attitude toward the Indian in recent decades as being characterized by a growing sensitivity to Indian cultural needs, and he finds Indians achieving in the 1970s a position of rapidly improving economic well-being, enhanced by access to educational opportunities and buttressed by legal protections accorded inherited tribal and individual rights. In short, he foresees a period of healthy coexistence between Indian and white, one which will make amends in some part for earlier efforts at total destruction or total assimilation of the Indian presence.

The Indian in America is a volume in the New American Nation series, a comprehensive and cooperative survey of the history of the area now embraced in the United States from the days of discovery to our own time. Each volume of the series is part of a carefully designed whole, fitted as well as possible to other volumes in the series; each is designed to be complete in itself. For the most part the series follows a chronological organization, but separate volumes, or groups of volumes, are devoted to special subjects as is this volume, and to such others as constitutional history, foreign affairs, and westward expansion. Other aspects of the interaction of Indian and white man will be considered in a forthcoming volume on Discovery and Exploration, and in the four volumes relating to the history of the West, of which the first two have already appeared in this series.

HENRY STEELE COMMAGER
RICHARD BRANDON MORRIS

Preface

THE present volume seeks to give a general impression of the character and experiences of the many Indian tribes and nations of the New World before, during, and after the shattering impact of their involvement with European settlers and their descendants. No attempt will be made to catalogue the separate characteristics or history of each Indian tribe. Instead, the elements of belief and behavior that most consistently characterized Indian groups will be isolated and emphasized. This study is not written in the "ethnographic present," assuming the continued existence of long-altered behavioral characteristics. Nor does it subscribe to what Murray Wax has called "the myth of the traditional Indian culture."[1] It has been estimated that between 1,000 and 2,000 languages existed in the Americas at the time of European contact, each mutually unintelligible with every other.[2] There was and is no single Indian culture. The languages, customs, personalities, and beliefs of Indians varied (and vary) widely, and have been subject to numerous modifications over time. Anthropologists are also discovering an increasingly wide range of individual behavior within the context of supposedly monolithic tribal cultures.[3]

Nevertheless, it is possible to isolate unifying and consistent

1. Murray L. Wax, *Indian Americans: Unity and Diversity* (Englewood Cliffs, N.J., 1971), Introduction, p. xiii.
2. Harold E. Driver, *Indians of North America*, 2d ed. rev. (Chicago, 1969), p. 25.
3. Marvin Harris, *The Rise of Anthropological Theory* (New York, 1968), pp. 403–419.

patterns of behavior among Indian individuals as well as among
Indian tribes and this study will attempt to describe these patterns.
The study is also concerned with describing the cultural changes
wrought in Indian life by outside pressures. Such changes were
sometimes brought about by other Indians, but the most radical
changes were induced by the immigrant white man and his prog-
eny. So pervasive were the presence and impact of the white man on
Indian life that it would falsify the record to try to deal with the
Indian as though the white man did not exist. Each influenced the
other.

In order to make sense of the rapid and varied historical changes
occurring in so many different and interacting cultures, I have
generally distinguished between Indian behavior when the Indian
existed on a plane of military equality with the white man and
Indian behavior after he was reduced to a position of dependence
and inequality. The early chapters deal with the Indian when he
lived and acted on a plane of equality with the white man. The
middle sections concern the Indian when his equality was being
challenged and destroyed by the white man. The final sections of
the book consider the Indian as he has since existed on a plane of
inequality, his destiny shaped largely by whites.

The term "the Indian" will be used in this book to reflect the
unities and similarities I see in many Indian cultures, although the
term should be understood to be simply a tool to facilitate exposi-
tion, not an anthropological or historical description of all Indians.
I will use the term "the white man" to reflect the unities and
similarities I see in the philosophies and actions of the representatives of the various European cultures, and their American off-
shoots, who dealt with "the Indian." It is certainly true that
Europeans shared more common characteristics than American
Indians. While Europeans fought over religion they were Christians
worshiping a common God. While they spoke different languages,
their educated men used Latin. The Indians, on the other hand,
"shared neither a universal language nor a known historical experience." They were "far more culturally diverse" than their discoverers.[4] Yet unifying patterns among the different Indian cultures
are evident, particularly as they changed under the impact of
European power and culture.

4. Hazel W. Hertzberg, *The Search for an American Indian Identity: Modern
Pan-Indian Movements* (Syracuse, N.Y., 1971), p. 1.

I have consciously avoided the term "primitive" in this book not because the term offends an increasingly sensitive minority, but because it confuses and distorts reality. Anthropologically, the term refers to individuals belonging to societies less complex in organization and structure than other more complex and elaborate societies, such as modern industrialized states. Anthropologists do not imply by the term "primitive" any concept of inferiority. Rather they mean the simple as opposed to the complex, the nonliterate as opposed to the literate. Sparse population, also, is usually characteristic of simple societies and dense population of complex societies. Some Indian societies, particularly in Mesoamerica (central and southern Mexico and Central America), were populous in number and complex in social organization, but most Indian societies in North America were sparse in number and simple in political structure.

The term "primitive," even if used nonpejoratively, as meaning merely nonliterate, relatively untouched by "civilization," or characterized by simple technological and subsistence practices, seems ineluctably to drag after it a conception of inferiority even if not racially defined. The term also fails to encompass the nonmaterial, nontechnological, nonpredictable characteristics of Indian life which are different from but not inferior to similar aspects in more sophisticated societies. Even in regard to such civilized problems as population control, so-called primitive peoples often provide examples to emulate. "Primitive" man, for example, seems to have curbed his intrinsic fertility to a greater extent than "civilized" man. Moreover, the possible favorable eugenic results of such "primitive" practices as polygamy, to say nothing of the egalitarian treatment of those children who are brought into the world in such societies, have attracted favorable "civilized" attention.[5]

The mental convolutions required in dealing with "primitive art" illustrate the difficulty inherent in both the theoretical and popular understanding of the term. In the 1950s many ethnological specimens, which documented everyday life in "primitive" societies, were extracted from their cases and displayed separately as "works of art." The movement was hastened by the trend in Western art to abstract and symbolic design, based in some degree on a sudden awareness and understanding of the art of Africa, the Pacific

5. James V. Neel, "Lessons from a 'Primitive' People," *Science,* CLXX (1970), 815–822.

islands, and pre-Colombian America. Normally such exhibits were labeled "primitive art" though the term was increasingly challenged either on the grounds that the art was not "primitive" but of the highest aesthetic and technical order, or that the objects were not made as works of art but for use and that they should not be wrenched from their context and made to carry a burden of meaning nonexistent in the societies from which they came. Present-day practice is to avoid--as much as possible—both the term "primitive" ("tribal" is sometimes substituted) and the term "art" and to let the objects speak for themselves. Behavior as well as material artifacts can be dealt with in the same way. Instead of talking about "savage" behavior or "primitive" artifacts, one can speak more precisely of Mohawk ritual cannibalism or Seneca false face masks.

The category "primitive," therefore, even though continuing in use (though with diminished frequency) by anthropologists, is rarely used hereafter in this book because the term seems to me to have lost the capacity words are meant to possess: to clarify, explain, and instruct—and serves rather to confuse, to mislead, and to distort.

Although the Indian's loss of independence and even equality at the hands of the white man might suggest a simple and unrelieved tragedy, no different from the history of many ethnic groups that have disappeared from the face of the earth, in fact the history of the American Indian has a brighter side to it. The Indian has fructified and regenerated the character of the larger society of which he constitutes a part, and in the process has established a degree of autonomy and pride missing among representatives of other groups who were forced to share their heritage with alien intruders. In strength the Indian inspired violence; in weakness charity. In both cases the American will and conscience were shaped by a living context within which an immigrant white society sought to establish itself. While the white man's will was harsh and his conscience weak, he nevertheless ultimately saw the Indian as a joint participant in the unified nation that emerged from the chaos of settlement and war. Sympathy and admiration eventually overcame hatred and contempt in the minds of white Americans and have guaranteed a permanence to the existence of different, but no longer alien, Indian cultures in the new American nation.

I owe a particular debt of gratitude to Dr. William C. Sturtevant, Curator of North American Anthropology at the Smithsonian Institution, who has been my mentor in matters ethnological since I came to the Smithsonian in 1958. On the subject of the law and the American Indian, I am in the debt of John T. Vance, Commissioner of the Indian Claims Commission, who has helped keep me abreast of the powerful role of law in Indian life. In matters of organization and style I am indebted, more than I can adequately express, to Richard B. Morris, who originally invited me to do this volume and who guided, shaped, criticized, and encouraged me in overcoming the many obstacles (too often of my own making) that stood in the way of its completion. Finally, I owe much to the many scholars, both Indian and white, in the growing field of Indian history, and to the institutions, such as the Newberry Library of Chicago (with its Center for the History of the American Indian) and the Smithsonian Institution (with its National Anthropological Archives and massive ethnographic collections), which have supported the growth of this interest. I must take responsibility for the weaknesses and errors that remain after all this generous help has been extended by these individuals and institutions.

W.E.W.

THE INDIAN IN AMERICA

CHAPTER 1

Origins of the American Indian

THE question of *where* the American Indian came from has fascinated Europeans since Columbus's time. The literature of speculation concerning Indian origins is enormous and has been dealt with in skillful fashion by a number of scholars.[1] Perhaps the most popular theory was the belief that the Indians were the descendants of the lost tribes of Israel.[2] That the Indians, including the Aleuts and Eskimos, came originally from Asia is now almost universally accepted. Even those who qualify their acceptance merely postulate the probability of additional transoceanic contact across the Pacific or Atlantic.

The question of *when* early men came to America is a more difficult question. The key to human movement into the New World was the glacial ice of the late Pleistocene period, beginning about 70,000 years ago, which lowered the sea level some 100 to 150 meters, creating a land bridge between Asia and America of considerable width. Animals, vegetation, and finally man moved across the bridge.[3]

1. The best study is Lee Eldridge Huddleston, *Origins of the American Indians: European Concepts, 1492–1729* (Austin, Texas, 1967). See also Robert Wauchope, *Lost Tribes and Sunken Continents: Myth and Method in the Study of American Indians* (Chicago, 1962).

2. James Adair devoted a great portion of his *History of the American Indians; Particularly Those Nations adjoining to the Mississippi, East and West Florida, Georgia, South and North Carolina, and Virginia* (London, 1775) to this subject. See Wilcomb E. Washburn, introduction to Adair's *History* in *The Colonial Legacy*, ed. Lawrence H. Leder, Vol. III (New York, 1973), 91–120.

3. James B. Griffin, "Eastern North American Archaeology: A Summary," *Science*, CLXVI (1967), 175–191, especially 175–176.

However, while serving to facilitate access from Asia by creation of a land bridge, the glaciation served also to block access into the continent at certain times. Movement south is generally assumed to have taken place east of the Rocky Mountains along a periodically ice-free corridor. The rugged fiordlike, beach-free indentations of the coastline of the northwest coast of North America would have impeded pedestrian travel along the coast, and evidence for navigation by boat along the northern rim of the Pacific is slim.[4]

There is a distinct possibility that, for at least a brief period—perhaps a hundred years—the open corridor east of the Rockies and the land bridge across the present Bering Strait to Asia may have coexisted. Whether or not these two major inducements to movement from Asia to America did so coexist, the possibility of movement by small boat across the narrow Bering Strait and consequent movement down the corridor, even when partially interrupted by the advancing glaciers, cannot be overlooked.[5]

The question remains as to *when* early man arrived in the New World. Scholars have suggested increasingly earlier dates. Dr. Louis S. B. Leakey suggested, on the basis of recent excavations of what he regarded as stone tools in California, the existence of early man in the New World even before the last ice age. Leakey's hypothesis has been vigorously challenged by those who assert that a selection of likely looking chipped stones cannot prove their human origin. Natural rather than human action may have caused the chipping upon which Leakey's conclusions rested.[6]

A less extreme estimate of the origin of early man in America is that of Alan L. Bryan, who believes that "man must have entered Alaska prior to 35,000 years ago in order to explain his presence south of the coalescent ice sheets 11,500 years ago." Bryan believes that American archaeologists have had difficulty finding conclusive evidence for the presence of man in America before 12,000 B.C. because they have considered as diagnostic artifacts only certain types of relatively sophisticated flaked stone projectile points. By

4. Alan L. Bryan, "Early Man in America and the Late Pleistocene Chronology of Western Canada and Alaska," *Current Anthropology*, X (1969), 339–348, at 339.

5. Comment of Wolfgang Haberland on Bryan article, *ibid.*, 352.

6. Report of L. S. B. Leakey, R. D. Simpson, and T. Clements, *Science*, CLX (1968), 1022–1023; Vance Haynes, "The Calico Site: Artifacts or Geofacts?" *Science*, CLXXXI (1973), 305–310.

considering other types of artifacts as diagnostic, such as large bifaces, blades, simple burins, pebble choppers, and other simple tools adapted from nature, the archaeologist can posit man in America prior to the period—roughly 25,000 years ago—when the corridor was closed by the ice sheet.[7] As in the case of Leakey's critics, opponents of the Bryan thesis deny that the simple stone artifacts (and animal bone fragments) interpreted as human tools can be so unequivocably designated. Those who have interpreted the modification of such stones and bones as the result of human action have asserted the need to push back the date of human occupation of North America. Others resist the tendency to see man in America at the time these "tools"—if they are such—were made. Much of the evidence for the antiquity of early man, as determined by the carbon 14 process and by amino acid racemization (which deal with organic materials), is questioned by scholars either because of doubts about the validity of the method or of the particular sample. Nevertheless, the number of sites claimed to be 13,000 years or older grows yearly despite continuing skepticism by some archeologists of the evidence for such sites because of possible distortion by "interpreter and experimenter effects."[8] Despite the uncertainties surrounding the dating of early man in America, one of the most respected scholars in the field, Gordon R. Willey, thinks it "likely" that man first crossed into America "as far back as 40,000 to 20,000 B.C."[9]

The clustering of undisputed sites of New World hunters in the period 11,500 to 10,500 B.C. has suggested to anthropologist Paul S. Martin that the appearance of Old World hunters in the New World was sudden and catastrophic for the megafauna of the hemisphere. Sweeping down from the north, destroying the unsuspecting fauna in a way that forestalled its survival, the discoverers of the New World hypothesized by Martin to derive from this

7. Bryan, *op. cit.*, p. 343; Robert F. Heizer, "The Western Coast of North America," in *The California Indians: A Source Book*, comp. and ed. R. F. Heizer and M. A. Whipple, 2d ed. (Berkeley, 1971), p. 132.

8. Paul S. Martin, "The Discovery of America," *Science*, CLXXIX (1973), 969–974, at 972. Jeffrey L. Bada, Roy A. Schroeder and George F. Carter, "New Evidence for the Antiquity of Man in North America Deduced from Aspartic Acid Racemization," *Science*, CLXXXIV (1974), 791–793.

9. Gordon R. Willey, *An Introduction to American Archaeology*, Vol. I: *North and Middle America* (Englewood Cliffs, N.J., 1966), p. 37.

period "triggered a human population explosion" that allowed their descendants to sweep from Alaska to the tip of South America in 1,000 years. With the destruction of the enormous food supply afforded by the vulnerable megafauna, the population explosion ceased and population declined. Martin's explanation is an imaginative hypothesis which remains to be tested, as do the many other guesses concerning the antiquity of man in America.[10] One critic, for example, has suggested that the megafauna of North America may just as readily have been carried off by new diseases sweeping across the northern land bridge to which American fauna were not resistant.[11]

The evidence of physical anthropology demonstrates that the earliest known immigrants to America were almost exclusively long-headed (dolichocephalic) types. A later set of migrants, represented by the Athapascan and Eskimo peoples, represented a more distinctly Mongoloid type than their predecessors. None of the early waves of emigrants derives directly from the stocks that produced the modern populations of Mongolia, China, and Japan. Rather, the American Indians stem from the ancestors of the marginal Mongoloid populations of southeast and west central Asia.

The possible migration of representatives of later and more sophisticated cultures, either from Asia, Europe, or Africa, bringing, in the several millennia before the birth of Christ, pottery, metallurgy, or cultivated plants, is a hotly debated subject upon which it is still impossible to speak with assurance. Scholars continue to place emphasis on the distinctness of cultural evolution in the Americas but seem increasingly willing to accept more direct and more significant importations of culture from outside the area.[12]

Because the principal route from Asia into North America was probably east of the great barrier of the Rocky Mountains, the spread of culture was more uniform east of the mountains than it was west. California, more than any other area, was difficult of access by aboriginal peoples and the explanation of its cultural development has sometimes been characterized as the "fish-trap theory" in order to account for the wide variety of linguistic, cultural, and somatic types who successively made their way into the

10. Martin, *op. cit.*
11. Letter of James W. Corbett, *Science*, CLXXX (1973) , 905.
12. Willey, *op. cit.*, pp. 20–24.

area without any significant outmigration. As has been pointed out, although movement along the northwest coast of North America is possible, the evidence—physiographic, archaeological, and cultural —suggests that coastal movements of migrating peoples were minimal. Thus movement into California required travel over formidable mountains or across fearsome deserts. Once located in the pleasant California valleys, the group that wished to reverse the course faced an equivalent difficulty.[13]

Whence came the Eskimos and Aleuts, legally classified as Indians yet biologically different in numerous respects? Archaeological investigation in the critical area of the Aleutian Peninsula where the warm Pacific waters are separated from the cold Alaskan coast suggests that the common ancestors of Eskimos and Aleuts must be found at a time earlier than 4000 B.C. that will allow for the gradual development of their characteristic subsistence patterns: the Eskimo exploiting the fish and mammals of the coastlines that freeze as well as the land animals in the adjacent tundra-covered territory, and the Aleuts exploiting the open waters of the Aleutian chain. The chance of the ancestors of Eskimos and Aleuts being found in Alaska seems less and less likely. That origin seems more remote in time and seems probably Asiatic in source, perhaps at the time when Alaska and Asia were one land mass.[14]

While the present volume does not seek to tell in detail the story of the prehistory of the present area of the United States, a brief survey of the prehistoric development of the southwestern and Mississippi Valley areas may help to demonstrate the patterns of change and continuity which marked the history of the original occupants of North America prior to the arrival of the white man. While evidence of prehistoric life is widespread throughout the continent, the Southwest provides particularly clear evidence of the stages of growth that mark early man's occupancy of the continent.

The Southwest is composed of desert, mountain, plateau, and plains segments and it was in the high mountain regions that the earliest developed cultures of the area are found. The earliest

13. Heizer, *op. cit.*, pp. 131–132.
14. D. E. Dumond, "Prehistoric Cultural Contacts in Southwestern Alaska," *Science,* CLXVI (1969) , 1108–1115. See also W. N. Irving and C. R. Harington, "Upper Pleistocene Radiocarbon-Dated Artifacts from the Northern Yukon," *Science,* CLXXIX (1973) , 335–340.

inhabitants, who occupied the eastern plains portion of the area by about 10,000 B.C., were primarily big game hunters. Many of the animals they pursued, such as mammoths, are now extinct, victims of their finely shaped spears and arrows.

The early hunters were followed by hunter-gatherers who moved into the basin and desert areas farther west. The evidence of the artifacts left by these early peoples indicates that grinding stones, choppers, and scrapers were more important than spear or arrow points. By 5000 B.C. the Desert culture, best exemplified by the Cochise culture, showed a gradual shift from subsistence activities based primarily on hunting to an intermediate form based on combined hunting and gathering.

The great breakthrough occurred with the introduction of agriculture which, deriving from areas to the south, begins to be represented by the evidence of corn in some of the caves of the Southwest about 2000 B.C. It is important to keep in mind that the transition from hunting to gathering to agriculture was neither swift and sudden nor precise and exclusive. All three modes of subsistence continued and continue simultaneously to the present, varying only in the emphasis placed on one or another in different parts of the continent. If any lineal evolution can be determined, it is a slow trend from a primary reliance on hunting to a primary reliance on agriculture, with gathering playing an important supplementary (in exceptional cases a primary) role.

The by-products of an agricultural, sedentary economy were as significant in the New World as in the Old, and in the final millennium B.C. one begins to find evidence of pottery vessels and house construction: artifacts missing in the caves and campsites of earlier hunter-gatherers. Storage pits to preserve the harvest became more common, while the evidence of burials suggests both greater stability and care in this as probably in other developing cultural patterns of the society.

With the development of these more elaborate cultural traits, the desert culture is often given the name of Mogollon culture. The undecorated, brown or reddish pottery of these people, probably introduced from Mexico, spread in much of the southwestern area, as did other aspects of Mogollon culture in the first centuries A.D. In the final centuries of the first millennium A.D. Mogollon culture was increasingly interacting with other southwestern cultures, such as

Hohokam and Anasazi. Hohokam culture, which developed side by side with Mogollon, began to rely almost exclusively in its desert home on irrigation agriculture. Hohokam culture produced a more highly developed pottery, clay figurines, even cast copper bells, and large ball courts. Cremation was favored over burial.[15]

In the plateau areas to the north, meanwhile, the Anasazi people (after a Navajo word meaning "the people who have vanished") felt the impact of Mogollon innovations about A.D. 600 in the form of pottery making and more permanent houses. The Anasazi culture, evolving from the Basket Maker culture, was less sophisticated than the cultures to the south, relying more on gathering and hunting. The Anasazi initially lacked the pottery of their southern neighbors but produced excellent baskets. They lived in caves or impermanent structures. Under the impact of Mogollon culture the Basket Maker culture, by about A.D. 800, had evolved into what is known as Pueblo culture. This evolution has most recently been documented by careful archaeological work carried out on Black Mesa on the Navajo and Hopi reservations of northern Arizona by a team of archaeologists under the direction of Robert C. Euler.[16]

As Pueblo culture flourished, pottery styles showed more elaborate decorations. Construction, including the building of large ceremonial chambers known as kivas, became more elaborate. By A.D. 1000 Pueblo villages were numerous and agriculture the principal means of subsistence, replacing hunting and gathering. The spreading Pueblo culture—which extended from the Rio Grande valley in New Mexico on the east to the Gila and Salt rivers in Arizona on the west and south—reached its greatest extent about A.D. 1200 and by 1400 was beginning to break up—for reasons that are not entirely clear—into the patterns with which the later white man became familiar: the Hopi country, the Rio Grande pueblos, the Zuñi-Acoma area, and the Little Colorado sites. Under the pressure of the warlike Navajo and Apache peoples after 1600, and of the Spanish and Americans, Hopi centers dwindled to their present extent.[17]

15. Willey, *op. cit.*, pp. 178–245: For a popular account of the history of archaeology in North America see C. W. Ceram, *The First American: A Story of North American Archaeology* (New York, 1971).

16. Robert Euler, "Exploring the Past on Black Mesa," *The American West*, X, No. 5 (Sept., 1973), 12–17, at 13.

17. *Ibid.*

Evidence of other important prehistoric cultures is scattered throughout the eastern United States, in particular in the Ohio and Mississippi valleys. The distinguishing feature of these cultures is earthen mounds, some of great size and complexity. In the northern areas the mounds most often formed burial chambers. Some formed huge effigies of animals: serpents, birds, bears, and the like. In the southern regions, centering on the Mississippi River basin, the mounds served as platforms for temples or residences of exalted persons. Thousands of such mounds exist (100,000 is the estimated number in the United States) and their discovery spurred efforts at excavation and analysis by some, and looting or destruction by others, in the nineteenth century.[18]

The first publication of the Smithsonian Institution's *Contributions to Knowledge* series, initiated by Secretary Joseph Henry in 1848, was a study of *Ancient Monuments of the Mississippi Valley: Comprising the Results of Extensive Original Surveys and Explorations.* The authors were Ephráim George Squier and E. H. Davis, a newspaper editor and physician, respectively, of Chillicothe, Ohio, in the heart of the mound country. Objects of great beauty were unearthed from the mounds of the Ohio Valley but theories about the origins of the peoples who inhabited the surrounding areas leave the matter uncertain and controversial. Spanning the period of roughly 1000 B.C. to A.D. 1700, the Mound Builders are generally placed in the context of the Woodland tradition which emerged about 1000 B.C. from the Archaic tradition preceding it. Characteristic of the Woodland tradition were pottery, ceramic figurines, the mounds, and plant cultivation. The two high points in the cultural development of the region were the material remains left by the Adena people of the Ohio Valley and those left by the Hopewell people who followed the Adena in the southern Ohio region, achieving their highest expression in the centuries 100 B.C. to A.D. 200. The details of these cultures are varied and complex and suggest either Asiatic or Mesoamerican origins. The evidence of burial mounds, while common to Asia and America, can more easily be derived from Mesoamerican sources, given the large geographic gap between known Asiatic mounds and those of the Eastern Woodlands.[19]

18. Ceram, *op. cit.,* p. 193.
19. Willey, *op. cit.,* pp. 246–341, especially 248–249, 273.

Agricultural innovations, principally the introduction of maize, beans, and squash, must be attributed to Mesoamerican influences. Hypotheses concerning the origins of Woodland pottery postulate either Siberian Mesolithic and Neolithic influences or Mesoamerican influences. Gordon Willey, in contrast to some authorities, believes that agriculture was more than a casual adjunct of Woodland economy and explains the existence of the economic surpluses necessary to support the development of the elaborate burial mounds with their ceremonial and mortuary functions.[20]

Perhaps most exciting of the precontact cultures of the eastern United States was the Temple Mound culture of the lower Mississippi Valley which flourished from A.D. 700 to 1700. Early French descriptions of the Natchez and other lower Mississippi tribes described peoples still living in this Mesoamerican-influenced (if not -derived) culture. The peoples associated with the temple mounds possessed large permanent towns, built around large rectangular plazas, practiced intensive maize agriculture, and were strictly distinguished by social class and function. Ceramic innovations (new vessel forms, new techniques of decoration, and the like) also marked their life. The influence of the Mississippian tradition (as the culture of the temple mound builders is known in contrast to the Woodland tradition) spread north into the Mississippi and Ohio valleys and east into Georgia and Alabama. It carried Mesoamerican influences with it to the Eastern Woodlands by diffusion, intermittent contact, and occasional emigration. Because these Mesoamerican influences were indirect and because the cultures they affected had, for the most part, evolved (or devolved) into the later Woodland cultures met by the first European explorers, Europeans failed to find in the present area of the United States the rich and complex living traditions discovered in Mesoamerica. Nevertheless, the evidence in both the Southwest and the Mississippi Valley demonstrates the important influences of the higher cultures of Mesoamerica in the present area of the United States.[21]

The "New World" was in fact a new world even before the Norsemen and Columbus first cast European eyes upon it. Man, whose age has been tentatively pushed back in the Old World by millions of years, can be identified in the New World only in terms

20. *Ibid.*, pp. 267–268.
21. *Ibid.*, pp. 249, 292–293.

of tens of thousands of years. The periodic advance and retreat of glaciers alternately facilitated and hampered movement into the New World and trapped most of its inhabitants once they had migrated south into the more temperate regions. The isolation of America and the Americans—despite the possibility of occasional transoceanic contacts in the millennia immediately preceding European contact—had important biological and cultural consequences. Those consequences were to become evident with the arrival of European men, European animals, and European diseases. America had been isolated from the knowledge, the diseases, and the competition of the Old World for too long and her earliest inhabitants fell victim to a new wave of immigration, this time from the east.

CHAPTER 2

Indian Personality

W HAT was the Indian like when the first white man set foot in the New World? Neither historian nor anthropologist can give a simple answer to this question. Not only are there hundreds of different cultural "styles" among the many nations of Indians, but the culture of every one was modified by the very process of observing and interacting with it. Nevertheless, there are certain persistent characteristics that distinguish Indian life from European life.

Virtually all Indians lived in close and intimate relationship with nature. To some extent, the European of the period did also, but not to the same degree. The Indian relied directly upon nature for his life, and, perhaps more important, was fully conscious of that dependence. Lacking the technical devices by which Western European man had overcome or manipulated nature—as by writing or by firearms—the Indian's mind was turned constantly toward the natural environment which was the source of life and death and of reward and punishment. The many and varied folk tales of the different tribes reflected this orientation—whether of fear, respect, or love—toward the forces and products of nature. Indeed, so close was the feeling of identity that the Indian in many ways saw himself as a fellow sharer of, or competitor for, the life which the giver of all life provided. The feeling suggested in Emerson's paraphrase of the Indian wisdom of the East—"I am the slayer and the slain"—is applicable to the red Indian. The prayer that the Indian hunter might say over his animal prey—to excuse the necessity of the taking or to justify the human need that required it—was an expression of a psychological oneness between the hunter and his quarry. The virtually universal character of such a ceremonial gesture was eroded rapidly with the introduction of European firearms and European values. The followers of Saint Francis gave a horrendous example of callous unconcern about the souls of the animals God had placed on the earth. Had not God, in the Christian's book, given animals to be useful to, and used by, men? The Christian had it in his book—in the written command of God. The Indian, on the other hand, had it in his oral tradition, learned perhaps in the open air rather than in the house or temple, that the animal had a personality and a soul that went through life as he did: with joys and sorrows, needs and desires.

The Indian view of the relationship between man and nature was well expressed in a belittling and condemnatory passage in the work of an early-nineteenth-century German philosopher, then president of Marshall (later Franklin and Marshall) College, in the German area of Pennsylvania. The Reverend Frederick A. Rauch, in his *Psychology; or a View of the Human Soul; including Anthropology*, 4th edition (New York, 1841), observed that:

The savage is so wholly sunk in the life of nature, that he does not distinguish between its activity and that of mind, but views both as merged into each other. We, accustomed from youth to separate soul and body, mind and nature, find it almost impossible to transfer ourselves into the life of the savage in this respect; and yet this sphere of thinking and feeling in reference to nature, constitutes the most essential portion of the intellectual existence of the savages.[1]

One of the lasting gifts of the Indian to the white man has been this perception of the place of man in nature, a gift more readily understood by a twentieth-century student than by a nineteenth-century university president.

Indian adults sought consciously to avoid antagonizing their associates. The traditional Indian attitude of dignity and aloofness, which stood in marked contrast to the noisy, quarrelsome behavior of the whites with whom the Indians came into contact, seems to

1. P. 68.

have derived from a training that began in the indulgence shown by Indian parents to faults committed by their young ones. The eighteenth-century Moravian missionary John Heckewelder explained its existence among the Delaware Indians in this way: "Parents had rather make good the damage than punish the children, for the reason that they think the children might remember it against them and avenge themselves when they have attained to maturity." The Indian parent did not attempt to establish his authority by harsh or compulsive means, according to Heckewelder, who observed that "no whips, no punishments, no threats are ever used to enforce commands or compel obedience." The consequences of such an upbringing, the anthropologist Anthony Wallace has noted, is that the Indian would not be likely to be governed by the "punishing conscience demanded by European society." Social cooperation would be achieved by a calculating avoidance of attitudes and actions which might antagonize his associates.[2]

The concept of a Jehovahlike God who chastised the wicked had little meaning to a Delaware brought up without the experience of punishment for faults. His God was rather the Great Spirit who upheld the natural order. Individually a Delaware might have a personal guardian, usually an animal spirit, who watched over him and who revealed himself in dreams or visions.[3]

A common experience among Indian children in many tribes was a "vision quest" during which a boy, on attaining puberty, went off by himself into the woods or onto a mountain to commune with the spirits, wait for a vision, ponder his dreams, perhaps mortify himself until, hopefully, he established a relationship with the supernatural or merely "found himself." This maturing experience, based on individual search rather than on community teaching or enforced obedience, helped to reinforce the spirit of freedom and independence so often noted by European observers of the Eastern Woodland Indians, and which was inculcated by the permissive and indulgent attitudes taken by parents in bringing up their children.[4]

2. Anthony F. C. Wallace, *King of the Delawares: Teedyuscung, 1700–1763* (Philadelphia, 1949), pp. 14–15, quoting Heckewelder. See also A. I. Hallowell, "Some Psychological Characteristics of the Northeastern Indians," in *Man in Northeastern North America*, ed. Frederick Johnson (Andover, Mass., 1946).

3. Wallace, *op. cit.*, p. 16.

4. Anthony F. C. Wallace, *The Death and Rebirth of the Seneca* (New York, 1970), p. 38; John Axtell, "The Scholastic Philosophy of the Wilderness," *William and Mary Quarterly*, 3d ser., XXIX (1972), 359.

Children among the Seneca Indians, Wallace has noted, "did not so much live in a child's world as grow up freely in the interstices of an adult culture." Children imitated adult behavior, as in hunting activities. Parents indulgently observed and quietly supported their children's progress. No casual or severe punishments, violent rages, or effusive demonstrations of affection characterized Iroquois behavior, as it often did white. The result of such upbringing, Wallace has pointed out, was "an early self-reliance and enjoyment of responsibility; the cost, perhaps, was a lifelong difficulty in handling feelings of dependency."[5]

A study of Indian personality, education, and administration carried on by a team of university-based anthropologists among Navajos, Sioux, Papagos, and Hopis showed closely related systems of child upbringing among these diverse Western tribes as well as remarkable similarities to childhood training among Eastern Woodland Indians in the historical period. In all the tribes investigated, whether of the traditionally hunting type (Navajos and Sioux) or of the traditionally farming tribes (Hopi, Zuñi, and Papago)

the usual pattern of nurturing and training the infant (except in the most acculturated families) is primarily an affectionate, relaxed, gentle and permissive one, the child being kept close to the mother or other female relative from whom he receives a good deal of attention; being nursed whenever he cries; encouraged but not hurried or forced toward learning to walk and talk; never addressed in "baby talk"; not trained in cleanliness until after he has begun to walk and talk, and not expected to acquire complete control of elimination until the third year; weaned gradually between the eighteenth month until the third year; and treated from birth as an individual who belongs to the group and has a place and role in it.

The Indian child was thus, Laura Thompson noted, allowed and encouraged to develop "according to the natural rhythms of his individual needs—physiological, psychological and social."[6]

The Indian child care practices normally discouraged competitive, egocentric, and defensive attitudes among children and among parents regarding their children, and encouraged cooperative, self-confident, and secure behavior. Corporal punishment was rarely, if

5. Wallace, *Death and Rebirth of the Seneca*, p. 34.
6. Laura Thompson, *Personality and Government: Findings and Recommendations of the Indian Administration Research* (Mexico City, 1951), pp. 172–173.

ever, used traditionally. The child was encouraged and disciplined not by his immediate biological family, but by relatives within the extended-family group, and by reference to supernatural agents. The child was brought into relationship with the larger society of which he was an intimate part: with public opinion and with supernatural powers as well as with the members of his immediate family.

The generalized love of children among Indians is indicated in an incident involving Father Le Jeune, a French Jesuit priest. Le Jeune, censuring an Indian shaman called the Sorcerer for bragging about his exploits with women, told him that it was not honorable for a woman to love anyone else except her husband. Were the women promiscuous, a father would not be sure that his reputed son was indeed his son. To his argument, the Sorcerer replied: "Thou hast no sense. You French people love only your own children; but we all love the children of our tribe." Le Jeune records that he began to laugh, "seeing that he philosophized in horse and mule fashion."[7]

While physical coercion of Indian children was rare, shame and ridicule often served to achieve the same ends. Anthropologists who have studied Zuñi child upbringing have asserted that ridicule was "quite possibly the most important single sanction in the upbringing of the Zuñi child, and more than any other one factor shapes overt behavior in later life." The Zuñi child's "hypersensitivity to shame" continued throughout his life and dissuaded him from behavior that would be laughed at by his fellow Zuñis. The possibility that one might be accused of being a witch also reinforced what Ruth Benedict, in *Patterns of Culture,* termed the Apollonian ideal of the Zuñi. No one wants to anger another, partly because of fear of ridicule or fear of being accused of improper behavior. The calmness of adult Zuñis and many other Indians can be related to fear rather than trust of their fellow tribesmen.[8]

A constantly noticed feature of the uncorrupted Indian was his faithfulness to his pledged word. That word was frequently pledged to white men and was maintained even to the disadvantage of his

7. Quoted in D'Arcy McNickle, *They Came Here First: The Epic of the American Indian* (Philadelphia, 1949), p. 128.

8. Dorothea C. Leighton and John Adair, *People of the Middle Place: A Study of the Zuni Indians* (New Haven, Conn., 1966), pp. 72–74. See also Frederick O. Gearing, *The Face of the Fox* (Chicago, 1970), pp. 47–49.

red brothers. The frequency of incidents illustrating this fact suggests that individual honor ranked above racial affinity in the mind of the Indian. John Heckewelder recalled how frequently whites were forewarned of impending war by Indian friends. Heckewelder knew of no case in which this trust had been betrayed. "The word 'Friend' to the ear of an Indian," Heckewelder noted, "does not convey the same vague and almost indefinite meaning that it does with us; it is not a mere complimentary or social expression, but implies a resolute determination to stand by the person so distinguished on all occasions, and a threat to those who might attempt to molest him; . . ." Heckewelder denied the suggestion that an Indian's friendship had to be purchased by presents and lasted only so long as such gifts continued. What was essential, Heckewelder observed, was that whoever chose to obtain the friendship of an Indian must treat him on a footing of "perfect equality." They did not forgive contempt any more than they forgot true friends.[9]

Instances of the behavior described by Heckewelder can be found among other tribes in other areas in every period of white-Indian interaction.[10]

The "silent Indian" is a frequent figure of comment by non-Indians, often being interpreted in terms of dignity on the one hand, or dullness on the other. The critical factor underlying this behavior is the character of the relationship of the person remaining silent to the persons with whom he is in contact. When that relationship is ambiguous and uncertain, the Apache and Navajo will customarily remain silent. This is so whether the situation is one of meeting strangers, courting, meeting one's children coming home after a long absence, or getting "cussed out." In each case, as Keith Basso has pointed out in his study of the Western Apaches, the person keeping silent is uncertain of his relationship with those with whom he is involved. He may spend days before speaking with a stranger. Lovers may spend months before they feel sufficiently at ease to speak with each other. Parents feel apprehensive that their children returning from school may have lost respect for their

9. Paul A. W. Wallace, ed., *Thirty Thousand Miles with John Heckewelder* (Pittsburgh, 1958) , pp. 124–125.
10. E.g., Arthur H. DeRosier, Jr., *The Removal of the Choctaw Indians* (Knoxville, Tenn. 1970), pp. 34–36; *Annual Report of the Commissioner of Indian Affairs for 1868*, p. 29.

native ways. In each case the reaction of the other party is uncertain or unpredictable and the Apache response to this uncertainty is silence. The close similarities of Navajo behavior to Apache and the historical evidence of similar behavior on the part of other tribes suggest that whether or not one interprets Indian silence as based on instinctive dignity, it can be said to be based on a caution which is at once related to fear of and to respect for the uncertain status of the other party.[11]

The same individual caution and desire to avoid conflict helps to explain the tendency, to be noted in the discussion of Indian consensus politics, of the individual Indian to withdraw from meetings or councils rather than to vote in the minority.[12]

The early explorers often assumed that the Indians lived without religion and without laws. The absence of a written code of laws, the absence of the paraphernalia of European religious and judicial institutions, all helped give some European observers the idea that they were dealing with savages who had no comprehension of law, justice, and the various institutional controls with which Europeans were familiar. Of course this impression was an incorrect one. Just as all Indian groups had a complex religious life, so too did their judicial systems show great variety and great complexity. That these systems were not written down was irrelevant. The Indian by training and custom knew what was expected of him, just as he could remember—better than the European—the conditions of the treaties he signed with the white man.

Central to the concept of Indian law was retributive justice. Indeed, the similarity between Jewish attitudes in this regard and Indian habits was one of the principal arguments used by men like James Adair, the eighteenth-century Indian trader and historian, to identify the Indians with the lost tribes of Israel. Mercy, for both, was a latter-day Christian corruption. Revenge was the form in which Indian justice was most often expressed. It was a noble passion, and an all-consuming one. A wrong *had* to be repaid, and it usually was, though it took years of patient effort to accomplish it. In the absence of complex formal legal machinery of the sort familiar to a European society, revenge or retribution was normally

11. Keith H. Basso, " 'To Give up on Words': Silence in Western Apache Culture," *Southwestern Journal of Anthropology*, XXVI (1970), 213–230.
12. See below, p. 48.

sought by the kin of the aggrieved party. Different crimes, such as adultery, murder, or theft, required different forms of retribution according to the different Indian cultures involved. But though the executioners of the sentence were private and interested parties, they acted in accordance with tribal custom and sanction. To exceed the bounds of that which was accepted as proper would in itself be a violation of the code and would subject the offender to further sanctions.

Adair, to illustrate the Indian concern for retaliation, recounted the case of a little boy who while shooting birds in a cornfield happened to wound another boy by chance. The one offended against bided his time until he was able to return the wound in an equal manner. Then, "all was straight," as the Indians put it. "Their hearts were at rest," Adair noted, "by having executed that strong law of nature, and they sported together as before."[13]

Indian justice was meted out not only for crimes committed against fellow tribesmen, but against whites as well. In a typical instance, reported by Governor James Glen of South Carolina in 1748, the Cherokees required one of their towns to put to death the murderer of an Englishman—"a worthless drunken fellow, a Pack-Horseman"—or risk total destruction of their town and all of its inhabitants. Though the murderer was a "Man of Note, a great Hunter and Warriour," he was executed and his body left to rot on the ground.[14]

Retaliation was carefully weighed and considered before being put into execution. The Seminoles on the Georgia-Florida border in 1817, for example, charged the Americans with having killed ten of their warriors and, in the phrase of General Edmund P. Gaines, the local military commander, "claim a balance of three to be due to them; they admit, by necessary implication, that they have killed seven of our citizens." Gaines noted that the Indians struck at particular individuals they accused of stealing their property or killing their young men.[15]

13. James Adair, *History of the American Indians; Particularly Those Nations adjoining to the Mississippi, East and West Florida, Georgia, South and North Carolina, and Virginia* (London, 1755), facsimile edition (New York, 1968), p. 150.

14. Public Record Office, London, C. O. 5/385, foll. 120v–121r.

15. Letter of Oct. 1, 1817, in *American State Papers . . . Indian Affairs*, 2 vols. (Washington, 1832–1834), II, 158–159.

The failure of the white legal system to meet Indian standards of retributive justice in interracial crimes frequently forced the Indians to seek justice in their own fashion. Nevertheless, the common folk knowledge that a white man would never hang for killing an Indian was not always true. The instances in which whites suffered the death penalty for murdering an Indian, while rare, do exist. Two examples can be cited, one in the Plymouth Colony in 1638, and the other in the state of Indiana in 1825.

In the Plymouth case a Narragansett Indian, who had been trading in Massachusetts Bay, was murdered in the woods by four Englishmen who accosted and befriended him. The motive was robbery, the English appropriating the five fathoms of wampum and three coats of cloth that the Indian was carrying. Although left for dead, the Indian survived long enough to identify his assailants, who were subsequently captured by other Narragansetts. The Narragansetts immediately suspected that the murder presaged an assault on them by the English as the Pequots had predicted when they had unsuccessfully urged the Narragansetts to join with them against the English a few years earlier. Roger Williams of Rhode Island, operating in his usual invaluable role of mediator between the Indians and the English, calmed their fears and promised that justice would be done. The crime having been committed in Plymouth Colony jurisdiction, the murderers were tried, condemned to death, and, with the exception of one who escaped, executed. This despite the fact that "some of the rude and ignorant sort murmured that any English should be put to death for the Indians." Yet, as Governor William Bradford pointed out in his history of the colony, to have ignored the crime might have raised a war. Some of the Narragansett Indians were present at the execution, which gave them "and all the country good satisfaction."[16]

In the Indiana case, on March 22, 1824, on Fall Creek (a tributary of the White River) nine friendly Miami and Seneca Indians were, in cold blood, deceitfully and brutally murdered by a group of white men who had obtained their aid for the ostensible purpose of looking for stray horses. The whites involved, when caught, pleaded the customary rationalization, that it was "no worse to kill an Indian than to kill a wild animal." With the fate of the entire

16. William Bradford, *Of Plymouth Plantation, 1620–1647*, ed. Samuel Eliot Morison (New York, 1952), pp. 300–301.

frontier—vulnerable to hostile Indian attack—in the balance, the authorities moved rapidly to bring the guilty parties to justice. Three hundred dollars' worth of goods were distributed to the families of the victims with the condolences of John Johnson, the Piqua, Ohio, Indian agent whose jurisdiction extended to the area. Governor William Hendricks of Indiana urged quick prosecution in order to satisfy the Indians that the government did not condone the crime. Secretary of War John C. Calhoun and Commissioner of Indian Affairs Thomas L. McKenney vigorously supported the efforts of the local authorities to make examples of "such monsters, to deter others from deeds so horrible." When friends of the defendants engaged competent legal talent in their behalf, a United States Senator, James Noble of Indiana, was induced to argue the case for the prosecution. In a series of trials, marked by a literal waving of the bloody shirts of the murdered Indians, appeals to the Indiana Supreme Court, an escape, and a last-minute reprieve of the son of one of the murderers who had been compelled by his father to join the murdering party, the principals were convicted of murder, sentenced to death by hanging, and hanged.[17]

The Plymouth and Fall Creek cases were exceptions to the rule that interracial justice was impossible to obtain in America. Perhaps the prosecution was successful in each case because the consequences of acquittal—in Indian reprisals against the rest of the white community—were greater than the consequences of conviction. But such a calculating expediency is not the sole explanation. In both communities there was the right combination of concerned officials who recognized the potential force of Indian revenge as well as the persisting requirements of Anglo-Saxon justice.

While the motive of revenge can be considered an expression of individual personality, it was also the formal expression of a sociopolitical system. Retribution, as a system of justice in societies based on kinship, served the same function that courts, police, and jails served in societies based on written law and the power of the state.

The generosity noted by almost all observers of the Indians must be seen in the light of its functional utility as well as in the light of abstract standards of justice. Among people dependent upon hunting for their subsistence, sharing is a functional necessity for

17. George Chalou, "Massacre on Fall Creek," *Prologue: The Journal of the National Archives*, IV (1972), 109–114.

survival. Because of the uncertain success of the hunter, the size of the animals taken in relation to the number of hunters, and the difficulty of preserving meat, patterns of sharing in Indian societies dependent upon hunting were normally liberal and generous. The ethic of sharing was inculcated into the society and few attempted to ignore it, although evidence does exist, as among the Copper Eskimos, that when the women could hide food (as they could do while cooking indoors in the winter but could not while cooking outdoors in the summer) they frequently did so.[18]

To point out the fact of Indian generosity is not to ignore the existence of attitudes of envy and greed. Indian generosity implied the expectation of similar generosity to oneself in time of need. Studies of particular individual Indian communities have usually noted the existence of grudges and animosities arising from a belief that the appropriate degree of generosity within this reciprocal relationship had not been extended. Failure to maintain the proper character of the reciprocal relationship tended to lead to realign. ment of the social units within the community, or resolution of the conflict by part of the community moving against or away from the nonconforming individual.[19]

The psychic income heaped upon the successful hunter normally made up for the deprivation he might otherwise have felt as a result of the obligation to share with the less successful and more dependent members of society. The great hunter was one of the most admired and honored members of the community. While the game he killed was "his" in a real sense—Indian societies did not normally practice economic communism—the rules of his society imposed the requirement of sharing his luck or skill with less fortunate or skillful members of the community.[20]

The term "Indian giver," used as a term of reproach, throws light on the nature of Indian exchange. In a society in which a market economy regulated by monetary counters does not exist, the more informal system of barter of roughly equal portions of goods or services must prevail. In the absence of precisely defined units of economic measurement, a vaguer form of ethical equivalence is

18. John H. Dowling, "Indian Ownership and the Sharing of Game in Hunting Societies," *American Anthropologist*, LXX (1968) , 502–507.

19. Joel S. Savishinsky, "Mobility as an Aspect of Stress in an Arctic Community," *American Anthropologist*, LXXIII (1971) , 604–618, especially 611.

20. Dowling, *op. cit.*, 502–507.

expected. When to the absence of a traditional market economy is added the cultural gap between those unable to communicate with each other effectively in precisely defined verbal units, the need for a silent—but still ethically and economically equivalent—exchange is evident. In early contacts between explorers and coastal Indians, when each party feared treachery by the other, the two parties often left equivalent amounts of goods to be taken by the opposite party after their departure. These early, silent exchanges at more than arm's length are useful models upon which an understanding of "Indian giving" may be based. The "gift" is freely extended, but an equivalent return is anticipated and, if received, evaluated in terms of the original gift. If seen as a psychological equivalent, whatever its monetary worth, the exchange is satisfactory. Satisfaction encompasses not only an economic return (perhaps the least significant) but, more important, a diplomatic and human response.[21]

The Indian's attitude toward goods was similarly incorporated in his attitude toward land, which is discussed in the following chapter.

Exploring the unconscious, particularly among persons long dead, is a risky business, and one steps cautiously in this field, but personality studies of the American Indian are becoming increasingly sophisticated. Perhaps the leading practitioner in the field is Anthony Wallace, whose analysis of the unconscious sources of Iroquois behavior has not been matched by equivalent studies of other Indian groups.

Behind the brave, independent, self-reliant Iroquois male was, in Wallace's interpretation, an unconscious craving to be cared for, to be passive. This craving was expressed by the Iroquois dream-guessing rite by which the dreams of any individual were hinted at before a council which in turn attempted to discover their meaning and to satisfy them. Wallace has noted that outwardly unallowable passive tendencies were concealed in dreams, which remained active in character, but were fulfilled by a passive receiving action. Like a baby, Wallace pointed out, the dreamer's real desires—often of a sexual nature—could only be hinted at until someone guessed what he wanted and the council gave it to him. Iroquois society thus

21. E.g., William Gerard De Brahm, *De Brahm's Report of the General Survey in the Southern District of North America*, ed. Louis De Vorsey, Jr. (Columbia, S.C., 1971) , pp. 108, 227–228.

socialized the process by which the individual faced his deepest needs and fears, and created a wonderfully effective remedy for individual and social disorganization.[22]

In a similar fashion the subconscious urges and fears of the outwardly taciturn and autonomous Iroquois found an outlet in rituals of the Society of Faces, whose members, concealed behind the contorted masks of mythical figures, could act out infantile or otherwise forbidden actions and in the process cure disease—perhaps psychosomatic in nature—and avert witchcraft. Behind the mask, the Iroquois man was allowed to act as he could not act in his everyday role. "With unconscious wisdom," Anthony Wallace has pointed out, the Society of Faces found a way of venting emotions of "rage and fear, lust and hate, boundless ambition and abject passivity, cold cruelty and noble altruism" without causing excessive fright to the patient. Under the cover of the false faces the Iroquois might indulge his longing to be passive, "to be an irresponsible, demanding, rowdy infant, and to compete with the Creator himself; . . ."[23]

The sophistication of Iroquois dream theory, as described by the Jesuit Father Ragueneau in discussing the Hurons in 1649, is evident in the language—which Anthony Wallace has compared to that of Freud himself—used by the priest. After commenting on desires that were expressed on the surface, Ragueneau noted that the Hurons

believe that our souls have desires, which are, as it were, inborn and concealed. These, they say, come from the depths of the soul, not through any knowledge, but by means of a certain blind transporting of the soul to certain objects; these transports might in the language of philosophy be called *Desideria innata,* to distinguish them from the former, which are called *Desideria elicita.*

Now they believe that our soul makes these natural desires known by means of dreams, which are its language. Accordingly, when these desires are accomplished, it is satisfied; but on the contrary, if it be not granted what it desires, it becomes angry, and not only does not give its body the good and the happiness that it wished to procure for it, but often it also revolts against the body, causing various diseases, and even death. . . .[24]

22. Wallace, *Death and Rebirth of the Seneca,* pp. 74–75.
23. *Ibid.,* p. 93.
24. Quoted in *ibid.,* pp. 61–62.

Ragueneau also described how certain medicine men acquired credit by their ability to interpret the hidden desires incorporated in dreams of children and sick persons.

Wallace has concluded that, intuitively, the Iroquois had achieved a great degree of psychological sophistication. They recognized conscious and unconscious parts of the mind. They knew the great force of unconscious desires, were aware that the frustration of these desires could cause mental and physical (psychosomatic) illness. They understood that these desires were expressed in symbolic form, by dreams, but that the individual could not always properly interpret these dreams himself. They had noted the distinction between the manifest and latent content of dreams and employed what sounds like the technique of free association to uncover the latent meaning. And they considered that the best method for the relief of psychic and psychosomatic distresses was to give the repressed desire satisfaction, either directly or symbolically. It would be fair to say that Iroquois and other Indian cultures in the seventeenth and eighteenth centuries possessed a deeper understanding of psychodynamics than most enlightened Europeans of the time.[25]

25. *Ibid.*, p. 63. Cf. Morris E. Opler, "Some Points of Comparison and Contrast between Treatment of Functional Disorders by Apache Shamans and Modern Psychiatric Practice," *American Journal of Psychiatry*, XCII (1936), 1371–1387.

CHAPTER 3

Indian Social Structure

THE Indian, wherever the white man found him, had effectively adapted himself to the environment in which he lived. On the frozen border of the Arctic Sea, the Eskimo survived and persevered by means of such devices as fur-lined "parkas" and snow-block igloos. Skillfully tapping the animal wealth of the sea and the adjoining land, the Eskimo met the demands of the environment.

Farther south, in the subarctic tundra and forest south and west of Hudson's Bay, Indian tribes such as the Chipewyan moved through the snowy terrain on snowshoes and toboggans hunting the caribou, an animal which supplied them with much of their material culture inventory as well as much of their food. Caribou skins were formed into a poncho-type garment the sides of which were sewn together with an awl to provide warmth and protection in summer and winter. Moccasins for the feet completed the outfit. The shelter of the Chipewyan similarly utilized sewn caribou skins which were arranged on a conical framework of poles set in a circle and bound at the top. Indian shelter, like Indian clothing, was frequently of an efficiency astonishing to the whites.[1]

At the other end of the climatic spectrum, the adaptability of the Indian to a hot, desert environment is illustrated by the Havasupais, who continue to occupy a site along the Colorado River that was probably settled about the time the Norsemen landed in

1. Wendell H. Oswalt, *This Land Was Theirs: A Study of the North American Indian* (New York, 1966), p. 23.

Vinland. Indeed, the two movements may well be related to the same climatic changes. The warming trend provided the Vikings with an ice-free access to the northern portions of North America. The same trend created drought conditions on the plateau above the deep canyon of the Colorado River which, along with the possible threat of hostile raiders, encouraged the Havasupais to descend to the river floor a mile below plateau level. Along the floor of the valley—with the aid of irrigation ditches—the Havasupais grew corn, beans, squash, and later a few European crop plants— apricots, figs, peaches, alfalfa—which they obtained from neighboring Indian tribes. The Havasupais—and others who joined them in the period A.D. 600 to A.D. 1100—continued to have access to the plateau, particularly in winter when hunting and food-gathering expeditions would be undertaken there. A Franciscan priest, Francisco Tomás Garcés, was the first white man to descend to the canyon floor and visit the Havasupais, a visit that took place in July, 1776. The physical isolation and cultural integrity of the tribe has continued despite the introduction of modern technology and the increasing contact established by the Havasupais with the Grand Canyon tourists who sometimes visit the Havasupai village.[2]

Although luckier than most Indian tribes in their isolation, the Havasupais, like the Eskimos of the Arctic and the Chipewyans of the subarctic, illustrate the ability of the various Indian groups effectively to adapt to the environment in which they have chosen to live.

The quest for food, whether by farming, by hunting, by fishing, or by gathering, was and is a central concern of all Indian groups, as it was and is of all human groups. For the North American Indian, this quest affected virtually every individual. While the white American of the twentieth century can rely on a small proportion of the population to produce the food which he purchases by exchange of money derived from industrial or other nonagricul-

2. The material on the Havasupais is derived from the research of Douglas W. Schwartz as reported in the following articles: "The Havasupai 600 A.D.–1955 A.D.: A Short Culture, History," *Plateau* (Museum of Northern Arizona, Flagstaff) , XXVIII (1956) , 77–85; "Prehistoric Man in the Grand Canyon," *Scientific American,* CLXXXXVIII (1958) , 97–101; "Nankoweap to Unkar: An Archaeological Survey of the Upper Grand Canyon," *American Antiquity,* XXX (1965) , 278–296; "Archaeological Investigations in the Shinumo Area of Grand Canyon, Arizona," *Plateau,* XXXII (1960), 61–67.

tural occupations, the Indian was and is more closely tied to the earlier pattern of direct engagement in agriculture, herding, fishing, hunting, and gathering. This direct involvement in subsistence activities has many consequences, not the least of which are the Indian's closeness to nature and his awareness of the uncertainty of nature's bounty.

Subsistence activities in the different parts of the North American continent have ranged from the most simple forms of gathering of nuts and roots to the most complex forms of irrigated agriculture. Examples of a few types of subsistence activities, and the social and political implications of those activities, will be discussed. Details of the character of specific tribal or areal subsistence patterns are available in traditional ethnographies.

While farming can be dated to 7000 B.C. in the New World—by independent invention according to some—and while a staggering list of plants have their origin and development in America, hunting, fishing, and gathering remained an important part of the life of the Indians occupying the present area of the United States at the time of the arrival of the white man. The anthropologist Harold E. Driver has estimated that farming was then practiced in less than half of the entire North American continent though horticultural products furnished about 75 percent of all the food consumed by American aborigines. The bulk of that food was produced in Mesoamerica among the dense populations of Mexico and the lands to the south. The principal agricultural areas in what is now the United States were the Southwest, the Prairies, and the East, but in the latter two areas Driver estimates that less than half the food supply was produced by agriculture. On the Plains, in the mountains, plateaus, and on the coasts, hunting, fishing, and gathering provided the principal source of food. In the two areas of most intense farming, Mesoamerica and the Southwest, men performed most of the agricultural tasks. In the areas where farming was less important than hunting and fishing, women tended to perform the agricultural tasks.[3]

In the great wedge-shaped central portion of the interior of North America east of the Continental Divide and extending into southern Texas lay the region of greatest hunting activity. Pedro de

3. Harold E. Driver, *Indians of North America*, 2d ed. rev. (Chicago, 1969), pp. 66, 81, 84.

Castañeda, a private soldier who accompanied Coronado on his expedition of 1539–1541 in the southwestern United States, described the Great Plains into which the expedition ventured as "nothing but cows and sky." In that "big sky" country the Plains Indians, then not mounted on horseback, sustained themselves almost entirely on the bounty of the cows, that is, the buffalos. As Castañeda described it:

With the skins they build their houses; with the skins they clothe and shoe themselves; from the skins they make rope and also obtain wool. With the sinews they make thread, with which they sew clothes and also their tents. From the bones they shape awls. The dung they use for firewood, since there is no other fuel in that land. The bladders they use as jugs and drinking containers. They sustain themselves on their meat, eating it slightly roasted and heated over the dung. Some they eat raw.[4]

Fishing provided a large measure of subsistence to the Indians living in the fish-abundant waters of the northwest coast where the fish runs helped determine the organization and character of native life. During the fish runs of the summer season, the Tlingits, for example, worked actively to catch salmon, cod, halibut, and eulachon for their year-round subsistence. The salmon were cut and dried in smokehouses for winter use. The winter season was reserved for handicrafts, trade, and ceremonial activities. During the winter the Tlingits lived in permanent villages of large wood-plank communal houses, containing from ten to forty related individuals. Summer fishing was conducted from summer camps near the fish runs.[5]

While agriculture in the desert areas was possible in the flood plains of a river or, in some cases, by means of irrigation ditches, the natural environment provided an astonishingly varied diet to Indians who merely gathered nature's bounty wherever it was to be found. An authority on the desert plant foods of the Cahuilla Indians of desert southern California, without being exhaustive, has discovered "not less than sixty distinct products for nutrition, and at least twenty-eight more utilized for narcotics, stimulants, or

4. Quoted in John A. Hawgood, *America's Western Frontiers: The Exploration and Settlement of the Trans-Mississippi West* (New York, 1967), p. 22.
5. Julia Averkieva, "The Tlingit Indians," in *North American Indians in Historical Perspective*, eds. Eleanor Burke Leacock and Nancy Oestreich Lurie (New York, 1971), pp. 318, 328.

medicines, all derived from desert or semidesert localities, in use among these Indians. . . ." Desert plants, which had developed protection against animals by poisons that they secrete, were utilized by Indians who leached away the poisons to obtain nutritious foods. Among the most famous desert plants are the algarroba, or honey mesquite, and the agave, which provided "pulque" and "vino mescale" for consumption by many desert tribes. In the higher mountain elevations the acorn of many species of oaks and the piñon, or pine nut, were major food resources to the local Indians.[6]

Even insects provided a significant portion of the food requirements of the Indians of California and the intermountain and desert areas of the West. While the litany of such food products—grasshoppers, maggots, caterpillars, larvae of bees, wasps, ants, and beetles, and the like—does not activate the salivary glands of modern man, the food they represent is not only harmless but wholesome. Grasshoppers were often captured in "surrounds"—reminiscent of similar practices used in hunting quadrupeds in other parts of the country—in which the swarms of grasshoppers were driven by an ever-contracting circle of Indians into a previously prepared coal-fire pit where they were quickly roasted and stored away for winter food. Caterpillars of the pandora moth, which feeds on the needles of the yellow pines of the Sierra and Cascade mountains, were often smoked from trees they infested by building a fire beneath until they dropped off into the hands of their captors. Boarding with the California Indians on the "American plan" in the early days, some whites reported, "was not so good."[7]

In the Upper Great Lakes region in particular and the Eastern Woodlands in general several different patterns of subsistence existed. All depended variously upon agriculture, hunting, fishing, gathering, and trading. That some tribes, such as the Ottawas, occasionally moved their agricultural villages through fear of hostile tribes or from the declining productivity of the soil should not imply that such Indians "roamed" the countryside. Nor should the

6. David Prescott Barrows, "Desert Plant Foods of the Coahuilla," in *The California Indians: A Source Book,* comp. and ed. Robert F. Heizer and M. A. Whipple, 2d ed. (Berkeley, 1971) , pp. 306–310.

7. E. O. Essign, "The Value of Insects to the California Indians," in *ibid.,* pp. 315–318.

traditional hunting parties which, in the case of the Ottawas, consisted of all able males and which left the village in both summer and winter give such an impression. Farther south the Miamis and the Potawatomis—of both sexes—lived in large permanent villages during the summer and in large, but temporary, hunting camps in the winter. Whether from fixed or shifting locations, the Indians effectively exploited the resources available to them. A significant portion of their subsistence needs were met by hunting.[8]

The role performed by women in most Indian societies—that of planting and tending the crops—was usually seen by Europeans as a demonstration of their degraded status in Indian societies. In fact the picture is distorted because of the failure to consider the nature of Indian agriculture in general and the nature of Indian subsistence patterns in particular. Among the Hurons, for example, the most difficult agricultural task was that of clearing the land. This work was done by men who cut down the smaller trees, girdled the large trees, and stripped off the branches, which they burned at the base of the larger trees in order to kill them. Crops were then planted between the stumps. Women worked the soil with wooden spades, kept the fields clear of weeds, and tended the crop of Indian corn, beans, and squash. Women also played a principal role in collecting acorns, walnuts, grapes, and other edibles, as well as gathering firewood for the lodges. The men's role was not to sit around and watch the women work, however. Hunting was an important male activity, one that had important noneconomic values as an exercise in the supremely important skills needed for war, and economic values as a supplier of important protein for the tribal diet and skins for clothing. The fall hunts kept the hunters out of the village for a month or more, usually in search of deer. Another activity of the male, usually underestimated in its importance by observers, was fishing. The Huron economy, in particular, relied heavily on fish taken from the lakes and waters surrounding Huronia on three sides. Again, fishing was the responsibility of the man. Other male activities included trading, the construction of palisades around the villages, and the manufacture of canoes.[9]

    8. James E. Fitting and Charles E. Cleland, "Late Prehistoric Settlement Patterns in the Upper Great Lakes," *Ethnohistory*, XVI (1969), 289–302.
    9. Bruce G. Trigger, *The Hurons: Farmers of the North* (New York, 1969), pp. 26–35.

We have no less than the early-nineteenth-century white captive of the Iroquois Mary Jemison as authority for the fact that the female agricultural role among the Iroquois was not severe. Indeed, Mary Jemison asserted that the cares of the Indian women were "not half as numerous, nor as great" as those of white women. Economic pursuits such as agriculture, as Mary Jemison noted, could simultaneously accommodate women's child-care responsibilities. Agriculture thus could be carried on more effectively by women with children than could hunting or fishing. That some native groups, such as the Chukchees of Siberia, divide the labor of summer herding of the reindeer according to child-watching and non-child-watching members of the group suggests the correlation between the agricultural tasks assigned Indian women and the special responsibilities of women for childbirth and child care.[10]

The explanation for the high status of women among the Iroquois has long been debated by scholars. There is no doubt that their power was exercised through control of the economic resources of the tribe. The agricultural lands adjoining Iroquois village sites were worked and controlled by the women, who were occasionally spoken of as "owning" the land, though most authorities assert that the land was communally and not individually owned. A Seneca woman might, Anthony Wallace has pointed out, "own" a plot of land that she cultivated, "but there was little reason for insisting on private tenure: the work was more happily done communally, and in the absence of a regular market, a surplus was of little personal advantage, especially if the winter were hard and other families needed corn." Hoarding brought recriminations. The Iroquois system was geared to cooperation in behalf of larger social units, not to individual competition.[11]

All accounts speak of the ample quantity of food stores produced by the woman-dominated Iroquois economy. Distribution of the food was at the discretion of the matrons, who might make available or withhold food for meetings of the Council and even for war parties, thus affecting the decisions of those bodies. Matrons nominated Council Elders—the highest governing body of the League—and had a voice in the conduct of war and the establishment of

10. Judith K. Brown, "A Note on the Division of Labor by Sex," *American Anthropologist*, LXXII (1970) , 1073–1078.

11. Anthony F. C. Wallace, *The Death and Rebirth of the Seneca* (New York, 1970) , p. 24.

treaties. As keepers of the longhouse, which symbolically represented the organizational structure of the League, they dominated
the domestic scene, seeing to it that tasks were appropriately
allotted and that the common stores were equitably distributed.

However exaggerated Father Joseph Lafitau's eighteenth-century
assertion that "all authority" is vested in the Iroquois women, there
is no question but that the Iroquois women played a significant role
in Iroquois life, more so than the women of other Indian nations.
Yet the role of women in other Indian societies was frequently more
significant than white observers realized, particularly in societies in
which agriculture played a central role.[12]

To the assertion that the American Indian had no conception of
private or exclusive individual ownership of land, Felix Cohen
responded that "there is probably no form of real or personal
property right in the whole range of ownership forms known to our
legal system that has not been lodged in some Indian tribe during
our national history."[13]

The truth of Cohen's assertion is attested by anthropological
studies. As Harold Driver has pointed out, "Property might be
owned by a single individual, two or more individuals, an entire
community, or a tribal group." Nevertheless, Indian concepts of
property showed strong differences from European concepts and the
difference was a frequent cause of friction between Indians and
whites. In general, there was a greater emphasis by Indians on user's
rights, and a lesser emphasis on the rights and power of nominal
owners, whether those nominal owners were individuals or the
tribe. The nominal owner was normally bound by the traditions
of customary use held by members of a kin group, whether the
group was a single family or a lineage segment. The owner could
not prevent such use or arbitrarily dispose of the property without
reference to those preexisting rights. The kinship groups which
possessed such usufructuary rights might be "patricentered,"

12. Father Joseph Lafitau, *Moeurs des sauvages ameriquains, comparées aux
moeurs des premiers temps* (Paris, 1724), quoted in Judith K. Brown, "Economic
Organization and the Position of Women among the Iroquois," *Ethnohistory*,
XVII (1970), 151–167, at 153.
13. United States Department of the Interior, *Federal Indian Law*, a revision
through 1956 of the *Handbook of Federal Indian Law* prepared by Felix S.
Cohen and first printed in 1940 (Washington, 1958), p. 590.

"matricentered," or "bicentered," depending upon whether descent and residence were determined through the male or female line.[14]

"Property" rights which existed among the Hurons illustrate the Indian land "holding" system. A man could clear as much land as he wished and the land remained in the possession of his family so long as they wished to cultivate it. However, once abandoned, it could be planted by anyone else. The communal emphasis of such a system was reinforced by the storage facilities in the longhouse shared by several Huron families where large casks to store corn were located in the porch or in some corner rather than in the divisions belonging to individual families. The traditions of reciprocity and sharing among the members of the longhouse encouraged the *de facto* pooling of all individual resources.[15]

Lewis H. Morgan, the pioneer American ethnologist, interpreted the frequency of joint tenement houses accommodating several families, tribal rather than individual ownership of land, and the acceptance of the "law of hospitality" among virtually all Indian groups as evidence of a primitive communism which was necessitated by the weakness of the family as an organization "to face alone the struggle of life." One need not accept Morgan's simplistic notions of stages of barbarism, in which he placed the various Indian nations according to the practices he discovered among them, or his overexuberant attribution of communism to aboriginal societies in order to appreciate the significance of his description of a system dominated by communal rather than individual goals. Nor did Morgan's recognition of the expedient value of hospitality—which provided "a final equalization of the means of subsistence"—diminish his honest admiration of the system. "I very much doubt," he wrote, "whether the civilized world have in their institutions any system which can properly be called more humane and charitable."[16]

Indian societies were (and to a large extent remain) oral or oral-aural cultures. An oral culture is a culture based on tradition. Nothing can be "looked up" as in the visual world of print. Tradition—knowledge based on experience—is passed down and around

14. Driver, *op. cit.*, pp. 269, 271.
15. Trigger, *op. cit.*, p. 28.
16. Lewis H. Morgan, *Houses and House-Life of the American Aborigines* (1881; reprinted, Chicago, 1965, with intro. by Paul Bohannan), pp. 51, 61–64.

by the members of the group and particularly by the storytellers and orators. How does one fix the traditions and customs of one's group in his head? To a great extent one organizes that tradition in a dynamic, event-filled account. That "moving" account of the world and the people's place in it can be communicated to all members of the group and indeed can be passed down from one generation to another with uncanny accuracy. Scholars who have studied the transmission of contemporary folk knowledge have demonstrated the ability of the tellers to remember and to transmit to equally receptive minds the story that "pictures" their world. The ability of the teller and the told to comprehend the coherent account of the world of the storyteller is aided by the dynamic, sequential, personal, and polemical quality of the story. Learning is communal and so is the action that derives from it. The passion for unanimity among Indian groups in council, the shaping of negotiations with the white man in terms of the familiar event-world of those who share the oral tradition, all derive from this basic context of Indian existence.

The white world view is visual rather than oral, static rather than dynamic, abstract rather than eventful. Learning that view tends to be an individual rather than communal activity. The individual scholar, the individual leader, can isolate himself from the group processes and, through the medium of the static visual record and the written word, organize and move the society of which he is a part. Originality emerges from such a culture because the individual is less bound to the group of which he is a part. The medium by which the individual, print-oriented person communicates does not require a sympathetic refrain from its audience. Writer and reader do not have to be in the physical presence of one another, as speaker and listener do. The written message does not have to be framed in traditional forms, perhaps with mnemonic devices such as the wampum belt which often punctuated the oral statements of Indians in negotiation with whites. It can be recorded coldly and abstractly. It can be forgotten until it is convenient to recall it. The creators of such written messages can be detached from their consequences. The speaker of an oral message, on the other hand, is a part of the message. Empathy and participation mark his expression.

Both views of life are coherent in their own right, though they are subject to larger influences that can in time change and invalidate their assumptions. In conflict, as they usually were in American history, they have resulted in continuing tragedy based on the inability of either side successfully to comprehend—let alone accommodate—the view of the other. The harshness of the conflict has somewhat abated as the Indian has become more visually oriented and script-minded, while the white man, in an era of instantaneous communication by telephone and television, has come increasingly to rely on oral-aural means of personal contact. Nevertheless, the gap between the oral and visual cultures of red man and white man continues to exist and to plague the relationship between the two peoples.[17]

Indian tribes were customarily divided into "clans" composed of individuals who believed themselves descended from a common ancestor. Among the Seneca Indians of New York there were eight clans, named, as was common among Indian nations, for animals: Wolf, Bear, Beaver, Turtle, Hawk, Snipe, Deer, and Heron. Members of a particular clan always married outside the clan. They could claim hospitality from their fellow clan members throughout the Iroquois Confederacy. In Seneca councils the clan was represented by its own chiefs, nominated, in the Iroquois fashion, by the most ancient and respected woman of the clan.[18]

The clan system, as described by Anthony Wallace in his discussion of Delaware culture in the seventeenth century, served, in the absence of any overall political organization, as "a sort of social cement, binding together, by ties of more or less obligatory friendship, sib [clan] members in widely scattered communities, and providing a measure for social classification in intercommunal religious and political meetings." Three clans or sibs were known throughout the Delaware country: Turtle, Turkey, and Wolf. Clan affiliation followed the female line. The clan system cut across the geographical extent of the East Coast region, from Manhattan to Delaware Bay, where the Delawares lived. The separate Delaware communities, or "nations" as they were usually called in colonial times, were composed of several lineages: groups of persons who traced their common descent through the female line from an

17. Based on Walter J. Ong, S.J., "World as View and World as Event," *American Anthropologist*, LXXI (1969), 634–647.
18. Wallace, *Death and Rebirth of the Seneca*, pp. 14–15.

actual female ancestor. (Clan members believed in their common descent without necessarily being able to trace that descent.) A maternal lineage might number fifty or more men, women, and children. Usually they lived together in a longhouse. Several lineages and their longhouses constituted the community or nation, of which the Delawares could boast thirty or forty prior to the arrival of the white man. The chief sachem of each community coordinated and presided over the deliberations of the community council, composed of the older and more distinguished leaders. Anthropologists have traditionally asserted that no overall political coordination existed except to the extent that the clan system served such a function, despite the ascription of political and geographical authority to the clan system by the Moravian missionary and historian John Heckewelder.[19]

The clan or sib system furnished a set of symbols for channeling behavior within a population too large for each member to have full knowledge of the personalities of each other member. The clan unified a larger territory than was possible without the device, inhibited intervillage hostility, and provided the possibility of unifying many villages into a form of nationhood. The larger political confederacies of the Iroquois and of the Southeast are hard to imagine without clans as a foundation. Clan members traveling from the Chickasaw country to the Creek country would be given hospitality by the totemic group among the latter having the same animal name. Individuals belonging to the same groups considered themselves relatives and received hospitality as such. Personal names were "owned" by the clan and those not in use were assigned by the clan as "titles."[20]

The clans or sibs were sometimes gathered into groups of related clans called "phratries" (if more than two groupings of clans) or "moieties" (if only two groupings of clans). In ceremonies, in games, even physically in the case of the Iroquois longhouse, the two sides sat opposite each other, planned together, or contested against each other. The moiety principle, Wallace has pointed out, "provides a

19. Anthony F. C. Wallace, *King of the Delawares: Teedyuscung, 1700–1763* (Philadelphia, 1949), pp. 8–11.

20. Elisabeth Tooker, "Clans and Moieties in North America," *Current Anthropology*, XII (1971), 357–376, at 358, 361; comment of Ernest L. Schusky to Tooker article, 372.

ready tool for the organization of reciprocal behavior on almost any ritual occasion."[21]

Anthropologists have expended enormous amounts of energy in determining the kinship relationships among the peoples they have studied. It has recently been argued that the European ethnocentric background of the anthropologists has led them to overemphasize the actual genealogical relationships involved in the so-called kin groupings among the Indians. In fact, Elisabeth Tooker has pointed out, "As a general rule, descent is little emphasized among North American Indians." According to Tooker the lack of interest in genealogical lineage may be based on the lack of inheritable property common among North American Indians. Wealth in the form of money, domesticated animals, land, and slaves was relatively unimportant for the Indian. In societies where such goods were significant, inheritance would take on greater importance, and with inheritance, genealogy. In fact, those Indians (e.g., certain Northwest Coast peoples) with the highest population density in North America and most productive areas of food supply did emphasize lineages more than did those peoples living in less productive areas in a more scattered fashion.[22]

In Tooker's hypothesis, the totem of the clan was not regarded as an ancestor, but "as a being with whom the members of the clan were particularly associated." "Thus, it is possible," she argues, "that these clans are not lineages for which the genealogical connections have been forgotten, but rather groups composed of lineages for which the genealogical connections never existed or were of incidental importance." Clans, in Tooker's analysis, "may be primarily a device for classifying people who are not well known, not a device for retaining knowledge of genealogical relationships." Tooker notes that the earlier historical literature often spoke of "tribes" or "nations" where the anthropologist would now refer to "clans." Possibly this older usage, Tooker asserts, is nearer the Indian perception of these social units. Not only were North American clans a "kind of nationality," Tooker suggests, but they were also a "kind of religious nationality." The Indian made no sharp distinction between the secular and sacred office. Tooker

21. Wallace, *Death and Rebirth of the Seneca*, p. 15.
22. Tooker, *op. cit.*, pp. 357–358.

hypothesizes that the similarity of clan organization throughout North America suggests the possibility of a former influence—by trade or war—from a powerful cultural center in Mexico. Mexican influences, which include the clan system, might have spread up the rivers of North America long before Europeans arrived, and influenced the native tribes.[23]

Tooker's warning against the overemphasis on formal genealogical relations has been echoed by Roger M. Keesing. In a provocative study, Keesing has asserted that anthropologists' concentration upon such relationships has led them to miss the true organizational features of the societies they study, particularly when that organization is loosely structured in terms of friendship rather than kinship and in terms of varying contextual situations rather than of inflexible genealogical relationships. Whatever the probability of a diffusion of clan and other cultural elements from Mexico, Tooker's argument for a consideration of clans and moieties as forms of organization related less to genealogy than to social utility is an important corrective to the frequent overemphasis by anthropologists on the role of genealogical descent in Indian society.[24]

Personal relationships were seen by most Indians in kinship terms, hence the frequent use of terms such as "grandfather," "father," "uncle," "children," in their interchange with whites. "Father" was regarded as a parent with both parental authority and parental responsibility. The term was often used to enforce the reciprocal responsibility that was implied by it. The word "children" implied subordination in similarly reciprocal terms: the loving parent might correct; he also should indulge the child. Parent-child relationships among Indians were considerably less harsh than among seventeenth- and eighteenth-century Europeans. "Uncles" provided support, assistance, and protection while "nephews" heeded their good counsel. "Brothers" were equal. Governor Thomas Dongan of New York addressed the Iroquois in 1687 as "brethren" with himself and other English "subjects" of the king, not as "children" of the king. A year later, in 1688, when Sir Edmund Andros assumed the government of New York for a

23. *Ibid.*, pp. 359–364.
24. Roger M. Keesing, "Simple Models of Complexity: The Lure of Kinship," *Kinship Studies in the Morgan Centennial Year,* ed. Priscilla Reining (Washington, 1972), pp. 17–31.

period, he addressed the Iroquois, who had greeted him as "Brother Corlaer," as "children." The Mohawks, in reply, informed "Corlaer"—a term for the governor of New York deriving from Arent van Curler, who made the first Dutch treaty with the Mohawks— that under the traditional covenant between themselves and the English they were called "brethren": "therefore lett that of Brethren continue without any alteration."[25]

In the petition of several Wyandot chiefs presented to the President of the United States, the Senate, and the House of Representatives, on February 28, 1812, protesting the constant demands for cession of their lands, the Indians noted how, while refusing to sell any more of their lands, they had, at a conference with Governor Hull of the Michigan Territory,

consented to make our Great Father a present of this land, in hopes that he would reciprocate with us, and let us keep the land out of which we sprung. Surely, since you call yourselves our Fathers, let your conduct answer to your professions. We have given you one hundred times as much, at the treaty of Brownstown, for nothing; we have always behaved like dutiful children; surely you will not, after this, treat us like a step father, but you will at least be the hundredth part as generous as we have been to you.[26]

Chief Justice John Marshall, in his opinion in *Cherokee Nation v. Georgia* (30 U.S. 1), in 1831, cited the fact that the Cherokee Indians addressed the President as "their great father" as one of the pieces of evidence indicating that the Cherokee nation was not a foreign nation but a "domestic dependent nation" whose relationship to the United States resembled that of "a ward to his guardian."[27]

Kin relationships were the basic building blocks of Indian society. Those blocks were formed into social and political structures ranging from nuclear families to vast empires. The Indians, in their initial attempts to establish a basis of cooperation with the immigrant whites, attempted to incorporate the newcomers into the

25. *The Livingston Indian Records, 1666–1723*, ed. Lawrence H. Leder (Gettysburg, Pa., 1956), p. 138; *Documents Relative to the Colonial History of the State of New York*, 11 vols. (Albany, 1856–1861), III, 559.
26. *American State Papers . . . Indian Affairs*, 2 vols. (Washington, 1832–1834), I, 795–796.
27. 30 U.S. 1 at 17.

familiar kinship system. When proffered marriage alliances were turned down by the whites, the Indians sought to establish relationships based on the reciprocal responsibilities of brother to brother, nephew to uncle, and, finally, children to father. The white man refused the proffered relationships, misinterpreted Indian speech as weakness, and increasingly imposed his will on the disheartened remnants of once proud Indian nations.

Students of the Indian have demonstrated the complex and smooth-working social organization of the tribes which functioned without the need for written laws or the paraphernalia of European civilization. In some cases, as noted earlier, humor and ridicule directed at an offender by his fellow tribesmen were sufficient to compel the desired behavior. In other cases more formal coercive mechanisms were necessary. Men's societies among the Hidatsas of the Plains, for example, served both to identify potential leaders and thereafter to utilize their ability to guide the behavior of others. As individuals demonstrated skill in warfare and growing maturity and judgment, they were able to join or purchase into the various societies until they reached the most responsible society—that entrusted with police duties for the tribe—the Black Mouths. The Black Mouths enforced the decisions of the older men in council on such matters as moving the village, deciding when to leave for the summer hunt, prohibiting movement from the village for warfare, and the like. Should an individual violate the regulations, he might be beaten and stripped of his goods, though if he was repentant and took the correction in good spirit he might be forgiven and rewarded for his good behavior.

The Black Mouths played a particularly important role in maintaining peace between the different villages of Hidatsas and Mandans. If a theft by an individual of one village against an individual of another village occurred, the negotiation would take place between the Black Mouths of each village and restitution or reparation would be made after justice had been enforced by the Black Mouths of the culprit's own village. The Black Mouths played a similar role in guaranteeing the safety of visiting tribal delegations come for trade or negotiation. Often this had to be done by satisfying the objections of those who had lost relatives at the hands of the visitors' tribes. Once received into the village the bonds of hospitality prevailed in a mutual obligation. If the village were attacked, even by members of the same tribe as those visiting, the visitors were obligated to join their hosts in repelling the attackers.

The Black Mouths also played an important role vis-à-vis the whites. Often they returned horses taken from traders. They similarly enforced the regulations against hunting or chopping wood by whites living with them when buffalo herds were moving into the area and all such activities were enjoined to prevent the herd from being diverted.[28]

One of the less common forms of punishment among Indians was whipping. Nevertheless, in the Plateau area, whipping was given and received in a formal manner as a means of social control. The whipping complex antedated the arrival of the Europeans in the Plateau area. Its origin is uncertain, but the Spanish Southwest mission culture would seem to be the logical source. Its spread into the Plains was probably through the agency of the Shoshonis. The Plains Indians used correctional whipping to enforce the strict discipline needed on the buffalo hunts.[29]

One of the most unusual mechanisms for mediating internal conflicts—found primarily among the Indians of the Southeast—was the designation of certain towns as towns of refuge or places of safety. Usually the privilege was designed for those who had killed a person by accident though the Cherokees in the eighteenth century allowed their town called Choate to protect even a willful murderer. Indeed, James Adair, the historian of the Indians of the Southeast, cited the example of an Englishman who fled to Choate after killing an Indian warrior in defense of his property. The Englishman remained at Choate in perfect safety even though the relatives of the deceased were required by Cherokee custom to avenge their kinsman's loss. The headmen of the town dissuaded the Englishman from leaving too soon and risking his security. Instead, they persuaded him to stay longer and to "wipe off the tears" of the incident with various presents until the passions raised by the affair were extinguished.[30]

28. Alfred W. Bowers, *Hidatsa Social and Ceremonial Organization*, Smithsonian Institution, Bureau of American Ethnology, Bulletin 194 (Washington, 1965), pp. 174–212.

29. Thomas R. Garth, "The Plateau Whipping Complex and Its Relationship to Plateau-Southwest Contacts," *Ethnohistory*, XII (1965), pp. 141–143.

30. James Adair, *History of the American Indians; Particularly Those Nations adjoining to the Mississippi, East and West Florida, Georgia, South and North Carolina, and Virginia* (London, 1775, facsimile ed. with intro. by Robert F. Berkhofer, Jr., New York, 1968), pp. 158–159.

To summarize, Indian methods of social control, though based on unwritten law and tribal custom, though ranging from humor and ridicule to whipping and death, provide a form of behavioral regulation as effective as that of any literate white society plentifully stocked with jails, churches, written codes, professional police, and the like. Indeed, white observers frequently remarked upon the greater effectiveness of Indian law than of white law in maintaining harmony within a society. When Indians lost their equal footing with whites, their systems of social control were challenged and eventually destroyed.

White assumptions about Indian political organization range all the way from the belief that they were totally autocratic to the conviction that they were totally anarchic. As usual the truth is complex and runs between these two poles. While some of the early explorers reported the Indians as living without laws and without religion, the early Spanish encounters with the complex empires of the Aztecs and the Incas—under their ruler-gods—encouraged a contrary view. Some Europeans imagined that all Indian nations were under the absolute control of their kings.

The European terms "king" and "emperor," used to refer to Indian leaders in the first few centuries of settlement, were replaced by "chief" and "headman" in later centuries after the independent power of the Indian had been neutralized or destroyed. John C. Ewers has asserted that "The concept of Indian 'kings,' as well as 'princesses,' was a white man's fiction," but one can go too far in dismissing the analogy. First of all, the concept of "king" or "prince" does not imply that Indian rulers possessed absolute power. Even in a Europe in which kings asserted absolute power royalty often struggled with the nobles and sometimes with the masses. A king might represent a nation both directly, as Louix XIV spoke of himself as the state, and indirectly as the spokesman of other classes or groups having power in the state. In the same sense Indian "kings," "emperors," and "princes" represented the powers inherent in Indian communities. True it is, as Ewers points out, that decisions affecting tribal policies were normally first made "in council" by talking things over until a "consensus" was reached. But one could also say much the same thing about European decision making in vital matters of war and peace. Both Indian and

European "kings" sought unifying agreement among all segments of society when faced with issues of survival. That the smaller Indian societies sought more general agreement and had fewer representative linkages between the individual warrior and the national leader does not alter this fact. Nor does the fact that Indian leaders could not easily control the warlike actions of youthful tribal members. Although discipline and control were perhaps more commonly accepted facets of European organization, white leaders were often unable to control the actions of their ordinary citizens.[31]

While Indian leadership lacked the coercive quality so familiar in European society, it achieved the same end by example and by persuasion. Among the numerous instances of Indian leaders eliciting a tribal response through personal example is the case of Salvador Palma, Captain of the Yuma tribe, as related in a petition to the Viceroy of New Spain, on November 11, 1776, requesting the establishment of missions in his territory. Palma, whose original Indian name was Olleyquotequiebe, recounted in the petition the fears of the Yumas in 1774 when they heard that Captain Juan Baptista de Anza was heading their way with a force of armed men. Palma, who claimed "the supreme rule" over the Yumas "by right of primogeniture inherited from my fathers and by these from my grandfathers," refused to accede to the wishes of most of the tribe that they meet Anza with weapons in hand prepared for a fight. Palma asserted that since the Yumas had never done an injury to the Spaniards nor the Spaniards to the Yumas they should be received in a friendly fashion. Palma went on to assert that

When I found them intractable I saw myself under the necessity of declaring that in spite of them I should defend the Spaniards with only those who might remain obedient to me; and though not a soul should follow me I alone would place myself at their side, even if it cost me my life. This threat had the desired effect, and not a single one disobeyed my orders.[32]

After meeting Anza at his invitation and being told of Christianity, Palma resolved to become a Christian. But "although in my

31. John C. Ewers, "When Red and White Men Met," *Western Historical Quarterly*, II (1971) , 134.

32. Herbert Eugene Bolton, ed., *Anza's California Expeditions*, Vol. V: *Correspondence* (Berkeley, 1930) , pp. 365–377, at 367–368. Reprinted in J. N. Bowman and Robert F. Heizer, *Anza and the Northwest Frontier of New Spain*, Southwest Museum Papers, No. 20 (Los Angeles, 1967) , pp. 148–155.

heart I was convinced, I wished nevertheless to talk it over with my people, not so much in order to obtain approval as to win them over to the same view." Palma obtained permission of Anza to go back to his people to tell them about the new religion. "And I found them so well disposed that they agreed unanimously to anything I might do." Even allowing for exaggeration—both of his former authority and his later persuasiveness—Palma's account of how he chose to exercise his claimed right of "supreme rule" over his people is instructive. The Indian leader had to persuade, convince, and set an example. He could not rely solely on peremptory command or unchallenged coercion.[33]

Whatever one calls those who led or spoke for Indian groups, however they assumed positions of authority, and whatever process was followed in effecting changes in leadership, Indian leaders performed the same leadership functions that leaders in European society performed. Moreover, native leadership was evident at every level of Indian social organization, even among the native peoples in the Arctic, Great Basin, Northeast Mexico, and Baja California, whose largest permanent unit at the time of European contact was the family, and who had no territorial organization larger than the residential kin group. Such groups are not considered by some anthropologists to have had "true political organization." Nevertheless, family and kin group heads provided the direction given by political leaders in tribes with more elaborate social structures.[34]

Numerous native peoples in the Subarctic, Northwest Coast, Plateau, California, and Southwest areas possessed (and some still possess) territorial organizations ranging from family groups through bands and tribelets to true tribes. Each such organization, whether or not designated political, was directed by a leader variously chosen (more often by ability than heredity) and variously obeyed (more often voluntarily than by coercion).

On the Plains, Prairies, and in the East true tribal organization was more frequent than elsewhere, although many Indians in these areas were organized in bands and village groups prior to the coming of the white man. True tribal organizations are associated with the more populous agricultural tribes or with those nomadic tribes who were once agriculturalists but turned to hunting after

33. *Ibid.*, p. 369.
34. Driver, *op. cit.*, p. 287.

ARCTIC OCEAN

ESKIMO

KUTCHIN

ARCTIC

ESKIMO

ALEUT

ESKIMO

ESKIMO

ESKIMO

ESKIMO

ESKIMO

ESKIMO

TLINGIT

SLAVE

NORTH

HAIDA TSIMSHIAN BEAVER

CHIPEWYAN

HUDSON BAY

BEOTHUK

BELLA COOLA

WEST

SIKSIKA
(BLACKFOOT)

SUBARCTIC

NASKAPI
MONTAGNAIS

BELLA BELLA

CREE

CREE

KWAKIUTL
NOOTKA

KAIGANI
(BLOOD)

PLAINS
CREE

MICMAC
MALECITE
PASSAMAQUODDY

COAST SALISH

KUTENAI

PUYALLUP COLVILLE
NISQUALLY SPOKAN COEUR
CHINOOK D'ALENE

PIEGAN

ASSINIBOIN

OJIBWA (CHIPPEWA)

ABENAKI
PENOBSCOT
PENNACOOK

PLATEAU

OJIBWA
WYANDOT

OTTAWA

HURON

TILLAMOOK

YAKIMA
WALLA WALLA FLATHEAD

NEZ PERCE

HIDATSA
MANDAN
GROS VENTRE (ATSINA)
ARIKARA

WINNEBAGO
MENOMINEE
SAC

MAHICAN

CAYUSE

CROW

NEUTRAL

IROQUOIS

MOHAWK ESOPUS
ONEIDA NIPMUC WAMPANOAG
ONONDAGA WECQUAESGEEK NARRAGANSET
CAYUGA HACKENSACK PEQUOT
SENECA RARITAN MOHEGAN
SUSQUEHANNOCK WAPPINGER
(CONESTOGA) DELAWARE
PAMUNKEY NANTICOKE
MATTAPONY POWHATAN
CHICKAHOMINY
OCCANEECHI PAMLICO
TUTELO NOTTOWAY
CHEROKEE TUSCARORA
YUCHI CATAWBA

YUROK
HUPA

KLAMATH
MODOC

BANNOCK

TETON
DAKOTA

SANTEE
DAKOTA

FOX

POTAWATOMI

NORTHERN
PAIUTE

SHOSHONI
(SNAKE)

YANKTON
DAKOTA

PONCA

IOWA

KASKASKIA MIAMI
PEORIA WEA

**EASTERN
WOODLAND**

WASHO

GOSIUTE

PLAINS

OMAHA

KICKAPOO

**CALI-
FORNIA**

GREAT BASIN

NORTHERN
CHEYENNE

PAWNEE

OTO

MISSOURI

ILLINOIS

UTE

PIANKASHAW
SHAWNEE

SOUTHERN
PAIUTE

ARAPAHO

KANSA

SOUTHERN
CHEYENNE

OSAGE

CHUMASH

HAVASUPAI NAVAHO JICARILLA
MOHAVE WALAPAI HOPI APACHE
YAVAPAI ZUNI PUEBLO

KIOWA

QUAPAW

CHICKASAW

CADDO

SOUTHEAST

CREEK YAMASEE

CAHUILLA

YUMA **SOUTHWEST**
COCOPA PIMA WESTERN
PAPAGO APACHE

KIOWA
APACHE

COMANCHE WICHITA

TUNICA CHOCTAW

NATCHEZ ALABAMA

ATLANTIC
OCEAN

MESCALERO
APACHE

MOBILE

SERI

TARAHUMARA

LIPAN
APACHE

SEMINOLE

PACIFIC
OCEAN

YAQUI **NORTHERN**

KARANKAWA

CALUSA

MEXICO

GULF OF MEXICO

TAINO

**TRADITIONAL
CULTURE AREAS
AND TRIBAL LOCATIONS
NORTH AMERICA**

CIBONEY

TAINO

CIBONEY

TARASCAN

YUCATAN
MAYA

TLAXCALAN
AZTEC

MESOAMERICA

acquiring the horse. Leadership structures among such tribes were more elaborate than among the simpler hunter-gatherer groups. Almost invariably a distinction was drawn between war chiefs and civil chiefs. Although bravery in war was a prerequisite to leadership among Indian tribes, those designated civil chiefs were concerned with maintaining peace within the society and arguing the case for peaceful settlement of disputes with outsiders. War chiefs were responsible for organizing and leading war parties in time of war. Such tribes were often task organized for movement or buffalo hunting, and usually contained men's societies to police and enforce the rules elaborated for the benefit of the society.[35]

It is difficult to find the type of virtually absolute power possessed by the rulers of the Aztec and Inca empires in Mexico and Peru wielded by the heads of Indian states in the present area of the United States. Nevertheless, near absolute authority was exercised by the rulers of the Natchez, in the Gulf Coast area, where the influence of Mexican priestly states was strong, and to a lesser extent it existed in Powhatan's "centralized monarchy" in Virginia and among the Calusa in Florida.[36]

The evolution of political organization in complex Indian societies has been documented in the history of the Cherokees. Cherokee political organization responded rapidly to the opportunities and dangers impinging upon the tribe. Until early in the eighteenth century, no formal political system united the then independent villages of Cherokees. The impingement of the English and, to a lesser extent, the French upon the Cherokees forced the creation of a tribal state which could respond to the whites, who through ignorance and convenience regarded all Cherokees as members of a single state. The Cherokee organization that evolved was essentially an aggregation or confederation of separate villages, using as a model the council organization that expressed the will of the individual villages. At first this organization took the character of a tribal priest state but as it showed its inability to prevent the

35. *Ibid.*, p. 299.

36. Christian Feest, draft article on "Virginia Algonquians" for forthcoming *Handbook of North American Indians*, Smithsonian Institution, Washington, D.C. See also John M. Goggin and William C. Sturtevant, "The Calusa: A Stratified, Nonagricultural Society (with Notes on Sibling Marriage)," in *Explorations in Cultural Anthropology: Essays in Honor of George Peter Murdock*, ed. Ward H. Goodenough (New York, 1964), pp. 179–219.

young warriors from harming traders, it was increasingly modified by the introduction of warriors into its councils who strove to introduce a more coercive discipline into Cherokee politics.[37]

The adaptability of Indian political organization is evident in the varied forms in which village organization was shaped to meet particular needs. These "structural poses," as anthropologist Fred Gearing has termed them, placed varying responsibilities upon the members of the community at various times. The hunt, for example, was a task neither for an individual family nor for the entire village. It was normally the province of an aggregate of independent households, particularly in the winter season, when groups of ten or so individuals would leave the village to hunt deer, a major food item and, in the form of skins, the principal trade item with which to obtain European weapons, paint, utensils, and clothes.

Another "structural pose" involved the response to a killing of, or injury to, a member of the village. For this purpose, the relationship of each individual to a particular clan was central. There were seven Cherokee clans—all matrilineal—and each village had all seven represented. The clansmen within each village formed a clan section. Allocation of garden plots, regulation of marriage, and revenge for injuries were the responsibilities of the clan sections. Murder required blood revenge, which all male clansmen of the victim's clan were required to see carried out. Should the object of the revenge flee to the house of the village priest chief he could not be killed. A hearing was usually conducted in the chief's house by the two clan sections and a settlement arranged. The system worked despite the fact that it was probable that one member of the revenging clan section was married into a household of a member of the clan section of the offender.[38]

Another structural pose was assumed by the Cherokee village through the village council, a body which made decisions concerning relations with neighboring tribes and with European colonies. For such decisions, the village acted as a single unit but with a body of elders—called by the Cherokees "the beloved men"—drawn from the seven clans. All male villagers could speak on matters discussed

37. Fred Gearing, *Priests and Warriors: Social Structures for Cherokee Politics in the Eighteenth Century,* American Anthropological Association, Memoir 93 (Menasha, Wisc., 1962) , p. 5.
38. *Ibid.,* p. 21.

by the council. When a village council decided on war, another structural pose was assumed by the community. A special war organization, including war chief, war priest, speaker for war, and surgeon, was elected by the warriors who in turn appointed eight officers from among the young men for various tasks. In addition there was a seven-man council for war, representing each of the clan sections, and other structured hierarchies based on the status and experience of the young warriors. Once dispatched, usually in bands of twenty to forty men, the war parties were virtually autonomous in carrying out their missions. No practical control was exercised over these parties by the body of elders. (The organization of the community for summer ball games with other villages resembled in many ways the organization for war.) On the return of the war party the warriors had to undergo ritual purification before rejoining the activities of the village.[39]

The values of Cherokee society in its war pose were quite distinct from the values revered in its peaceful pursuits. Peace was the normal state; war the abnormal. The good man, in Cherokee thought, avoided conflict, neither expressed anger nor gave occasion for it. This attitude formed the basis for the famed "unanimity" principle common to many Indian groups by which they sought to achieve harmony and agreement at virtually any cost. Often this unanimity was more a matter of appearance than of reality (though effective nevertheless) in that the individual failing to obtain assent to his own views would retire without expressing dissent from the views of others. A good man would avoid a confrontation even by withdrawal.[40]

The Cherokee method of command was, in a similar fashion, governed more often by invisible bonds than by overt authority. The independence of the Indian warrior was often noted by Western observers. A warrior might even "desert" his fellows should his dreams impel him to withdraw, yet such behavior seems rarely to have been triggered by the motives that might have activated a white soldier. The Cherokee war organization was so carefully determined by reference to accomplishments in the past and by agreement of the warriors involved as to provide a firm basis for mutual trust among the members of a war party. Yet the war chief

39. *Ibid.*, pp. 27, 61.
40. *Ibid.*, pp. 31–32.

was not without coercive power, however much that power was resident in the hearts of his men and the customs of the villages to which the warriors must return.[41]

Gearing has asserted that the war organization of the Cherokees was "incompletely and imperfectly institutionalized" and, in fact, "not workable," but in fact the organization can be asserted to have met Cherokee needs admirably. The inability of the Cherokees to resist white encroachment and domination should perhaps be attributed not to any defect in Cherokee organization but to superior power and numbers in the whites.[42]

As white pressure increased, Cherokee political organization expanded to form a loose confederation of the independent fraternally related villages. In response to the demands of the English, particularly those of South Carolina, for protection of English traders operating among the Indians and for punishment of Cherokees for offenses committed against the colonists, an "emperor" of all the Cherokees was selected from among the village chiefs. The English refused to accept the Indian system as they found it and the Indians accommodated themselves to the English demand. The Cherokee federation was neither so ancient nor so carefully structured as the Iroquois Confederacy but it functioned effectively during the last half of the eighteenth century, even in a losing cause.

A recent study of Cherokee law by a legal scholar has concluded that

It is too strong a term to call the Cherokee nation a confederacy of towns. At best, it was a collection of towns populated by a common people. At worst—in times of strife—it was anarchy. Yet we cannot conclude that there was no national government. When the headmen of certain towns furnished a leadership that others would follow, the nation became a functioning reality, and this occurred as often as not.[43]

The lack of agreement on the degree of political coherence of an Indian "nation" affects jurists as well as historians and anthropologists. In a split decision of the Indian Claims Commission, three commissioners asserted that the Treaty of Greeneville of 1795 and

41. *Ibid.*, p. 49.
42. *Ibid.*, p. 47.
43. John Phillip Reid, *A Law of Blood: The Primitive Law of the Cherokee Nation* (New York, 1970), p. 33.

numerous other treaties made with the Potawatomi nation or parts
thereof, living in separated villages along certain rivers in the
present states of Wisconsin, Illinois, Indiana, and Michigan, cor-
rectly recognized the political unity of the nation. Two commissioners dissented, asserting that while the nation might have existed
culturally and linguistically it did not exist politically as a unit.
That General Anthony Wayne at Greeneville insisted on treating
the several "bands" or groups of Potawatomis as members of a
single nation demonstrated, in the eyes of the minority, "the
Government's complete ignorance of the Potawatomi political
structure, and its insensitivity to Potawatomi pronouncements that
they constituted separate groups and that they should be treated as
such." The minority asserted that the determining factor in the case
was the *de facto* Potawatomi political structure, rather than the
United States' refusal to deal separately with the separate Potawatomi political elements at that treaty.[44]

Certainly the Potawatomis, scattered over the Old Northwest
territory, existed in bands whose chiefs exercised authority separate
and distinct from the authority exercised by other chiefs of other
segments of the Potawatomis. But, in the face of the United States
claims to land possessed by many of the Potawatomi bands, and in
the context of the United States tendency to treat with the Indians
in national, or tribal, guise, a national consensus was both elicited
and achieved. That this consensus did not take the European form
of a permanent national ruler, whether that of a crowned head or
a parliamentary body, did not mean that a political unity, for purposes for which political unity was required, did not exist. In this
sense the United States helped the Potawatomis, as they did other
tribes earlier and later, to achieve a stronger tribal unity. In the
same sense, modern governmental policy has elicited and developed
a pan-Indian unity among modern Indian tribes which display the
same divisions and looseness of organization that characterized the
Potawatomis at the turn of the nineteenth century.[45]

44. *Citizen Band of Potawatomi Indians of Oklahoma, et al., Potawatomie
Tribe of Indians, the Prairie Band of Potawatomie Indians, et al., Hannahville
Indian Community, et al.,* v. *the United States,* decided March 28, 1972, 27 Ind.
Cl. Comm. 187 at 194, 212–214, 359, 381, 391, 471.
45. Vine Deloria, Jr., *Custer Died for Your Sins: An Indian Manifesto* (New
York, 1969) , especially chap. 9; and Vine Deloria, Jr., *We Talk, You Listen:
New Tribes, New Turf* (New York, 1970) .

William T. Hagan has made an instructive analogy between the autonomous Greek city-states and the individual Indian bands or villages. One could extend the analogy to point out that the Greek city-states could and did join together as Greeks for peaceful pursuits, such as the Olympic games, or for military defense against non-Greek invaders. Unity among all Greek communities was as difficult to achieve as it was among related Indian communities. But both tribal and intertribal (or national and international) unity was obtained for particular purposes and for particular periods among related groups of Indians and among Greeks.[46]

To summarize: Political organization among Indians varied from the simple family groups of the remote Arctic and desert West to the complex confederacies of tribes in the East and autocratic states of Mexico and their imitators in the Gulf coastal areas. Indian political organization was designed to meet various challenges, including the challenge of European expansion, which altered the political structure of many tribes. Since Indian purposes and Indian values differed from those of the whites, Indian political structures differed also. The subjugation of the Indians should not automatically be taken to demonstrate the inefficiency of Indian political organization. The overwhelming force of numbers and technology brought against the American Indian would have destroyed any political system that could not draw upon equal resources.

In the materialistic world in which most whites find themselves, the idea of a people attached by strong bonds to the spirit world is sometimes hard to imagine. Yet almost all Indians of the past were, and, indeed, many in the present are, strongly bound by such a belief. The importance of establishing proper relations with the supernatural power, or essence, or beings who were believed to influence, if they did not determine, human actions, was a major and continuing concern. Such a relationship, on the part of hunters or those with a strong hunting tradition, as in the northern and western portions of the continent, was often sought through individual withdrawal experiences and vision quests. Withdrawal often occurred at times of biological crises, as at birth, puberty, and death. At such times those affected were particularly subject to the

46. William T. Hagan, *The Indian in American History*, American Historical Association, Pamphlet No. 240 (Washington, D.C., 1971), p. 4.

supernatural force that pervaded the universe. Girls would withdraw for varying periods at puberty, for example, so that this strong supernatural force would not endanger themselves or others, particularly men. The bereaved after a death, or killers, often withdrew to minimize the desire of the soul of the departed one, or the one killed, to take a loved one, or the persons responsible for his death, with him to the afterworld.[47]

Vision quests to tap the spiritual power resident in the universe were another form of recognition of the reality of the supernatural. Individual men, usually on the approach of manhood (though the experience was not limited to youths or to men), would make a solitary quest in some remote natural place, such as a mountainous area, where they would seek to make contact with the supernatural force and obtain from it some element of its power. The token obtained was often a song or a fetish which, duly solemnized through ritual, would provide a guardian spirit to the youth. Individual vision quests were particularly common among hunters of the north and the west who depended upon their individual skill and luck in achieving survival. As an authority on Ojibwa religion has put it: "The hunter felt himself a soul at bay, against cosmic forces personalized as cynical or terrorizing."[48]

Some individuals achieved more effective contact with the supernatural than others. Those most attuned to the spirit world were shamans, or medicine men, who functioned in one form or another throughout native North America. The shaman, by virtue of his superior contact with the supernatural, was called upon to cure diseases and exorcise evil spirits. Sufficient belief in the curative power of shamans remains so that some contemporary medical doctors utilize the assistance of shamans in effecting their cures among Indians.[49]

Each Indian culture defined the spirit world in its own fashion and sought to establish the proper relationship between man and that world in appropriate ways. The Winnebago Indians of the Great Lakes area, for example, believed in a large number of spirits,

47. Ruth Underhill, "Religion among American Indians," in Roger C. Owen, James J. F. Deetz, Anthony D. Fisher, eds., *The North American Indian: A Sourcebook* (New York, 1967), pp. 96–108, especially pp. 97–98.
48. Ruth Landes, *Ojibwa Religion and the Midewiwin* (Madison, Wisc., 1968), p. 7.
49. Underhill, *op. cit.*, pp. 103–104.

most of whom were seen as animals or animal-like beings capable of taking any form they wished. The supreme deity was Earthmaker. Each Winnebago hoped to possess a personal guardian spirit whom he sought—usually as a child between the ages of nine and eleven—by fasting. The Winnebago's relationship to the deities was a personal one which gave him support and protection that he might otherwise lack. Indeed, the absence of such a support left him weak and vulnerable. So important was this spiritual relation to the Winnebago that, as the anthropologist Paul Radin has pointed out, "When they lost their belief in the efficacy of fasting and the spirits no longer vouchsafed them visions, Winnebago culture rapidly disintegrated."[50]

While religion among those cultures strongly influenced by hunting placed greatest emphasis on individual efforts to achieve an acceptable relationship with the supernatural, tribes with a firm agricultural tradition developed communal appeals to the spirits through standardized rituals. The anthropologist Ruth Underhill has pointed out that the different approach of the agriculturalist tribes reflected the different economic and social needs of an agricultural society. The need for communal work in the fields, the importance of weather, the uncertainty of plant growth, all called for an approach to the spirit world different from that pursued by hunters. The more elaborate ceremonies of the agriculturalist tribes included pleas for rain and rituals associated with planting, green corn, and the harvest.[51]

The most elaborate, formal, and ritualistic religious practices were found among populous, agricultural, hierarchical societies like the Hopis of the Southwest or, preeminently, the Natchez of the lower Mississippi Valley. The Natchez, though destroyed utterly by the French in the eighteenth century, did not disappear before their culture was described by attentive observers, though the suspicion remains that the delineation of the character of the Great Sun, the god-king of the Natchez, may have owed something to the familiar attributes of Louis XIV, *Le Roi Soleil,* under whose aegis French contact with the Natchez was established. Although the religious

50. Paul Radin, *The Trickster: A Study in American Indian Mythology* (New York, 1956), pp. 115–116.

51. Underhill, *op. cit.,* pp. 104–106. See also Ruth M. Underhill, *Red Man's America: A History of the Indians in the United States,* rev. ed. (Chicago, 1971), p. 101.

observations of the Natchez centered on an elaborate temple, specialized priests, and complex ceremonies, they derived, as did the religious practices of the simple hunter societies, from an all-powerful Great Spirit who created the Natchez theocratic state. In that state the Great Sun was linked functionally to the Great Spirit, the sun was venerated, and a sacred fire preserved continually in the sacred temple. Shamans also played a religious role among the Natchez, as did the lesser spirits who suffused the spirit world.[52]

In southern Arizona among the Papago Indians one finds equally developed the communal ceremonies characteristic of the Pueblo Indians (designed to bring rain and therefore food) and the vision experiences common among the Plains Indians (designed to bring power to the individual). By both individual quest and communal ceremony the Papagos sought rain and food, and their product: health, fertility, and life.[53]

Among the warlike Plains Indians numerous ceremonies were designed to obtain the favor of the Great Spirit. The bull dance of the Mandans involved an ordeal of self-torture: the deliberate running of skewers through the legs, arms, and bodies of the young participants who were then pulled up by two cords lowered from the top of the lodge beside which the ceremony was conducted. The torment was extreme: the blood poured from the open wounds. Bystanders placed upon the splints each man's shield, bow, and quiver, and sometimes the skull of a buffalo was attached to the arm or leg. The painter George Catlin noted:

The unflinching fortitude with which every one of them bore this part of the torture surpassed credulity; each one as the knife was passed through the flesh sustained an unchangeable countenance; and several of them, seeing me making sketches, beckoned me to look at their faces, which I watched through all this horrid operation, without being able to detect anything but the pleasantest smiles as they looked me in the eye, while I could hear the knife rip through the flesh, and feel enough of it myself, to start involuntary and uncontrollable tears over my cheeks.

The one ordeal was followed by another: the voluntary offering of one or other of the fingers of the left hand to be chopped off as it was extended upon a dried buffalo skull. No attempt was made to

52. Oswalt, *op. cit.*, pp. 485–488.
53. Ruth M. Underhill, *Papago Indian Religion* (New York, 1946), pp. 17, 21.

bandage the wounds or stop the flow of blood. It was left to the Great Spirit to cure. A by-product of this religious ceremony was the evaluation by the chiefs of the tribe of the strength and character of the initiates. From that assessment, they knew whom to appoint to lead their war parties.[54]

Preparations for war as well as for life required religious sanctification. The eighteenth-century trader and historian James Adair compared the ceremonies of purification observed by the Southeastern Indians bent on war with those of the ancient Israelites, from whom he believed the American Indians descended. When a skilled Indian orator had convinced a number to join him in a warlike enterprise, the party, before setting out, purified itself by fasting for several days in a sacred place with the consecrated contents of the Indian ark, a small wooden chest that Adair equated with the Hebrew ark, but which the modern anthropologists equate with the "medicine bundles" better known in the North and West. The Indian, in his preparatory purification and throughout the campaign, would abstain from sexual intercourse, even with his own wife. In sum, in war as in the hunt and in other activities of life, the Indian voluntarily underwent trials which demonstrated his spiritual capacity and commitment to the end he sought to achieve.[55]

"Animals and human beings," Harold Driver has pointed out, "were spiritually equated by the Indian as they are physically equated by biologists today." The almost universal belief among Indians in animal souls (as in human souls) encouraged rules for the taking and consumption of the food lest the animal, improperly killed, butchered, or eaten, inform his fellow creatures, who might thereupon avenge themselves on the responsible hunter. Fishing, on the other hand, was less regulated by taboos than hunting. Driver's hypothesis for the difference is, first, that fish were less important in the Indian diet for the North American continent as a whole and, second, that fish are farther removed from man biologically than mammals and resemble man much less in appearance and behavior. In those areas, as in the Northwest Coast and Plateau, where

54. George Catlin, *Letters and Notes on the Manners, Customs, and Condition of the North American Indians*, 2 vols., 3d ed. (London, 1842), I, 171–172, 180–184. See also Catlin's *O-kee-pa: A Religious Ceremony and other Customs of the Mandans*, ed. John C. Ewers (New Haven, Conn., 1967), especially pp. 54–62.

55. Adair, *op. cit.*, pp. 159–169; personal conversation with William C. Sturtevant, Smithsonian Institution, Washington, D.C.

fishing, and particularly salmon fishing, provides the principal food resource, elaborate ceremonials concerning the catching of salmon do exist. Particular importance was placed on the importance of catching the first salmon in a formal and correct manner so that its soul would tell other salmon, who would then follow, assured of the same respectful treatment.[56]

The Teton Sioux of the Great Plains performed rituals and ceremonies of a similar character to assure that the supply of buffalo would continue. The buffalo hunters often apologized to the Great Unseen Buffalo—a sort of leader of all the buffalo—for having to kill the buffalo. The hunters also took care not to be wasteful, lest the buffalo leave and bring starvation to the tribe.[57]

There exist sufficient examples of Indian concern for killing only so much as he needed and only in the proper manner to support the assertion that the Indian was the first ecologist. (Some authorities, however, disagree.) This concern can be documented not only by the observations of anthropologists, but from the historical record. It was expressed directly by Hendrick Aupaumut, chief of the Mahican Indians, originally from the upper Hudson River and later resident in Stockbridge, Massachusetts, in his *History of the Muhheakunnuk Indians* written in the last decade of the eighteenth century and transcribed by John Sergeant, missionary to the tribe, in 1822. Hendrick wrote:

It was a law among them not to kill any more game than was necessary for their own use—none even to barter, which might have produced a temptation to waste their animals. By this regulation their game was preserved undiminished, the consumption being no greater than the natural increase. This law continued in force, until the *Chuckkathuk,* or *white* people, came to his island.[58]

Belief in life after death was and is characteristic of most Indian societies. When a person was about to die among the Hidatsas of the Plains, for example, it was customary for those who had lost loved ones shortly before to bring messages to the one about to

56. Driver, *op. cit.,* pp. 98–100.

57. Clark Wissler, *Indians of the United States,* rev. ed. (New York, 1966), p. 171.

58. Quoted in *First Annual Report of the American Society for Promoting the Civilization and General Improvement of the Indian Tribes in the United States* (New Haven, Conn., 1824), p. 42.

depart to carry to the spirit world. Murderers were excluded from the villages of the dead, and became wanderers in the afterlife. The world of the dead was, in some measure, a duplication of the world of life, the murderer being excluded from the company of the community in death as he was in life. Among the Hidatsas there was some disagreement as to whether suicides were condemned to wander aimlessly as were murderers. Many Hidatsas, particularly women, among whom the incidence of suicide was greatest, believed that the suicide did not suffer from exclusion as did the murderer, and in periods when the tribe was decimated by epidemics, many people committed suicide merely to catch up with and rejoin their recently deceased relatives.

Many Indian origin myths, for example that of the Hidatsas, conceived of the original members of the tribe emerging from underground to the surface of the earth. According to Hidatsa tradition, one woman heavy with child broke the vine by which the people were ascending, thus separating the people. Many Hidatsas believed that on death the individual returned to his people in the land below. Others believed in an opposite process whereby the first people descended from the sky and returned to the sky.[59]

The Pueblo Indian anthropologist Alfonso Ortiz, in describing how he climbed Tsikomo, the mountain of the west, in 1964, reported that his Tewa informants regarded the almost perpetual presence of clouds overhead and the greater frequency of rain at the higher elevation as signs of unusual sacredness: "The spirits were unusually active here because this was where they lived." The Tewas—like other Pueblo Indians—are involved in an unceasing quest for rainfall. The source of this moisture, as a result, achieves a level of sacredness.[60]

Many American Indians conceived of a bipolar spiritual universe influenced by two great spirits, one a good spirit, often called by northern Algonquian-speaking Indians a Manitou, and the other an evil spirit known by the term "Windigo." The former spirit tended to be remote and abstract and not directly involved in affairs on earth. The latter tended to be down-to-earth, personalized, and directly involved in human affairs. The northern Indians,

59. Bowers, op. cit., pp. 172–174.
60. Alfonso Ortiz, The Tewa World: Space, Time, Being and Becoming in a Pueblo Society (Chicago, 1969), p. 25.

who lived in fear of occasional starvation, seemed to be more concerned with the power of the evil spirit than with the beneficence of the good spirit. The fear that the evil spirit would possess one was ever present, and its actuality, as expressed in dreams, had terrifying results. Despite the dramatic character of the "psychosis," as it might be termed in European-based psychiatric thinking, the number of individuals affected was small. Nevertheless, the existence of even one person affected by the evil spirit—which usually expressed itself in the form of an uncontrollable urge to consume human flesh—was a danger to the entire community, which usually met the challenge by condemning the unfortunate one to die. Death was often requested or welcomed by the one "possessed," whose craving was as repellent to himself as to the community which sought to save itself from his passion.

It is not an easy matter to decide what this Windigo "psychosis" was caused by and what it meant. There are many different theories, but analogies to the phenomenon of self-confessed witches in European and American society in colonial times can be made. The origin of the Windigo psychosis among the northern Algonquian-speaking Indians may similarly derive from a self-generated fear among some who lived in a harsh environment in which the possibility of defeat in the fight for survival added an obsessive anxiety to traditional factors of concern.[61]

The prevalence of the Windigo psychosis among northern Algonquian-speaking societies but not among many other societies is hard to explain in view of the fact that the impulse to cannibalism is not associated solely with those affected by the Windigo disorder. An explanation of the difference has been offered by a scholar, Thomas Hay, who points out two significant distinguishing features of northern Algonquian Windigo behavior. One is "the extraordinary importance attached to following one's dreams without consulting others." The other is "the absence of alternative patterns for displacing cannibal desires from members of the band or for expressing them symbolically." Comparison with Iroquois practices is instructive. The importance of dreams among the Iroquois was

61. Raymond D. Fogelson, "Psychological Theories of Windigo 'Psychosis' and a Preliminary Application of a Models Approach," in Context and Meaning in Cultural Anthropology, ed. Melford E. Spiro, in honor of A. Irving Hallowell (New York, 1965), pp. 74–99.

equally as important as among the northern Algonquians. But the Iroquois dream was under social control. The dreamer hinted at the nature of the dream and the tribal leaders then attempted to interpret it and decide what must be done to satisfy it. Similarly, the inclination to cannibalism among the Iroquois was institutionalized and displaced in the practice of cannibalism following success in war. For the northern Algonquians, on the other hand, "there were no institutionalized patterns for directing the cannibal impulses toward outsiders." Lacking such alternatives, the northern Algonquian often had to meet his inclination to eat human flesh by indulging his passion.[62]

An insight into the origins of Indian religious thought is provided in the Trickster figure, derived from a myth common among Indians, as indeed among the ancient Greeks, the Chinese, the Japanese, and in the African and Semitic worlds. Though often depicted in the form of an animal, as raven, coyote, hare, or spider, Trickster is of no fixed form. As Paul Radin, who studied the myth among the Siouan-speaking Winnebagos of central Wisconsin and eastern Nebraska, put it, Trickster is "primarily an inchoate being of undetermined proportions, a figure foreshadowing the shape of man." Trickster is both culture-hero and trickster, benefactor and buffoon, god and man. In the majority of Trickster myths, which are spoken narratives owned as property by talented individuals and passed by word of mouth from generation to generation, Trickster is seen as the creator of the world and bringer of culture. At the same time he is often unaware of ethical values, unconscious of the effects of his actions, and possessed of an enormous sexuality. The tales of his doings are outrageous in a Rabelaisian sense, and often inexplicable in a moral sense. Radin saw his divinity as secondary and as an accretion supplied by a priest-thinker to an original myth which, he asserted, "began with an account of a nondescript person obsessed by hunger, by an uncontrollable urge to wander and by sexuality." The Trickster embodies, Radin asserted, "the vague memories of an archaic and primordial past, where there as yet existed no clear-cut differentiation between the divine and the non-divine." The ribald tale of Trickster's progress

62. Thomas H. Hay, "The Windigo Psychosis: Psychodynamic, Cultural, and Social Factors in Aberrant Behavior," *American Anthropologist*, LXXIII (1971), 1–19, at 8 and 10.

can scarcely be matched in the rawest drugstore paperback sex novel of today. Yet mixed in with the cycle of salacious and scatological accounts of Trickster's unprincipled and irrational doings is frequently another cycle of events, that of the culture-hero or Transformer—Trickster in another form—who brings fire, flint, tobacco, or cultivated plants to the people, who regulates the seasons and the weather, and destroys monsters.[63]

Carl Jung, in commenting on the Trickster myths, has noted that even while "so-called civilized man" has forgotten the Trickster, inwardly civilized man is still a primitive, "profoundly disinclined to give up his beginnings," and can never forget or really give up the psychic reality expressed in the Trickster myth. "The trickster is a collective shadow figure, an epitome of all the inferior traits of character in individuals." The Indian, more attuned to the unconscious and undifferentiated in man than his more "civilized" brother, has created, and retained, in the Trickster myths a recognition of man's inner nature.[64]

The religious outlook of many Indian groups, as noted earlier, was strongly influenced by dreams. Indeed, a Jesuit missionary among the Senecas in the seventeenth century complained bitterly that

The Iroquois have, properly speaking, only a single Divinity—the dream. To it they render their submission, and follow all its orders with the utmost exactness.

Whatever they thought they had done in their dreams, they felt obliged to carry out in their waking hours. While other nations, the Jesuit noted, might follow those dreams they considered most important, "This people, which has the reputation of living more religiously than its neighbors, would think itself guilty of a great crime if it failed in its observance of a single dream." The Jesuits worried that their death might be contemplated by an Iroquois dream and labored mightily but unsuccessfully to destroy the Indians' confidence in dreams.[65]

Dreams among the Mohave Indians in the twentieth century, by

63. Radin, *op. cit.*, Prefatory note, x, pp. 124, 165–168.
64. C. G. Jung, "On the Psychology of the Trickster Figure," in Radin, *op. cit.*, pp. 206–209.
65. Wallace, *Death and Rebirth of the Seneca*, pp. 59–60.

contrast, found a sympathetic observer in a psychiatrically trained anthropologist, George Devereaux, who noted that the Mohaves derived their " 'theory of the universe' from the psychodynamics of dreams, instead of deriving a theory of dreams from a 'theory of the universe' based upon (supposedly) different types of data and considerations." The Mohaves, in effect, reversed the process of medieval Christians who formulated a conception of human nature in terms of "a theological *imagery* whose dream sources were deliberately denied," and instead developed "a theological imagery consciously correlated with dream experiences." The Mohaves were able to do so because of their ability to recognize and to understand the "logic of the unconscious" by which repressed urges and fantasies strove to express themselves. Thus, though the Mohaves believed that ghosts, witches, and non-Mohave individuals could cause illness and misfortune, they also believed that the psychosis was not "injected" by these external agents, but was a product of the interactions of these forces and the individual's psyche. Despite the Mohave Indian's " 'clinical' acumen and capacity for empathy" as well as his tendency to " 'psychologize' the universe," Mohave psychiatry, Devereaux concluded, is "still" methodologically "supernaturalistic" and thus "appears to represent a second step in the development of psychiatry."[66]

To the Indian, men, animals, and objects might be the possessors of powers beyond normal human comprehension. To the Blackfeet, for example, the horse—introduced to America by Europeans—was a gift to their people from sky and water spirits. In less than two centuries, anthropologist John Ewers noted, "The European horse became so completely integrated into the religious beliefs of these Indians that historically acceptable traditions of its first acquisition were lost."[67]

Indian religion, in sum, comprised a vast range of beliefs and practices explaining and prescribing man's relationship to some unknown or unknowable power that affected his life. Whether he

66. George Devereaux, *Mohave Ethnopsychiatry: The Psychic Disturbances of an Indian Tribe*, Smithsonian Institution, Bureau of American Ethnology, Bulletin 175 (Washington, 1961, reprinted 1969) , pp. 495–500.

67. John C. Ewers, "The White Man's Strongest Medicine," Missouri Historical Society, *Bulletin*, October 1967, pp. 36–46 at 37; see also John C. Ewers, *The Horse in Blackfoot Indian Culture*, Smithsonian Institution, Bureau of American Ethnology, Bulletin 159 (Washington, 1955) , pp. 291–298.

sought understanding and help from the supernatural powers inhabiting the universe as an individual, as did many of the hunters,
or through prescribed communal rituals, as did many of the agriculturalists, he almost invariably was a believer in some force outside
himself. Yet, at the same time, he often recognized, through dreams,
the unconscious forces within himself which seemed to link him
with the larger forces of the universe. His ability to empathize with
other humans and with nonhuman living creatures who seemed to
share the same life force provided the Indian with a coherent and
meaningful world view.

Games of challenge and games of chance throw light on the social
structure of many North American Indian tribes. Lacrosse, javelin
throwing, foot races, and various games of chance were absorbing to
the entire Iroquois community, for example, and reminded Lewis
Henry Morgan of the classical games of the Greeks and the Romans.
Indeed, to Morgan, the games, rather than serving an innate
competitive spirit, represented a humanistic concern which showed,
he believed, "that the American wilderness, which we have been
taught to pronounce a savage solitude until the white man entered
its orders, had long been vocal in its deepest seclusions, with the
gladness of happy human hearts."[68]

Games were an activity for which preparations and ritual similar
to those used in going to war were necessary. Indeed, in the Southeast, team games between towns were explicitly recognized as replacing warfare. Elaborate rites were performed in the days before
the game, including a ball dance the night before. Extensive wagers
were made on the outcome of the contest, which was begun after a
short harangue by one of the old men of the town. Play was
extremely rough, with players frequently put out of commission by
the opposing side. The same qualities of physical prowess, swiftness,
and intelligence admired in a warrior were admired in an Indian at
play.[69]

Among the Western mounted hunting tribes the character of
games varied somewhat from those in the East. Among the Chey-

68. Lewis H. Morgan, *The League of the Iroquois* (1851; reprint ed., New
York, 1962, with intro. by William N. Fenton) , pp. 291–312, especially 312.
69. John R. Swanton, *The Indians of the Southeastern United States*, Smithsonian Institution, Bureau of American Ethnology, Bulletin 137 (Washington,
1946) , pp. 674–686.

ennes, for example, horse races, foot races, wrestling matches, target shooting with guns or arrows, swimming, and jumping were often the object of competition between men representing the different warrior societies. If a band of Sioux happened to camp nearby, competition was often joined between representatives of the two tribes. Betting was an integral part of the procedure. Everything might be bet: guns, ammunition, bows and arrows, blankets, horses, robes, jewelry. The stakes were usually piled on a blanket, matched articles facing each other. The winners took all.[70]

Games of chance—usually involving the casting of some form of dice—were common among American Indian cultures, and were outgrowths of religious ceremonies in which divination—the desire to discover the probable course of future events—was the principal concern. Thus the Micmac bone dice game was played in a ceremonial bowl also used for divination. Incantations, exorcisms, fasting, sexual continence, and other ceremonial acts continued to be associated with the games even when their basic divinatory character had been lost. Although games of pure skill and calculation, such as chess, are asserted to have been absent among American Indians, it is important to remember that the player of traditional "dice" games considers that he is in fact engaging in a game of strategy in which he possesses the same ability to control the situation that the chess player has. Games of physical skill such as lacrosse involve a similar relationship between the player, a limited set of actions, and an "unambiguous symbol system" which capture the player and absorb him in a "state of monistic awareness."[71]

Games of chance and games of skill were, in summary, pervasive in aboriginal America. They were interwoven into the religious and kinship systems of the Indians and often inculcated warrior virtues.

Those who sympathize strongly with the wrongs suffered by the Indians at the hands of the white man often ignore or forget the fierce intertribal conflicts that characterized life in the present area of the United States before the arrival of the white man. Where tribes, bands, or individuals lacked true political organization,

70. Karen Daniels Petersen, *Howling Wolf: A Cheyenne Warrior's Graphic Interpretation of His People,* intro. by John C. Ewers (Palo Alto, Calif., 1968), p. 54.
71. Mihaly Csikszentmihalyi and Stith Bennett, "An Exploratory Model of Play," *American Anthropologist,* LXXIII (1971), 45–58, especially 47, 56.

anthropologists are reluctant to term the conflicts carried on among them true warfare, but violence did, nevertheless, exist. Murder seems to have been particularly prevalent in the Arctic region. One anthropologist discovered that every mature Eskimo man of thirty or older in a northern Canadian village he studied had killed at least one Eskimo man during his life. Far from suffering a stigma for such activities, a man's prestige was often raised by it. The principal cause of conflict in the Arctic was disputes over women. Such disputes also embittered the relationship between the Eskimos and their immediate neighbors to the south, the Athapascan Indians.[72]

Fighting over women, material possessions, or hunting rights extended to most of the other culture areas of North America, where other *casi belli* presented themselves. Plunder, adventure, and revenge were common causes of warfare throughout virtually the entire North American area. Prestige was a frequent motive, particularly among Indians of the Eastern Woodlands and the Plains and Plateau areas. Slaves were often the object of raids by Northwest Coast tribes. The enlargement of a tribe's physical boundaries was very rarely a motive in North America, though territorial conquest was not unknown. The sparseness of the Indian population of North America, combined with the vast resources of land and animals available for exploitation, made such European-style causes less necessary.

So central a concern of Indian life was warfare that among the most warlike—the Plains tribes—a graded set of war honors was established, participation in warlike activities was mandatory for any male desiring to be fully accepted into the tribe, and public recounting of one's deeds served to validate and disseminate the achievements of the participants. An action such as touching an enemy—a coup—without harming him but at the risk of one's life was often rated higher than killing or scalping an enemy. Horse stealing was another act of valor. Harold Driver has estimated that a hundred times as many horses were stolen on the Plains as were obtained in legitimate trade.[73]

To what extent were economic motives vital in precipitating Indian warfare? Driver has asserted, "In order to call the attention

72. Driver, *op. cit.,* pp. 310–311.
73. *Ibid.,* p. 323.

of the reader to the game aspect of war, the function of war as a ranker of men and creator of social solidarity within the political unit, and the religious functions of war, some anthropologists have disparaged the economic aspect." In fact, he maintains, the economic motive, even in the areas north of Mesoamerica, was strong and became stronger with the growing influence of European demands and values.[74] Although Indians gradually adopted white motives for making war, as they did white material culture, I believe that traditional motives—particularly prestige and revenge—dominated Indian belligerency throughout the period of Indian-white warfare.

74. *Ibid.*, p. 328.

CHAPTER 4

Indian-White Relations in the Context of Equality

THE first and most direct consequence of Indian-white contact was change in the material culture of the Indian tribes. That change was effected by trade and was built on aboriginal subsistence and intertribal trade patterns. Trade with the white man was initially supportive of—not destructive of—Indian life.

The material culture of the Indian at the time of white contact was closely related to traditional methods of obtaining his subsistence. The varying sources of that subsistence—buffalo, acorns, fish, corn, caribou, and the like—all required different techniques of gathering or capturing, with resultant differences in tools and technologies. Even within the same culture area—the Plains, for example—different tribes used different methods for taking the buffalo. Some used horses, some did not. Buffalo might be driven into a buffalo pound, driven off cliffs, encircled with fire, or surrounded by mounted hunters using bows and arrows. Similarly, fresh-water fish might be caught by the use of weirs, scooped up and clubbed, hooked, speared with wooden sticks, shot with arrows, or trapped in basketry traps.[1]

Because of the variety of natural resources and native talents in North America constant exchange took place among individuals and tribes both prior to and after the arrival of the white man. Harold E. Driver has concluded, "Probably every family in aborigi-

---

1. Robert H. Lowie, *Indians of the Plains* (Garden City, N.Y., 1963) , pp. 15–20.

nal North America exchanged something of value with another family at least a few times a year." Driver has also concluded that aboriginal trade was engaged in by all but one North American group or tribe: that group being the isolated Polar Eskimos "who thought they were the only people on earth when discovered by John Ross in 1818."[2] Trade contacts facilitated the diffusion of cultural traits outward from their source. Prized objects—natural or manufactured—were exchanged over vast distances and helped fashion a rough material unity despite the diversity of ethnic and cultural groups. Intertribal trade between the Southwest and the Plains prior to the arrival of the Spanish in 1540, for example, has been demonstrated by ethnohistorical and archaeological evidence showing the substitution of leather footgear for yucca fiber sandals in the Pueblo area, particularly in the Pueblo settlements in the upper Rio Grande area. The evidence suggests that a regular trade was carried on between the Rio Grande Pueblo villages and the Plains Indians in which buffalo hides and deerskins were exchanged for corn and blankets.[3]

Anthropologists have tried to set aboriginal trade in a structural model that recognizes the complex social, ceremonial, and psychological context within which the exchange of goods and services takes place. Indian trade should be studied with such a perspective. The phrases "gift and countergift," "more gift than barter," "ritual trading partner," and "ceremonial trade" that occur in the monographs on trade systems suggest the nonmaterial significance of trade among nonindustrial peoples. American Indian trade with neighboring tribes almost invariably took place in the context of ritual and ceremony. Navajo trading trips, for example, were usually timed to coincide with the ceremonies of those visited. Ritual trading partners were chosen and subsequent trading was in the form of an exchange of gifts. The trade between the Chilkat Tlingit Indians of Northwest British Columbia and the inland Athapascan Indians of the southern Yukon Territory reflected even more clearly the ceremonial aspects of the "trade." Games, dances, and even guest prostitution greeted the arrival of the Tlingits

2. Harold E. Driver, *Indians of North America*, 2d ed., rev. (Chicago, 1969), pp. 208, 211.
3. Bert Salwen, "The Introduction of Leather Footgear in the Pueblo Area," *Ethnohistory*, VII (1960), 206–238.

among the Athapascans.[4] The activities of buyers and sellers at these trading rendezvous have been compared to the activities of modern businessmen at a convention.[5]

Among the Huron Indians, trade visits to foreign tribes were akin to diplomatic visits, with speeches, feasts, and gifts preceding the actual exchange of goods. The Hurons refused to haggle, as they accused the French of doing. The profit motive was low in their priority of values. Nevertheless, the profits of the trade did enrich some individuals (those who had pioneered a particular trade had authority to exclude others from it) but without creating a gap between rich and poor because of the Indian sense of communal responsibility. No one must go hungry, not even the stranger visiting the Huron village. He who gained much in the trade gave much to honor the Huron ethic. He could not violate it with impunity.[6]

Anthropologists have defined three types of aboriginal reciprocal trade relationships: (1) generalized, or ostensibly altruistic "gift-giving"—characteristic of the family or inner group; (2) balanced reciprocity, or direct exchange—characteristic of more distant but still intratribal exchanges; and (3) negative reciprocity, or the attempt to maximize one's own economic advantage by haggling or even theft—characteristic of intertribal trade.[7]

Perhaps no more famous example of reciprocal exchange can be cited than the potlatches of the Northwest Coast. The term "potlatch" comes from Chinook jargon and means simply "to give." Earlier interpretations of the potlatch emphasized the destructive behavior of the participants (even to the killing of slaves) and the apparent paranoia of the participants over the possibility of being outdone in their generosity. More recent scholarship has distinguished between rivalry "gestures"—the presentation and destruction of a single item or lot of goods to embarrass, belittle, or offend some person—and rivalry "potlatches": meetings at which conflicting claims to the same specific right or set of rights were asserted. The function of the potlatch as a technique for social integration

4. Karl G. Heider, "Visiting Trade Institutions," *American Anthropologist,* LXXI (1969), 462–471. See also Marshall Sahlins, *Stone Age Economics* (Chicago, 1972).

5. Driver, *op. cit.,* p. 213.

6. Bruce G. Trigger, *The Hurons: Farmers of the North* (New York, 1969), pp. 38–41.

7. Heider, *op. cit.,* p. 462.

rather than as a socially disintegrative phenomenon has also received more attention in recent studies.[8]

The potlatch was a festival or feast given by one social unit, acting as host, to one or more guest groups. The host group displayed its hereditary possessions—which might include dances, songs, and carvings—and presented certain of its members as entitled to traditional ranks and privileges because of their inheritance of a new position, the birth of an heir, or the like. Gifts were distributed to the guests, who were thereby considered formal witnesses to the claims of the persons presented. The potlatch did not give, or create, social status, but confirmed or validated it. It might resolve conflicting claims of presumptive heirs, much as a court of law would do in white society. The potlatch also provided a substitute for physical violence among rival tribesmen and an emotional release for the participants.[9]

A recent study of potlatches among the Tlingits and Kwakiutls has demonstrated the close relationship between particular forms of potlatching and tribal social structure. Potlatches occur at "critical junctures which mark the rearrangement of the social structure, . . ." and are, in effect, *rites de passage* for the society. In Tlingit society there is a rule of marriage but no rule of succession. In Kwakiutl society, there is a fixed rule of succession but no rule governing the choice of spouse or group affiliation. Among the Tlingits, potlatches concern succession and occur at funerals. Among the Kwakiutls, potlatches occur at marriages or on occasions when the individual is initiated into a group, but not at funerals.[10]

Thus, while potlatching may incorporate elements of shaming, conspicuous consumption, redistribution of goods, and even megalomania envisaging destruction of one's enemies—elements which have formed the basis for earlier hypotheses about the meaning of the institution—the potlatch can now be seen more clearly as a way of reaffirming the structure of native society during periods of uncertainty and change. The guests who witness the ceremony validate the shift to a new stability, whether in the form of the

8. Philip Drucker and Robert F. Heizer, *To Make My Name Good: A Reexamination of the Southern Kwakiutl Potlatch* (Berkeley, Calif., 1967), pp. 8, 118–123, 133.

9. *Ibid.*, pp. 8, 133–134.

10. Abraham Rosman and Paula G. Rubel, "The Potlatch: A Structural Analysis," *American Anthropologist*, LXXII (1972), 658–671, especially 669.

succession of a new chief or the incorporation of an individual into a group.[11]

Although the frequency of potlatching increased after contact with white traders, when material wealth multiplied and positions were more often vacant or in dispute as the result of increasing mortality brought on by white diseases, the practice was eventually restricted by Canadian administrative regulations in the last quarter of the nineteenth century.[12]

Efficient as was the aboriginal Indian's utilization of his natural environment, both for direct exploitation and for purposes of trade with his neighbors, the introduction into the continent of European man, European animals, and European goods created a revolutionary change, sometimes in advance of the actual appearance of the white man. The anthropologist Leslie Spier recorded the reputed dream of an upper Chinook prophet—long before the appearance of the whites—in which he saw strange people and heard new songs. The prophet predicted the arrival of the whites and their marvelous possessions. Deward E. Walker, Jr., has pointed out the parallel between the Chinook prophet's prediction of the arrival of a new race with wonderful implements and the well-known "cargo cults" periodically reported among islanders of the Pacific Ocean. Undoubtedly, Indian observation of white material culture among other Indian tribes inspired such anticipations.[13]

The white man did in fact alter the environment—cultural and physical—in which the Indian lived. The more efficient, nature-dominating tools of the whites lessened the need to make an accommodation with nature. Directly, the white man brought war, trade, enslavement, and expulsion to many Indian groups. Indirectly, European tools and weapons gave the white man an advantage over the native in the competition for the animals of the forest and the fish of the rivers.

The utility of European firearms, metal knives and fishhooks, iron cooking pots, and similar tools was quickly recognized and these were eagerly sought after by the Indians. The common assumption that Indians, through their naïveté, were cheated by

11. *Ibid.*
12. Drucker and Heizer, *op. cit.*, pp. 26–27.
13. Deward E. Walker, Jr., "New Light on the Prophet Dance Controversy," *Ethnohistory*, XVI (1966), 245–255, especially 251–252.

unscrupulous white traders does not give an accurate picture of the exchange. The Indians valued the trader's commodities highly and were willing to exchange what was necessary to obtain them. Sometimes Indians then sold the newly acquired goods to other Indians at high "mark-ups."[14]

While less spectacularly revolutionary than metal tools, European dress was no less pervasive in its appeal. Lieutenant Henry Timberlake, in his *Memoirs* recounting his travels to and from the Cherokee country in the period 1756–1765, noted that the males wore a collar of wampum (beads cut out of clamshells), a silver breastplate, bracelets on their arms and wrists of the same metal, a bit of cloth over their private parts, a shirt of English make, "a sort of cloth-boots," moccasins ornamented with porcupine quills, and a large mantle or match-coat thrown over all. The women, he noted, wore their hair long and ornamented with ribbons of various colors, but the rest of their dress resembled that of the Europeans. The old people, Timberlake noted, "still remember and praise the ancient days, before they were acquainted with the whites, when they had but little dress, except a bit of skin about their middles, mockasons, a mantle of buffalo skin for the winter, and a lighter one of feathers for the summer."[15]

European trade goods acquired by Indians were not always used in the European way. Copper or brass thimbles were more frequently used as costume ornaments than for sewing, while mirrors were frequently used as signaling devices, particularly on the Great Plains. Glass beads were used not only for adornment, but for ceremonial purposes, as at treaty talks, and as grave furniture. Copper kettles were often cut up to make projectile points; sword blades and steel files were made into knives; and gun barrels were made into scrapers.[16]

Many trade items were designed specifically for, and received warmly by, the Indians. "An Iroquois man dressed in a linen breechcloth and calico shirt, with a woolen blanket over his shoul-

14. John C. Ewers, "The Influence of the Fur Trade upon the Indians of the Northern Plains," in *People and Pelts,* ed. Malvina Bolus (Winnipeg, 1972), p. 3.

15. Henry Timberlake, *Lieut. Henry Timberlake's Memoirs, 1756–1765,* ed. Samuel Cole Williams (Johnson City, Tenn., 1927), p. 77.

16. Kenneth E. Kidd, "European Trade Goods as Artifacts," draft of article for new edition of *Handbook of North American Indians,* in preparation, Smithsonian Institution, Washington, D.C.

ders, bedaubed with trade paint and adorned with trade armbands and earrings, carrying a steel knife, a steel hatchet, a clay pipe, and a rifled gun felt himself in no wise contaminated nor less an Indian than his stone-equipped great-great-grandfather."[17] Not all Indians, however, accepted or approved Indian utilization of the white man's culture—either material or political. "The Great Mortar," a Creek headman who was a constant thorn in the side of the English of South Carolina in the mid-eighteenth century, scorned a commission from any European, "even comparing an Indian with a Hat to a Mushroom," reported Edmund Atkin, the king's superintendent for Indian affairs in the southern colonies.[18] Nevertheless, the threat to withhold, or the promise to provide, trade goods was a powerful weapon in the hands of whites dealing with the Indians.

Many tribes prospered by virtue of finding themselves in a middle-man position. In the colonial Southeast, for example, the Catawbas and Occaneechis, occupying strategic positions in the Piedmont area between the coastal settlements of the English and the interior fastnesses of the Cherokees, at first prospered by virtue of the trade between the two groups, though their fate was eventually little different from that of the coastal nations crushed earlier by the English. English traders from Charleston and Virginia, at times licensed and at other times unlicensed, often resided with these Indians, and pack-horse trains of visiting traders were joyfully welcomed by the natives. The Catawbas and Occaneechis discouraged other Indians from attempting to make direct contact with the English. The Iroquois in the Northeast, in a similar manner, jealously guarded their trading role with the Dutch and later the English at Albany. With the guns obtained in trade—often illicitly—the trading Indians tyrannized those Indians lacking access to the refinements of civilization. By the late seventeenth century most of the hill tribes of the lower Appalachians had firearms. Yet the corrupting effect of the traders, often loose in their morals and unscrupulous in their dealings, hastened the destruction of the affected tribes. By encouraging the trade in Indian slaves, the traders induced wars among the red men. By bestowing their

17. Anthony F. C. Wallace, *The Death and Rebirth of the Seneca* (New York, 1970) , p. 25.
18. Atkin to William H. Lyttleton, Governor of South Carolina, Nov. 30, 1759, Lyttleton Papers, William L. Clements Library, Ann Arbor, Michigan.

powerful favors where they would be reciprocated, they sometimes altered the traditional social and political structure of the Indian communities to the detriment of the Indian community as a whole. By means of liquor and lust, they helped to debauch the morals of the tribe. The stresses and strains introduced by the English traders created, in the opinion of one scholar, the nativistic movements which underlay most of the conspiracies and wars on the southern colonial frontier in the late seventeenth and early eighteenth centuries.[19]

The European demand for fur to meet the needs of fashion and utility in Europe had profound effects on Indian life and social organization. In the long strip of Algonquian territory running down the east coast of North America, the beaver was the most highly prized fur-bearing animal. European demand for fur put an immediate premium on trapping the beaver. When Champlain visited the Penobscot Indians in 1604 the Penobscots welcomed him and invited French settlement in their country "in order that in future they might hunt the beaver more than they had ever done, and barter these beaver with us in exchange for things necessary for their usage."[20]

The effect of the European demand for furs was to make possible more permanent Indian settlements inland along the major rivers and to cause a decline in the number of seacoast settlements to which the Indians had been wont to resort when their economy was directed more fully to the fruits of the sea. In addition to encouraging movement inland, the European demand for furs helped to cause a formalization and elaboration of the Indian method of exploiting the fur-bearing environment. The extent to which the family hunting territories of the Algonquian Indians are of pre-Columbian origin and the extent to which they owe their development to the European fur trade is in dispute among scholars. The general view is that such family hunting territories—carefully delineated areas within which a particular family had exclusive authority to hunt—derive from European-induced consequences of trade and colonization. Such hunting territories were characterized

19. Charles M. Hudson, *The Catawba Nation* (Athens, Ga., 1970), pp. 32–33, 40.

20. Quoted in Dean R. Snow, "Wabanaki 'Family Hunting Territories,'" *American Anthropologist*, LXX (1968), 1143–1151, at 1149.

by a concept of land ownership by individuals or families, well-defined boundaries, restrictions on trespassing, right of the proprietor(s) to sell, lend, or otherwise dispose of the land, patrilineal inheritance and patrilocal residence.[21]

Although the exact character of the family hunting territories varied within the Northeastern Algonquian area it tended to have some or all of these characteristics. The fact that the family hunting territory focused on the most sedentary of the fur-bearing animals, the beaver, and was related to the abundance of the game rather than to any arbitrary territorial measure raises questions concerning the origin of this feature of Indian organization. Undoubtedly the beaver played a significant role in precontact Indian life but not the dominant role that emerged with the introduction of European demand and European techniques, like the steel trap, for taking the beaver. Indeed, the fact that the beaver is trapped rather than hunted gives the concept of a "hunting" territory a more sedentary, stable aspect. Also significant is the fact that the strength of individualized landholding patterns among the western Montagnais, in the words of Eleanor Leacock, "decreases not only northward toward the tundra where the Naskapi depend almost entirely upon the migratory caribou, but also *outward from the center of the earliest and most intense fur trade*." In Leacock's view, the essential element in the development of family hunting territories was the substitution of production for exchange in place of production for use, along with a shift from reliance upon migratory to sedentary animals.[22]

Leacock, and a majority of anthropologists who have considered the matter, see the gradual emergence of the concept of private property among the Indians as spurred by the introduction by Europeans of a capitalist economy. However, a minority of anthropologists think that European influences merely intensified and formalized the family hunting territories which, in their view, preexisted white contact. Dean Snow has pointed out that much of the discussion concerning hunting territories ignores the fact that many of the northeastern Algonquian tribes were localized in river valleys separated from one another and that their "territories" were more akin to paths up and down the river valley and its watershed

21. *Ibid.*, 1143; Driver, *op. cit.*, p. 275.
22. Quoted in Snow, *op. cit.*, 1145. Italics Leacock's.

than to blocks of land unrelated to this drainage pattern. The family hunting territory was perhaps as much a path or road as a territory. Moreover, the bounds of these territories were less sharply defined as the upper reaches of the rivershed were reached and the "borders" of a neighboring tribe in a different watershed approached.[23]

With the advent of European demand for furs, not only did a more precise localization of family territories develop as the wealth of the interior was more fully tapped, but the small hunting bands developed into more elaborate kin units and eventually, in the case of the Wabanakis of Maine, for example, coalesced in the formation of the Wabanaki Confederacy, modeled after the League of the Iroquois.[24]

With the introduction of efficient trapping methods and the lure of European trade goods "beaver trapping became the ladder by which the Indian could climb to a higher living standard, and also equip himself for defense from neighbouring tribes already armed with guns." As a result, the beaver was exterminated in area after area, which in turn spurred on the search for new sources of beaver. It was in this fashion that "the map of Canada was unrolled—slowly at first, then faster following the British takeover in 1763."[25]

The destruction wrought by the white hunters and traders and their Indian clients has perhaps been underestimated by white historians because of what one has called "the conquistador mentality that has so long dominated the writing of much American history." By killing off, or causing to be killed off, certain forms of wildlife, the white man forced the Indian to alter his pattern of living. In its most destructive form, the trading activity of the white caused starvation. In its least destructive it reshaped the social organization of the tribes and altered their economic subsistence patterns. Yet because the fur trader has always achieved a romantic image in the works of historians—particularly the followers of Frederick Jackson

23. Snow, *op. cit.*, 1150.
24. *Ibid.*
25. Eric W. Morse, *The Exploration of Canada: Some Geographical Considerations*, The James Ford Bell Lectures, Number 9 (Minneapolis, 1971) , p. 6; Robin F. Wells, "Castoreum and Steel Traps in Eastern North America," *American Anthropologist*, LXXIV (1972) , 479–483. The intimate relationship between the exploration of Canada and the search for furs and fur trade routes was convincingly made by Harold Innis in his *The Fur Trade in Canada* (1930) and has not been successfully contradicted.

Turner—the destructive impact of his work, and particularly the
ecological hazards he engendered, have gone largely unnoticed.[26]

The vital significance to the Indian of articles of European origin
is most dramatically illustrated by the effects of the acquisition of
the horse and the gun by tribes of the Great Basin and Plateau
areas of the West. The great intermountain area was the principal
channel of trade and communication between white men and
Indians in the area. Contact with Spanish culture in the Southwest
influenced most notably the Shoshoni-Comanche group who were
probably a united group in 1700, when both were on the northern
borderlands of Spanish settlement in the Southwest. Later in the
century, the Shoshonis separated from the Comanches and pushed
north, bringing with them culture traits suggestive of Spanish
influence. Most important of these acquisitions was the horse.
Stealing or trading horses from the Spaniards, the Shoshonis were
the agents for spreading horse culture farther north. The Comanches, too, were able to move out onto the Plains and adopt High
Plains culture patterns by means of the horse. Yet many of the close
linguistic relatives of both the Shoshonis and Comanches (for
example, the southern Paiutes) remained poor Great Basin
gatherers.

The Nez Perces got horses from the Shoshonis about 1730, before
many of the Plains Indians received them. Lewis and Clark reported the presence among the Shoshonis of large amounts of
Spanish goods as well as horses and mules having Spanish brands.
The northern Shoshonis also greeted Lewis and Clark, who brought
Sacajawea, their long-lost cousin, with the Spanish *abrazo* (embrace).[27]

About 1730 the Blackfoot Indians were attacked by their traditional rivals, the Shoshonis. In this attack the Shoshonis rode horses
and scattered their brave enemies. The Blackfeet, alarmed, sought
help from the friendly Crees and Assiniboins, who supplied them

26. Wilbur R. Jacobs, "Frontiersmen, Fur Traders, and other Varmints: An
Ecological Appraisal of the Frontier in American History," American Historical
Association, *AHA Newsletter*, VIII (1970), 5–11, quoted portion at p. 7.
27. Thomas R. Garth, "The Plateau Whipping Complex and Its Relationship
to Plateau-Southwest Contacts," *Ethnohistory*, XII (1965), 141–170, at 148;
Alvin M. Josephy, Jr., *The Indian Heritage of America* (New York, 1968),
p. 119.

with another secret weapon: ten firearms which could kill a man at a distance. The next meeting with the Shoshonis—in which both parties were on foot—resulted in the Shoshonis fleeing in disorder under the deadly fire of the new weapons. The several Blackfoot tribes soon acquired both firearms and horses and began their career of dominance on the northern Plains.[28]

When white traders finally came among the Blackfeet they were at first treated with friendship and respect. Gradually, however, in the last decade of the eighteenth century and first decade of the nineteenth, disagreements and disputes arose. During the Lewis and Clark Expedition, a fight occurred between some Piegans (one of three Blackfoot tribes) and Lewis's company. One Indian was killed. The movement of traders and explorers thereafter was fraught with danger.[29]

The geographic proximity of some tribes to the source of European trade goods was an advantage understood and utilized by the Plains Indians. The strategic position of the Blackfoot Indians between their enemies and the source of Canadian trade goods, for example, was carefully defended by the former. As early as 1795 the Kutenais tried to induce the Blackfeet, with presents of horses, to let them visit Fort George on the Saskatchewan to trade. The Blackfeet refused, fearful that their superior position would be jeopardized should the Kutenais obtain firearms from the white traders. The approach of American traders from the south, following the route blazed by Lewis and Clark in 1804–1805, however, provided an alternate source of trade goods for the enemies of the Blackfeet, a source that the Flatheads and Shoshonis were quick to utilize. Blackfoot reaction included attacks on individual American traders and attempts to block Canadian traders from penetrating beyond their traditional outlets.[30]

After terrorizing small parties of American trappers for years the Blackfeet came to an accommodation in the winter of 1830–1831 with Kenneth McKenzie, a Scot long engaged in the Canadian fur trade who had entered the service of the American Fur Company. McKenzie established peaceful relations with the Blackfeet by

28. John C. Ewers, *The Blackfeet: Raiders on the Northwestern Plains* (Norman, Okla., 1958) , pp. 21–22.
29. *Ibid.*, pp. 49–50.
30. *Ibid.*, pp. 51–56.

adopting the Canadian system of allowing the Indians themselves to collect the furs and barter them for trade goods at the posts of his company. The policy of the Blackfeet was clearly expressed to Major Sanford, Indian agent for the upper Missouri tribes: "If you will send Traders into our Country we will protect them & treat them well; but for Trappers—Never." Trade was established, though precariously, with the construction of a trading post in the Blackfoot country in 1831.[31]

The early trade in the upper Missouri was normally carried out in terms of native gift exchange. The trader was a guest in the village. Often he was embarrassed by being expected to validate his high status (for the things he brought were powerful "medicine") by generosity. Some, like Antoine Tabeau, a trader to the Arikaras in the early nineteenth century, refused to comply with native customs.

I made few presents beyond the ordinary and I even aspired to free myself from making them to villages that had nothing to offer in return. I refused to establish in my lodge a public smoking-room, an abuse consecrated by its age and expensive as it is tiresome. I did not pay back invitations with feasts, still less the dishes brought with interested designs. I did not keep twenty persons in the lodge of my host and I did not divide my daily fare with twenty parasites.

Eating alone behind a locked door, Tabeau was characterized as a miser, a hard man, and a glutton but, he asserted, his behavior was eventually accepted. From Tabeau's point of view, the Indians' failure to grasp "our ideas of interest and acquisition beyond what is necessary" led them to act outrageously. Specifically, their principle "that he who has divides with him who has not" made a mockery of the white man's trade.[32]

With the invention of the silk hat in the 1830s, the demand for beaver declined. Increasingly, however, buffalo robes supplanted beaver pelts as the principal article of trade, and American traders, utilizing the broad Missouri and Mississippi rivers, obtained an advantage over their British rivals of the Hudson's Bay Company

31. *Ibid.*, p. 57; John C. Ewers, "Folk Art in the Fur Trade of the Upper Missouri," *Prologue: The Journal of the National Archives*, IV (1972) , 99–108.

32. Quoted in Preston Holder, "The Fur Trade as Seen from the Indian Point of View," in *The Frontier Re-examined*, ed. John Francis McDermott (Urbana, Ill., 1967) , p. 134.

who had to transport their furs by lightweight canoes that could be carried over the necessary portages between northern watercourses.[33]

By the 1850s, the Blackfoot tribes, who had by that time been trading for three-quarters of a century with the whites, had become "completely dependent upon the traders for many articles which they now considered necessities, such as guns and ammunition, metal tools, and utensils." Indians born in the 1850s could not remember the use of stone arrowheads by their tribe, nor did they know how they were made. Iron arrow points, of which several dozen could be obtained in exchange for a single dressed buffalo skin, had made the laboriously chipped stone arrow point outmoded. Similarly, metal kettles, unbreakable and serviceable, replaced the fragile pottery vessels formerly made by the Indians. Dependence upon such necessities bound the Indian in an intimate and often vulnerable relationship with the white man.[34]

To sum up, the trade relationships which the Indians of North America developed with the white settlers were an extension of preexisting trade relationships among themselves. There was nothing inherently evil or corrupting about the material culture that was obtained from this new source (with the exception of certain dietary innovations such as distilled liquors, which will be discussed in another place). Horses, guns, metal tools, European cloth, and many other products were eagerly sought by the Indians and rapidly replaced less efficient traditional equivalents. The meeting of two contrasting economic systems caused adaptation on both sides: Europeans adapted themselves to the diplomatic, gift-giving nature of Indian trading habits; Indians came increasingly under the influence of European concepts of price as a function of scarcity and began to savor the attractions of individual material income in a money economy in contrast to the traditional psychic income of a sharing or barter economy. Some natives and some scholars have mourned the loss of traditional practices and virtues caused by the introduction of new goods, but the process was inexorable because it was welcomed, rather than resisted, by most. Those critical of the trade have often identified undesirable change in Indian society with the objects introduced rather than with the will of the persons

33. Ewers, *The Blackfeet*, p. 64.
34. *Ibid.*, p. 70.

desiring the objects. Others have overlooked the fact that some Indian groups, such as the Plains warriors, achieved their greatest power and fame as a direct consequence of such trade.

Late in 1608, Captain Christopher Newport returned from London to Virginia for the second time bringing instructions from the royal council for Virginia to crown the Indian leader Powhatan with a copper crown sent from England and to present him with a red woolen robe and an English bedstead. The hope was to cement relations between the English and the Indians by proclaiming Powhatan a subject-king under the overlordship of James I of England. The precise meaning of the "coronation" of Powhatan was less certain in the eyes of the Indians and of the English in the colony. Captain John Smith was reluctant to accord Powhatan the dignity such a coronation was bound to confer. He suggested that Powhatan be invited to Jamestown to receive his "presents." Newport agreed and Smith attempted to induce the Indian emperor to come to Jamestown for the purpose, not mentioning the coronation ordered by the council. Powhatan's response reflected the recognition of his dignity which Smith was hoping to overcome:

If your King has sent me presents, I also am a King, and this is my land. Eight days I will stay [here] to receive them. Your father [Newport] is to come to me, not I to him; nor yet to your fort. Neither will I bite at such a bait.

Powhatan prevailed. Newport made the wearisome journey and presented the bed and other furniture plus a scarlet cloak, which Powhatan put on only reluctantly, and finally the copper crown, which the English attempted to force on Powhatan's head. The Indian king, however, refused to bow his head and it was only with difficulty that the "coronation" was accomplished. The English believed they had achieved a symbolic recognition of Powhatan's dependence. To Powhatan, on the other hand, a few interesting but odd gifts had been received from a fellow sovereign.[35]

The "coronation" of Powhatan epitomizes the character of early political negotiation between Indians and whites in English America. First of all, it formally acknowledged both the military power and legal existence of the Indians. Second, it demonstrated

35. Philip Barbour, *Pocahontas and Her World* (Boston, 1970), pp. 36–42.

an inclination to circumvent and circumscribe that acknowledgment as time and opportunity might allow. If these attitudes can be called principles, it can be asserted that both principles were pursued throughout the course of English (and American) dealings with the Indians of North America. Even after the military power of the Indians was broken, their legal political existence as distinct political bodies, at least for particular purposes, continued.

The status of the Indian nations was determined not only by the power they could bring to bear against those who sought to change that status, but also by the legal status accorded them by the white nations with which they were in contact. What that status was and how it changed is complicated and subject to dispute. What are accurately described as the "speculative grants" of the European powers, by which the latter asserted absolute sovereignty over territories of unknown dimensions peopled by unknown numbers of unknown peoples, are customarily taken to represent the prevailing legal assumption of the period and to imply that Europeans felt no need to acknowledge native rights to land discovered by Europeans. Because these speculative grants were later realized in fact, undue emphasis has been given to their exaggerated claims. Nevertheless, it is inaccurate to assert that Europeans unhesitatingly assumed that their claims possessed either legal or moral validity, either against other European powers or against the native Americans.[36]

Indian nations were recognized in fact as independent powers, to be dealt with as other powers were dealt with: by the arts of war and peace in order to obtain food, shelter, and land. Increasingly in theory, however, whites made a distinction between the rights of the European rulers to "dominion" over the lands claimed by them in America, and the "possessory rights" of the Indians to the lands actually occupied by them. As European power waxed and Indian power waned, Europeans were able to delimit the areas and the privileges held by the native occupants of the soil and to maintain and expand the rights and privileges of the European sovereigns and their agents.[37]

36. Wilcomb E. Washburn, *Red Man's Land/White Man's Law: A Study of the Past and Present Status of the American Indian* (New York, 1971), pp. 1–46.
37. John Thomas Juricek, "English Claims in North America to 1660: A Study in Legal and Constitutional History" (Ph.D. diss., University of Chicago, 1970).

Students of the subject as diverse as Thomas Jefferson and Felix Cohen have agreed that most of the lands acquired from the native inhabitants of the present area of the United States were acquired by purchase from their original possessors. However, the details of this monetary recognition of Indian landholding rights are subject to dispute. The early history of Virginia is marked with periods in which perpetual war was declared on the Indians and no recognition of their ownership of the land, or even of their right to exist, was accorded. There was no agreement in theory or practice in seventeenth-century America on the nature of the Indians' right to the lands they occupied or claimed.[38]

Both the Pilgrims at Plymouth in 1620 and the Puritans in Massachusetts Bay in 1630 stepped into physical areas that seemed to have been "providentially" cleared of their Indian inhabitants by a guiding hand. Reasoning from Biblical precedent and the law of nature, New England leaders denied the right of the Indians to assert hegemony over lands that they did not occupy. The critical question was how to define the word "occupy." The Puritans chose to interpret the word in terms of a settled agricultural people and to deny Indians ownership of areas over which they merely hunted or fished. Not that the Puritans applied such severe standards to themselves. They eagerly asserted dominion over "vacant" lands in anticipation of their own future use of those lands, whether or not they occupied them in the strict sense required of their Indian fellow inhabitants.

Although it has customarily been believed that the early New England settlers respected the rights of the Indians and purchased land from them, Francis Jennings has asserted that this was not, in fact, the case, until 1633. He can locate no bona fide deed preceding that year. He asserts, moreover, that the only reason the Indians' right to convey the land they occupied was acknowledged then was in response to three challenges. One was the Dutch move up the Connecticut Valley and purchase, on June 8, 1633, from the grand sachem of the Pequot Indians, of land for a trading post near the present site of Hartford, Connecticut. The validity of such Indian

38. Washburn, *Red Man's Land*, pp. 109–110; Wilcomb E. Washburn, *Virginia Under Charles I and Cromwell, 1625–1660*, Jamestown 350th Anniversary Historical Booklets, Number 7 (Williamsburg, 1957); Wilcomb E. Washburn, *The Governor and the Rebel: A History of Bacon's Rebellion in Virginia* (Chapel Hill, N.C., 1957).

conveyances could best be countered—in the absence of Dutch willingness to recognize English sovereignty over the area—by obtaining similar grants from other Indians. Second, Roger Williams, the stormy petrel of Massachusetts, in 1633 wrote a treatise denying that a royal patent could convey lawful possession of the American soil. The magistrates of Boston saw to it that Williams's challenge to the validity of the king's patent and his additional challenge to the magistrates' authority over the town of Salem were refuted. Nevertheless, Williams had thrown a scare into the leaders of the colony, who thereafter took pains to acquire Indian title when they could in fact do so, even while denying fundamental Indian rights in theory. Finally, in 1641, Governor John Winthrop of the Massachusetts Bay Colony, in a title dispute in the Narragansett Bay country, found it expedient to support the authority of conveyances of land by Indians in the area to *some* Englishmen against conveyances obtained by *other* Englishmen less kindly disposed to the Bay Colony.

For all these reasons, according to Jennings, the presumed virtue of New England in purchasing the land acquired in its early years cannot be sustained. Jennings's analysis is challenged by another historian, Alden Vaughan, who asserts that the absence of deeds showing land purchases from the Massachusetts Indians prior to 1633 does not prove that such purchases were not made, but only that English-style written deeds were not considered necessary—until the events of 1633—to formalize the purchase.[39]

Jennings's criticisms of Puritan treatment of the Indians echo those of the commissioners chosen by Charles II to accompany the fleet sent to conquer New Netherlands in 1664. The commissioners also examined New England's treatment of the Indians. In the course of this examination they considered Massachusetts's law regarding Indian tenure, which cited Psalm 115, verse 16: "The heaven, even the heavens, are the LORD'S: but the earth hath he given to the children of men." The commissioners commented acidly: " 'Children of men' comprehends Indians as well as English; and no doubt the country is theirs till they give it or sell it, though it be not improved." The commissioners, in considering a tract of

39. Francis Jennings, "Virgin Land and Savage People," *American Quarterly,* XXIII (1971), 519–541; personal conversation with Alden T. Vaughan, Columbia University.

land called Misquamicut, claimed by Massachusetts by conquest of the Pequots, noted that the land had been conquered from the Pequots by the Narragansetts several years before the Pequot War and that "no colony hath any just right to dispose of any lands conquered from the natives, unles both the cause of the conquest be just and the land lye within the bounds which the king by his charter hath given it, nor yet to exercise any authority beyond those bounds." The commissioners declared void all grants made by "the usurped authority called the United Colonyes."[40]

While the Crown had to enforce a more liberal policy in New England, in Pennsylvania the founder—William Penn—acknowledged the Indian right in the land from the beginning. Penn's policy has been expressed in graphic form in the various representations of his initial treaty with the Indians, often, as in the paintings of William Hicks, showing that the lamb can lie down with the lion and still live to tell the tale. So long as Pennsylvania's policy was suffused by the spirit of the Society of Friends and controlled by the hand of the proprietor, Indian-white relations existed on a plane of equality and mutual respect. The relationship demonstrated that accommodation between the two races was possible so long as there was enough land for all *and* goodwill on both sides. Such a spirit did last until eroded by the pressures brought on by the Great War for Empire between the French and the English in the eighteenth century, by the influx of non-Quaker colonists, by the spread of settlement into the interior, and by the loss of proprietary control by Penn's successors. Penn's successful Indian relations depended upon his recognition of the Indian as the true owner of the soil, whose right had to be acquired fairly despite the king's apparent disposal of the soil without reference to the native inhabitants in his royal charters and grants to proprietary lords.

Penn summarized his legal case thus:

Whosoever buyeth any thing of the true Owner, becomes rightful Owner of that which he bought; and that the Indians are true Lords of the Soil, there are 2 Reasons; 1st because the Place was never conquer'd. 2dly That

40. *Records of the Governor and Company of the Massachusetts Bay in New England,* ed. Nathaniel E. Shurtleff, 5 vols. (Boston, 1853–1854), IV, pt. 2, 176, 213; *The Colonial Laws of Massachusetts: Reprinted from the Edition of 1660, with the Supplements to 1672,* ed. William H. Whitmore (Boston, 1889), p. 160. Quotations expanded and modernized.

the Kings of England have alwaies commanded the English to purchase the Land of the Natives . . . which it is supposed they would never have done, to the prejudice of their own Title, if the Right of the Soil had been in them, and not in the Natives.[41]

The period of Indian-white equality did not depend primarily upon white recognition of that equality, however. It was based first of all upon the power of the Indians to maintain that equality. No Indian nation demonstrated the capacity to maintain its equal status better than the Six Nations, or Iroquois Confederacy, south of Lake Ontario. Both in the period of Dutch rule at New Amsterdam and at Albany following the colony's conquest by the Duke of York in 1664 the Iroquois Confederacy possessed the requisite power and political organization to command respect from all interested European governments. While European nations occasionally asserted a proprietary interest over Iroquois lands and actions, the assertion was rarely to the faces of the Indians and when it was it was rejected by them. The relationship between the Iroquois and the Europeans was in the form of agreements or understandings which shifted in character and varied from formal alliances against other European or Indian foes to more informal arrangements—usually designated by the term "covenant chain"— by which the policies of the two peoples were coordinated and the peace maintained.[42]

When the Iroquois went to negotiate a treaty with the French in 1684, they pointedly rejected the English argument that they were subjects of the King of England and the Duke of York. They were, they asserted, "brethren." "We must take care of our selves," they pointed out. During the negotiations with the French, the Iroquois also set the latter straight when they talked of the Iroquois country

41. William Penn's Instructions to Captain Markham respecting Lord Baltimore, *ca.* 1683, MS., Cadwalader Collection, Historical Society of Pennsylvania, quoted in part in Francis Jennings, "Glory, Death, and Transfiguration: The Susquehannock Indians in the Seventeenth Century," American Philosophical Society, *Proceedings,* CXII (1968) , 15–53, at 46. Jennings notes: "This is an extraordinarily important document which seems to have been overlooked in historical discussions of Indian land transactions." The portion quoted is from a draft of Jennings's forthcoming volume tentatively entitled "The Invasion of America: Myths and Strategies of English Colonialism in the Conquest of the Indians," chap. 19, footnote 24.

42. Francis Jennings, "The Constitutional Evolution of the Covenant Chain," American Philosophical Society, *Proceedings,* CXV (1971) , 88–96.

as though it belonged to the King of France. Garangula (or Otreouti), an Onondaga chief, asserted that the Iroquois had permitted both the French and the English to come to their country to trade but asserted pointedly:

We are born free, We neither depend upon Yonnondio [New France] nor Corlaer [New York]. We may go where we please, and carry with us whom we please, and buy and sell what we please. If your Allies be your Slaves, use them as such. Command them to receive no other but your People.

When chided by the English later for making peace with the French, the Iroquois asserted that they made it with the left hand while "the covenant chain with your Excellency [Dongan] has always been kept in our right hand fast and firm."[43]

One of the forms in which negotiations were carried on between Indians and whites was by exchange of gifts. Freely offered gifts, or tribute, represented a pledge, an agreement, and a symbol of political relationship between two peoples. It did not necessarily imply subjection by one party to the other; merely the acknowledgment of a relationship which was, often, that of a more powerful to a less powerful nation. That relationship involved obligations on both sides, usually protection by the more powerful party against attacks on the weaker by a third party, while the weaker might concede certain rights, such as aid in war or free passage through its territories, to the other. Often a more powerful nation, such as the United States, paid tribute to a weaker nation in order to facilitate its purposes in the territory of the latter.

Presents from Indians to whites often represented substantial economic sums to colonial governments, as well as serving to cement diplomatic alliances. Governor Sir Nathaniel Johnson of the colony of South Carolina bitterly complained when the Commons House of the Assembly in 1706–1708 attempted to supplant him and his council in the regulation of the Indian trade. One of the consequences of such a shift in control would have been that Indian presents would have gone to the public treasury rather than to the governor. Johnson noted that Indian presents were the only considerable source of his income, implying that they exceeded his £200 sterling annual salary. The Commons House, despite the governor's

43. Jennings, unpublished MS. cited in footnote 41, chap. 19, pp. 19–20.

opposition, passed a bill authorizing commissioners appointed by the Commons to regulate the trade; however, they provided a £200 annual grant to the governor in lieu of the presents he customarily received from the friendly tribes.[44] Generous gifts cemented relationships; inadequate gifts caused alliances to disintegrate. Indian support in wartime—indispensable in the American forests—often depended upon the skill with which one or the other European power had previously taken care of its Indian friends. Even the conspiracy of Pontiac has been attributed "to a surprising degree" to "the lack of presents after 1763."[45]

When the generosity of one colony toward one tribe exceeded that of another toward a different tribe trouble was often the result. In 1747 the South Carolina Assembly, which had been appropriating about £1,500 a year in presents to the Indians surrounding the colony, asked the king to defray the expense in the future. Three thousand pounds were thereupon provided annually by the English government to be distributed in presents to the Indians adjoining the two colonies of South Carolina and Georgia. The plan to allow Georgia to distribute one-half the presents was bitterly resented by South Carolina, which pointed out that it was in contact with a great number of the Indian nations while Georgia had relations primarily with the Creeks. The effect of the unequal distribution of presents (the Creeks received half the presents received in 1749, for example) was to give the Creeks an advantage over their traditional enemies, the Cherokees, who, with the other Indian nations adjacent to South Carolina, were not so well supplied. The Creeks were thus, in the years following, better armed than their Cherokee rivals. The power supplied to the Creeks combined with the jealousy created in the minds of the Cherokees may well have stimulated the warfare that broke out between the two nations and which in turn led to border clashes between white settlers and the Cherokees.[46]

So aggrieved did the Cherokees feel that they sent delegations to the Virginia government in the spring of 1751 complaining of the arming of their enemies the Creeks and of the niggardliness of

44. M. Eugene Sirmans, *Colonial South Carolina: A Political History, 1663–1763* (Chapel Hill, N.C., 1966), pp. 90–94.

45. Wilbur R. Jacobs, *Wilderness Politics and Indian Gifts: The Northern Colonial Frontier, 1748–1763* (1950; reprint ed., Lincoln, Neb., 1966), p. 12.

46. *Ibid.*, p. 36.

South Carolina; to meet their needs they requested that traders from Virginia be sent among them. The Virginia Council responded favorably to the request and presented £200 to the Indians as a gift out of which a handsome present was to be made to the Cherokee "Emperor" resident at Choate, one of the principal Cherokee towns. South Carolina, suffering from frontier attacks by Cherokees of the Lower Towns, complained bitterly. Relations between the two colonies continued to be strained over "Cherokee policy" for many years.[47]

Farquhar Bethune, the English representative to the Choctaws during the American Revolution, expressed it well when he said:

Reason and Rhetoric will fall to the Ground unless supported by Strouds and Duffells. Liberality is alone with Indians true Eloquence without which Demosthenes & Cicero, or the more modern orators Burk and Barre might harangue in vain.[48]

In a period when the Indian nations felt equal in dignity and power to the white colonial governments, gifts—mutually exchanged—provided the political cement that linked the two races in a common interest. The Indians expected what the whites had in abundance: European tools, weapons, clothes, food, and drink. They gave what they had in abundance: furs, hospitality, information, and brave fighting men in time of war.

A traditional method of extending European control over the unconquered natives was by building forts in the Indian country. The building of such forts was not always resisted. Sometimes it was allowed willingly, at other times grudgingly. At times, it was begged or demanded. The Cherokees, subject to the incursion of the "French Indians" from the north in the eighteenth century, repeatedly asked the governor of South Carolina to build a fort in their country to intimidate their enemies. Governor James Glen alternately promised to build the fort (which his Assembly was reluctant to finance) and threatened the Cherokees with not build-

47. *Ibid.* See also Lawrence H. Gipson, *The British Empire before the American Revolution*, Vol. IV: *Zones of International Friction: North America, South of the Great Lakes Region, 1748–1754* (New York, 1939), 63–73.

48. Bethune to Alexander Cameron, Aug. 27, 1780, quoted in James H. O'Donnell, III, "The Southern Indians in the War of Independence, 1775–1783" (Ph.D. diss., Duke University, 1963), p. 240. The quotation, in slightly revised form, appears in the published version of the thesis, *Southern Indians in the American Revolution* (Knoxville, Tenn., 1973), p. 101.

ing it unless they were more cooperative. The geopolitical significance of such a fort was well understood by Glen. In a letter to the Board of Trade, July 15, 1750, the governor asserted that a fort in the Cherokee country "would not only prove a Bridle in the Mouths of Our Indians, but would really attach them more Firmly to Us, and would soon attrack all the Indians on this part of the Continent into Our Alliance, and instead of finding them chargeable by Presents they might easily in a little time be made Tributaries, by obliging each Town in every Nation to pay an Annual Acknowledgment of a few Skins for their Protection." In a time when the king provided several thousand pounds' sterling worth annually of Indian presents, the implications of reversing the tribute flow were not entirely ceremonial.[49]

A fort, named Fort Loudoun, was built in the Cherokee country in 1756 under the direction of the military engineer William Gerard De Brahm. Many years later, in 1795, in order to refute the charge that the Cherokees had ceded away an extensive portion of their territory, De Brahm, as "the only one who remains of those that officially know of this matter," declared that the Cherokees ceded to the Crown of England in 1756 "700 acres only, and no more," for a fort and garrison to defend the Cherokee nation against the Shawnees.[50]

The forts which Europeans built close to, and sometimes in the midst of, Indian country were elements in the complex diplomatic game played by all the contending parties in the New World. Often they were a bridle to prevent Indian attacks on the settlers; sometimes they were designed to assist Indian allies against hostile Indians or Europeans. Whatever their initial purpose, they introduced military power in the midst of the Indian country, overawed the increasingly outnumbered Indians, and provided a legal basis for ever-escalating European claims to sovereignty over the interior.[51]

49. Public Record Office, London, C. O. 5/385, fol. 23.

50. Letter "To the President of the United States," printed in the March 12, 1795 edition of the *Georgia Gazette*, quoted in William Gerard De Brahm, *De Brahm's Report of the General Survey in the Southern District of North America*, ed. Louis De Vorsey, Jr. (Columbia, S.C., 1971), pp. 265–266.

51. For an account of the establishment of nineteenth-century forts see Francis Paul Prucha, *Broadax and Bayonet: The Role of the United States Army in the Development of the Northwest, 1815–1860* (1953; reprint ed., Lincoln, Neb., 1967).

While gifts of practical value were highly esteemed by Indians, gifts of political significance were valued even more highly. One of the principal examples of such political gifts was the Indian peace medal, an engraved or struck medal which European powers, and the United States, in its turn, presented to heads of various Indian nations with which they came into contact. Similar in purpose to the formal commission or certificate given to friendly Indian leaders, the medal, which normally depicted the image of the head of state, had much greater significance among the illiterate tribesmen than did its literary counterpart. Of what symbolic and practical meaning were these medals? Thomas Jefferson, in answering Spanish charges that the United States was aggressively giving medals to Indian nations in the Spanish sphere of influence in the region of Florida in 1793, pleaded "ancient custom from time immemorial" as practiced by both England and Spain. "The medals," he asserted, "are considered as complimentary things, as marks of friendship to those who come to see us, or who do us good offices, conciliatory of their good will toward us, and not designed to produce a contrary disposition towards others." "They confer no power," Jefferson went on, "and seem to have taken their origin in the European practice, of giving medals or other marks of friendship to the negotiators of treaties and other diplomatic characters, or visitors of distinction."[52]

Jefferson's professions of innocent intent were more diplomatic than just. The medals were in fact designed to suggest a commitment ranging from formal allegiance on the one hand to informal inclination on the other. Nowhere is this more clear than in the area west of the Mississippi following the Louisiana Purchase. Lewis and Clark, on their great expedition, carried eighty-seven silver medals of four sizes to be given to chiefs of varying importance on the trip. The medals were given out with appropriate ceremony and speeches. The first presentation took place on August 3, 1804, at Council Bluffs, to a group of Oto and Missouri chiefs. Lewis and Clark informed the Indians that the "great chief of the Seventeen great nations of America" had replaced the French and the Spanish in the territory west of the Mississippi and had adopted them all as his children. They had been sent, the American explained, "to clear

52. Francis Paul Prucha, *Indian Peace Medals in American History* (Madison, Wisc., 1971), p. 8.

the road, remove every obstruction, and to make the road of peace"
between the United States and the Indians. A flag, medal, and some
clothes were to be presented, Lewis and Clark explained, and
"when you accept his flag and medal, you accept therewith his hand
of friendship, which will never be withdrawn from your nation as
long as you continue to follow the councils which he may command
his chiefs to give you, and shut your ears to the councils of Bad
birds." The American emissaries made it plain that the Indians
should not wear or keep the flags and medals they had received
formerly from the French and Spanish, since it would not be pleas-
ing to their new great father that they continue to wear those
"emblems of attachment" to any other great father. Upon the
response of the chiefs, Lewis and Clark presented a "Medal of
Second Grade" to one of the Otos and to one of the Missouris and
medals of the third grade to two inferior chiefs of each of the tribes.
Even in this first encounter, Clark spoke of giving medals to those
"we *made* Chiefs," though the implication was not clear to the
Indians themselves.[53]

The extensive use of peace medals by Lewis and Clark (their
supply was nearly exhausted on their return) was undoubtedly one
of the principal reasons their expedition through 2,000 miles of
uncharted continent succeeded so well. The proffer of this important symbol was understood and honored by the natives, who would
hardly have reacted as they did without such a gesture.

Zebulon Montgomery Pike, in his march to the source of the
Mississippi in 1805, found a constant demand among the Indians
for the recognition accorded by the medals. Pike not only lacked
American medals to distribute but discovered that British fur-
trading companies were presenting British medals and flags to the
Indian chiefs of the area. Pike enforced a promise from the British
agent to cease such activities and made an agreement with the Sioux
to turn in their British medals and flags, informing them in the
process that "traders have no authority to make chiefs; . . . It is
only great chiefs, appointed by your fathers, who have that authority." The Chippewas also promised to give up their English medals
but, as one of their chiefs (Obequette) noted, "If I have received a
medal from the English traders, it was not as a mark of rank or
distinction, *as I considered it,* but merely because I made good

53. *Ibid.,* pp. 17–18.

hunts and payed my debts." Pike's promises to supply American medals in the place of the English medals could not be quickly fulfilled and, in Pike's words, left a number of the Sioux and Chippewa chiefs "without their distinguishing marks of dignity" and caused them to question his honor and the faith of the government. A few replacements were made before the War of 1812 but many were not replaced until late in the 1820s when they could overcome the legacy of bitterness only with the greatest difficulty.[54]

The role of the white man in "making" tribal leaders is nowhere more evident than in the actions of Governor Lewis Cass of the Territory of Michigan and Thomas McKenney during the negotiations leading to the Treaty of Butte des Morts on the Fox River near Green Bay, August 11, 1827, which concerned the boundaries between the Chippewas, Winnebagos, Menominees, and the New York Indians. On the first day of the council, Governor Cass told the Menominees of the difficulties the Americans had experienced in dealing with them because of the fact that there seemed to be "no one to whom we can talk as the head of the nation." The Menominees, he noted, "appear to us like a flock of geese without a leader." He would, he asserted, on the opening of the council the following day, "appoint a principal chief for the Menomonies." Inquiries would be made to find a suitable person. Then, "We shall give him the medal and expect the Menomonie nation to respect him as the head man." A principal chief and a secondary chief were subsequently selected and medals and robes bestowed upon them.[55]

Though implying subordination in the American mind, the presentation and acceptance of medals were seen by the Indians as a mark of recognition of authority for the individual Indian involved, particularly in the necessary negotiations with the white man. While often forced upon the Indians, as by Cass, they were more often demanded by the Indians themselves. To the Indian mind, Thomas L. McKenney, head of the Indian Office, noted, medals were "tokens of Friendship," "badges of power," and "trophies of renown." "They will not consent to part from this ancient *right,* as they esteem it," he warned.[56]

Peace medals, however bizarre they may seem to us today, helped

54. *Ibid.,* pp. 25–32.
55. *Ibid.,* p. 47.
56. *Ibid.,* pp. 103–104. Italics McKenney's.

facilitate the adjustment between white man and red in the vast territories west of the Mississippi, usually to the white man's advantage. They provided the diplomatic, or political, dimension to what might otherwise have been a totally unregulated exploitation of the red man by the white. They helped to clarify relationships and minimize misunderstandings between the races, and thereby to reduce the number of incidents that might have led to violence and bloodshed.

An important but little utilized political relationship between Indians and whites was intermarriage. Such a course was urged upon the first Virginia colonists by the Indians but discountenanced by the zealous ministers of the colony. The few exceptions authorized were quite explicitly political matches: the Pócahontas-John Rolfe match was approved by the government of Virginia not because it was an ideal love match, but because it offered practical advantages of both a defensive and offensive nature to the colony. The most perceptive observers of the Virginia scene, including William Byrd, Robert Beverly the historian, and Thomas Jefferson, felt such an amalgamation to be advantageous to both races and to the peace of the country and regretted that it had not been officially encouraged.

The Iroquois in the North chided the French Jesuit priests who came among them with the plea: "If you love, as you say you do, our souls, love our bodies also, and let us be henceforth but one nation." The French *coureurs de bois* acted on this advice and achieved closer bonds of friendship with the native inhabitants of America than did the English.[57]

In retrospect it is easy to see that a great opportunity was lost when extensive intermarriage between whites and Indians—particularly on a political level—did not take place. Given the basic, if sometimes grudging, admiration of the white man for the Indian and the ultimate national approval of the goal of assimilation of the Indian into white society, it is unfortunate that the mechanism to achieve such an end was not put into operation at an earlier date. Many wars and much bitterness might have been avoided, and the nation strengthened morally and physically.

Some Indian nations maintained their independence by moving

57. Quoted in Wallace, *Death and Rebirth of the Seneca*, p. 43.

physically from place to place and in and out of alliances with other nations. No tribe illustrates this phenomenon better than the fiercely independent Kickapoos. The name of the tribe derives from the Algonquian word meaning "he moves about," and the Kickapoos moved at various times, in response to different pressures, from and to Wisconsin, Illinois, Indiana, Ohio, Michigan, New York, Pennsylvania, eastern Iowa, Missouri, Kansas, Oklahoma, Texas, and northern Mexico. In their incursions against the southeastern Indians they penetrated also into the area south of the Tennessee River.

When the French first encountered the Kickapoos in the seventeenth century in the Great Lakes area they found them receptive to French blandishments, unlike many of their Algonquian brothers. When the French began to supply the Sioux (and the Dutch and English the Iroquois) with arms and ammunition in exchange for furs, the Kickapoos found themselves pressed between two hostile forces whose capacity to destroy them had increased immeasurably. The Kickapoos suffered several massacres at the hands of their powerful neighbors. They fled to the forests around Green Bay. Allying themselves with the Fox and Mascouten Indians they formed a confederacy which, late in the seventeenth century, was respected and feared by Sioux and Iroquois alike. In their raids against both and against the French trading parties who supplied the Sioux with guns, they provided an effective example of guerrilla warfare in the interior. Their rejection of Catholicism and their hatred of the French were legendary. Yet the bitter opposition of the Kickapoos to the French was suddenly turned around in 1729 with the exchange of a French party they had captured for women and children of their own who had been captured by the French. With the exchange, effected by an understanding Jesuit Father— Michel Guignas, one of those captured by the Kickapoos—the Kickapoos reversed their position of hostility to the French and began to assist them against their former allies, the Fox, the Chickasaws, and other enemies of the French in the New World in the eighteenth century.[58]

The Kickapoos provide perhaps the best example of an Indian nation constantly on the move. A more famous example, however, is

58. Arrell M. Gibson, *The Kickapoos: Lords of the Middle Border* (Norman, Okla., 1963), pp. 1–22.

the Tuscarora nation, which after being defeated by North Carolina in the Tuscarora War of 1711–1712 moved north to become a
part of the Iroquois Confederacy. Thereafter the Five Nations were
called the Six Nations.

The ability of some Indian tribes to move from place to place (as
demonstrated by the Kickapoos and Tuscaroras) enabled them to
preserve their equality with the white man longer than they might
have been able to do had they been rooted in one spot. At the same
time, the ability of Indian tribes to make alliances with white men
against Indians, and with Indians against white men, with little
concern about the racial identity of their allies, provided another
element of flexibility in the Indian response to white expansion.

A logical extension of the practice of sending explorers, em-
bassies, commissioners, or other representatives of English or American governments on periodic visits to Indian nations was the
provision for official representatives to be stationed permanently
among them. While some white traders had from the earliest times
made their permanent homes among the Indians, marrying Indian
women and, as did James Adair among the Chickasaws in the mid-
eighteenth century, occasionally undertaking official missions for
colonial governors, the idea of a permanent political representative
resident among the Indians was of later origin. Until resident
agents became the norm most of the negotiations between the
independent Indian nations and European and American governments were carried on by commissioners designated for the task.
When the structure of "Superintendents of Indian Affairs" for the
Northern Department and the Southern Department of North
America was created in the mid-eighteenth century, the superintendents, Sir William Johnson in the North and Edmund Atkin in the
South, became responsible for carrying on many of the negotiations
with Indian nations in their areas, although by no means all.
Johnson was outstandingly successful in the new role. Appointed by
Governor George Clinton in 1746 as commissary of the stores and
provisions for England's Iroquois allies engaged in warfare with the
French and Indian enemies of the English, Johnson was instructed
to reside with the Mohawks. (Earlier commissioners had merely
made brief visits to the Indians from their Albany or New York
homes.) One hundred miles from the conjunction of the Mohawk
and Hudson rivers, on the present site of Johnstown, New York,

William Johnson built a fortified house close to the Mohawk Indians. At "Mount Johnson," or Johnson Hall, in the building completed in 1750, Johnson dispensed gifts and advice to visiting Indian delegates, effectively cementing a relationship of friendship between the colony and the Iroquois Confederacy. Johnson's house —located neither in the established European settlements nor in the midst of an Indian community—marks a midpoint in the evolution toward a resident agent living side by side with the Indians. No such physical proximity was achieved by Atkin, the southern superintendent, who traveled throughout the Southeast convening Indians in large congresses at various sites.[59]

Following the American Revolution, the United States increasingly saw the value of resident agents among the Indian tribes. The desirability of such a representative was noted by Secretary of War Henry Knox in 1792. Knox was particularly anxious to discover the true feelings of the Creek leader, Alexander McGillivray, toward the United States. Earlier approaches to the Creeks had been "external only," and United States actions toward the Creeks had been based on false or imperfect information. Knox believed that if men of talent and integrity were once established among the Indians, "They would possess the opportunity, and most probably the power, of regulating events as they should arise." With the knowledge gained of the chiefs would develop "the proper modes of managing them." United States agent Benjamin Hawkins was to provide the eyes and ears among the Creeks envisaged by Secretary Knox.[60]

Despite the growing number of resident agents to the Indian tribes in the nineteenth century, special commissioners for particular negotiations continued to be appointed. Often the commissioners were generals and territorial governors who had direct responsibility for, and knowledge of, Indian affairs in their jurisdictions. Negotiations were usually carried on in the home territory of the Indians, but occasionally such meetings took place in Washington, New York, or Philadelphia.

Contrary to popular assumptions, such negotiations were often conducted on a high intellectual plane. When United States Com-

59. Jacobs, *Wilderness Politics*, pp. 79–80.
60. *American State Papers . . . Indian Affairs*, 2 vols. (Washington, 1832–1834), I, 259–260.

missioners Duncan G. Campbell and James Meriwether attempted in 1823 to convince the Cherokees to relinquish their land in Georgia, they asked the council of the Cherokee nation to consider this:

The State of Georgia, in 1810, contained 242,433 inhabitants; in 1820, 344,773; showing an increase in ten years of 92,340; and yet the present settlements of Georgia do not very greatly exceed the Cherokee nation in extent, which contains about 12,000 inhabitants. This difference is too great ever to have been intended by the Great Father of the Universe, who must have given the earth *equally* to be the inheritance of his white and red children.

The Cherokee council, in responding to this letter, retorted:

We do not know the intention of the *Supreme Father* in this particular, but it is evident that this principle has never been observed or respected by nations or by individuals. If your assertion be a correct idea of His intentions, why do the laws of civilized and enlightened nations allow a man to monopolize more land than he can cultivate, to the exclusion of others?

The council communicated "the fixed and unalterable determination of this nation never again to cede *one foot* more of land."

The formal, written negotiation with "a government regularly organized, composed of Indians," for the extinguishment of the Indian title to the lands they possessed within the state of Georgia was "probably a novel procedure," Commissioner Campbell reported to Secretary of War John C. Calhoun. Yet, Campbell noted, this method of negotiating was preferred on both sides.[61]

The principal method of negotiation between whites and Indians was by treaty. The treaty process was maintained until 1871 when Congress undertook to legislate directly for the tribes. The change was precipitated by the growing irritation of the House of Representatives at being unable to "advise and consent" to Indian treaties as the Senate was constitutionally able to do. The House, which had to initiate all revenue bills, attached a rider to the annual Indian appropriations bill, announcing the change in policy. The Senate was thereafter forced to concede a greater measure of responsibility in Indian matters to the other house. Treaties have sometimes been regarded as legalistic anachronisms or

61. *Ibid.*, II, 462–464, 468–469. Italics in correspondence.

meaningless exercises imposed by a more powerful people on weaker peoples. In fact, however, they represented, more often than not, the bargain struck by two autonomous forces who weighed carefully the advantages accruing to each from the agreement. While a preponderance of power was increasingly on the side of the whites, often this power was potential, or local, and the advantages of avoiding its costly use by extending satisfactory treaty terms to Indian adversaries were apparent. From the Indian point of view the treaties made with the United States often provided positive advantages such as security guarantees, annuity payments, and promises of nonaggression in return for the surrender of some of the Indians' vast landed estate.

In general, treaties with Indians may be divided into several major categories: treaties of peace and friendship, treaties acknowledging United States sovereignty, treaties of cession, treaties of removal, and treaties of allotment. In some cases treaties provided for more than one of these purposes. Some treaties were negotiated with the Indians on a basis of equality; some were dictated to no longer powerful tribes. Some treaties followed a successful war; others an unsuccessful war.[62]

Treaty negotiations had a style of their own, full of symbols the meaning of which provides a fascinating study in psychology, communications, and mnemonics. One of the most famous symbols was the peace pipe, which was smoked by those in attendance as a symbol of the reconciliation achieved by the negotiations. Lieutenant Henry Timberlake, in his negotiations with the Cherokee leader Ostenaco during the Cherokee War of 1761–1762, was one of many white men who solemnly accommodated himself to the requirements of the custom. "The ceremony I could have waved," Timberlake noted later in his *Memoirs,* "as smoaking was always very disagreeable to me; but as it was a token of their amity, and they might be offended if I did not comply, I put on the best face I was able, though I dared not even wipe the end of the pipe that came out of their mouths; which, considering their paint and dirtiness, are not of the most ragoutant, as the French term it."[63]

62. G. E. E. Lindquist, "Indian Treaty Making," *Chronicles of Oklahoma,* XXVI, No. 4 (Winter 1948–1949) , 416–448; Cyrus Thomas, article on "Treaties" in Frederick Webb Hodge, ed., *Handbook of American Indians North of Mexico,* 2 vols. (Washington, 1907–1910) , II, 803–814.

63. Timberlake, *op. cit.,* pp. 60–61.

Wampum, woven into belts, provided another symbolic system of certifying and communicating agreements reached with the white man. Wampum, derived from certain types of seashells, was gathered along the entire east coast of the United States but the richest concentrations, particularly of the quahog clam which produced the most desirable purple wampum, came from Long Island at Gardiner and Oyster bays and from Narragansett Bay in New England. The shells were drilled through from opposite ends with metal drills and strung together or woven into belts. The Iroquois, who became the most famous users of wampum belts, seem to have obtained wampum from their neighbors the Mahican or River Indians who had access to the coast. There is no evidence of true wampum in upstate New York among the Iroquois before 1600. However, the Iroquois brought to a high point the technique of utilizing such belts during treaty talks with the whites. The belts helped to objectify the metaphors which provided both the substance and poetry of treaty talks. An oval figure represented a tribal council fire; a square or parallelogram a town or nation; a white line a path; a row of linked diamonds the chain of friendship; and the tree of peace the League of the Iroquois. Men with and without hats represented whites and Indians. The native orators manipulated these symbols and called forth a responsive use of them by the European governors with whom the Iroquois dealt.[64]

Indian eloquence was so frequently noted by white observers as to need little comment. A doctoral dissertation on the subject of Iroquois "persuasive speaking," based on an examination of 258 speeches by Iroquois at treaty councils between 1678 and 1776, concluded that Iroquois rhetorical skills were close to those recommended by the classical writers of antiquity, though no direct influence is to be ascribed to this source. Although utilizing the traditional appeals based on *ethos, pathos,* and *logos,* the Iroquois, the study concludes, gave "primary emphasis" to ethical proof—that is, establishing their goodwill and probity by argument and tactful usages—employed "a considerable amount" of pathetic proof—that is, by appeals to the emotions for sympathy—and "relied but little" on logical arguments. The logical arguments utilized by the Iro-

64. William N. Fenton, "The New York State Wampum Collection: The Case for the Integrity of Cultural Treasures," American Philosophical Society, *Proceedings*, CXV (1971), 437–461.

quois were directed to expediency and self-interest. Only one moral
or humanitarian premise—that of universal brotherhood—was used
as a basis of logical argument. The homely images for which Indian
orators were famous were drawn from their close observation of the
natural environment, the animals of the forest, and their fellow
Indians with whom they rubbed shoulders almost constantly in the
communally organized longhouses. The Iroquois child grew up, in
fact, hearing orators and storytellers speak at close range and with
great frequency. The most apt students became the orators of following generations.[65]

White negotiators, when they realized their opportunity, strove
consciously to break down Indian self-respect and confidence. James
Duane, a member of the Committee on Indian Affairs of the Continental Congress in 1784, advised the governor of New York prior to
the treaty talks with the Iroquois at Fort Stanwix to deny their
expectations of equal status and to treat them instead as inferiors.
Alluding to the century-long practice of conducting Indian negotiations in terms of Indian rhetoric and ritual, Duane urged: "Instead
of conforming to Indian political behavior We should force them to
adopt ours—dispense with belts, etc."

I would never suffer the word "Nation" or "Six Nations," or "Confed-
erates," or "Council Fire at Onondago" or any other form which would
revive or seem to confirm their former ideas of independence, to escape
. . . [Duane went on]; they are used to be called Brethren, Sachems &
Warriors of the Six Nations. I hope it will never be repeated. It is sufficient
to make them sensible that they are spoken to without complimenting
twenty or thirty Mohawks as a nation, and a few more Tuscaroras &
Onondagas as distinct nations . . . they should rather be taught . . . that
the public opinion of their importance has long since ceased.[66]

Too frequently treaties were negotiated with one portion of a
tribe and rejected by another portion. With the signatures of some
Indians on the document, American negotiators usually discounted
the opposition of the nonsigners. A typical example was the action
of a Kickapoo band of about 250 warriors under Chief Mecina

65. Wynn Robert Reynolds, "Persuasive Speaking of the Iroquois Indians at
Treaty Councils, 1678–1776: A Study of Techniques as Evidenced in the Official
Transcripts of the Interpreters' Translations" (Ph.D. diss., Columbia University,
1957) , pp. 3, 326–332.
66. Quoted in Wallace, *Death and Rebirth of the Seneca*, p. 197. Duane's
philosophy was implemented at the Treaty of Fort Stanwix.

which refused to abide by the Treaty of Edwardsville, signed on July 30, 1819, by which most of the Kickapoos agreed to exchange their tribal lands in Illinois for new lands on the Osage River in Missouri. Chief Mecina vigorously denied that any of the tribal lands and the resting place of "the bones of their ancestors" could be signed away by a portion of the tribe. Mecina's braves refused to move and continued to harass the white settlers who came into the ceded area.[67]

Another Kickapoo leader, Kennekuk, who claimed supernatural powers, led about 259 followers into an exile on the Vermillion River, where he preached his doctrine that the Indians must abandon their native superstitions, live virtuously, avoid whiskey and quarrels, and abide by the white man's law. Should they so do they would at last inherit the earth, clear of enemies. The peaceful, assimilative nature of Kennekuk's message won support among the local white population. For fifteen years Kennekuk avoided compliance with the treaties of Edwardsville and Fort Harrison (July 30, 1819, and August 30, 1819), by which the Kickapoos agreed to remove to Missouri from their tribal lands in Illinois and Indiana. The contrasting courses of action followed by the two Kickapoo leaders, Mecina and Kennekuk, illustrate the opposite paths which equally talented and spirited Indian leaders might follow. The Indians' misfortune was that, under the enormous pressure of the white advance, few of their options were permanently viable.[68]

Some treaties were honorably negotiated; some were imposed. Increasingly throughout the nineteenth century, prior to the abolition of the treaty-making process in 1871, treaties were imposed. An example is the treaty with the Osages of 1808. Peter Chouteau, the American commissioner appointed to negotiate treaties with the tribes of the area, assembled the chiefs and warriors of the Great and Little Osages in council and explained the substance of the treaty he had been instructed by Governor Meriwether Lewis of Louisiana Territory to offer to them.

Having briefly explained to them the purpose of the treaty, he addressed them to this effect, in my hearing [that of George C. Sibley, factor at Fort Osage], and very nearly in the following words: "You have heard this treaty explained to you. Those who now come forward and sign it, shall

67. Gibson, *op. cit.*, pp. 80–86.
68. *Ibid.*, pp. 88–91.

be considered friends of the United States and treated accordingly. Those who refuse to come forward and sign it shall be considered enemies of the United States and treated accordingly." The Osages replied in substance, "that if their great American father wanted a part of their land he must have it, that he was strong and powerful, they were poor and pitiful, what could they do? he had demanded their land and had thought proper to offer them something in return for it. They had no choice, they must either sign the treaty or be declared enemies of the United States."[69]

During the rapid movement west across the Great Plains and Rocky Mountains in the 1840s and 1850s, treaties were often made, often modified, often ignored, and often broken. The Treaty of Fort Laramie of September 17, 1851, with the Cheyennes, Arapahos, Crows, Assiniboins, Gros-Ventres, Mandans, and Arickaras, for example, set boundaries between the tribes and authorized roads and military posts within their territories in consideration of a grant of $50,000 a year for fifty years. The Indians did not surrender, however, the right of "hunting, fishing or passing over" any of the tracts of land described in the treaty. Despite the treaty, much of the land of the Cheyenne and Arapaho nations was overrun and occupied when gold and silver were discovered in the mountains of Colorado. The Senate, in ratifying the treaty, moreover, struck out the term of fifty years and substituted ten for it, although authorizing the President to continue the annuities for five years longer if he saw fit. Even after the Cheyennes and Arapahos were prevailed upon to accept a smaller reservation along the Arkansas River near Fort Lyon by the Treaty of Fort Wise, Kansas, on February 18, 1861, they were not for long left in peaceable possession. War broke out in 1864–1865. After the expenditure of $30 million, the destruction of many border settlements, and the withdrawal of 8,000 troops from duty in the South fighting the rebellion, the Indian war was finally settled by another treaty in October, 1865, calling for the removal of the Cheyennes and Arapahos from Colorado to a reservation partly in southern Kansas and partly in the Indian Territory. The Senate, in ratifying the treaty, emasculated it by insisting that the President designate a reservation outside the state of Kansas and not within any Indian reservation except with the consent of the tribes concerned. Despite the Senate's amendment,

69. Quoted in Laurence F. Schmeckebier, *The Office of Indian Affairs: Its History, Activities and Organization* (Baltimore, 1927), pp. 59–60.

the treaty brought the bitter war immediately to a halt. "What 8,000 troops had failed to give, this simple agreement, rendered nugatory by the Senate, and bearing nothing but a pledge of friendship, obtained."[70]

Treaties were, in sum, the principal legal link between the Indian nations and the white governments with which they dealt. Indian treaties, by definition, implied a contractual relationship between two autonomous parties. As the power balance shifted away from the Indians and toward the whites, the equality of the contracting parties became more formal than real, and in 1871 the form was abandoned altogether. The student of Indian-white relations must guard against the assumption that, because the treaty system was eventually abandoned, it reflected only insincerity or play-acting on the part of the whites. Indeed, agreements, such as the Great Sioux Agreement of 1889 (25 Stat. 888), negotiated after the end of treaty making, have been held to be legally binding in much the same way that earlier treaties are still binding.[71] The sanctity of treaties was recognized by whites as well as by Indians at the time they were made. Unfortunately for the Indians, their power to uphold by force the sanctity of the treaties they had made with the whites was insufficient to prevent later generations of whites from ignoring the treaties when it proved in their interest to do so.

Testimony is well nigh universal of the healthy physique of the Indian prior to extensive contact with the whites. William Gerard De Brahm, Surveyor-General for the Southern District of North America in the late eighteenth century, noted that in his frequent travels throughout the Indian nations of the Southeast, he had "never met with an Indian who was born a Cripple, but observed them to be all well made, tall and robust, neither very lean, nor inclining to Fatness, of the latter, he saw in all, only three, two Men and one Woman, all three Creeks, who were corpulent." He even reported that an Indian, running on foot, kept up with him for three hours while he kept his horse at a constant gallop. De

70. Report of Indian Peace Commission to President Andrew Johnson, Jan. 7, 1868, in *Annual Report of the Commissioner of Indian Affairs for 1868*, pp. 26–50, at 36.

71. Vine Deloria, Jr., ed., *Of Utmost Good Faith* (San Francisco, 1971), pp. 52, 63.

Brahm was one of countless observers who commented upon the physical well-being of the Indians met by the early explorers and settlers.[72]

The virtually unanimous ascription of fine health and sound bodies to the American Indian populations met by Europeans may seem to be belied by the historically documented fact that Indians, such as those New England Indians taken prisoner in King Philip's War, sickened and died under conditions of prolonged and heavy labor in the plantations and cane fields of tropical America. By contrast, imported African slaves survived and multiplied under a regimen that destroyed Indians. Commentators have tended to explain this phenomenon in cultural terms by ascribing a passionate love of freedom, or a will to self-destruction under the restraints of slavery, to the Indian. However, it is possible that the physiological superiority of melanization (the development of a black tinge to the skin as in African and other truly equatorial peoples) over keratinization (the development of a yellowish tinge as in the Mongoloids of Asia and the Americas) in tropical areas may account for the ability of the one group to withstand extensive exposure to solar ultraviolet light resulting in excessive doses of vitamin D and the inability of the other group to do the same. There is no agreement on this question, however. It is of interest that the only exception to the correlation between latitude and skin color in the Old World is the Eskimo. While most northern peoples have developed light skins to admit as much of the infrequently appearing sunlight as possible and thereby to prevent rickets, the Eskimo diet—rich in fish oil and meat high in vitamin D (the "sunshine" vitamin)—has made it unnecessary in all probability for the Eskimo to evolve a white skin.[73]

Despite the apparent good health of the Indian population of America, no influence brought by Europeans was more destructive than European diseases against which the Indians had no or little immunity. Why were the Indians without immunity to the European diseases brought by the first settlers? T. Dale Stewart has pointed out that the isolation of the American Indians, and the

72. De Brahm, *op. cit.,* p. 108.
73. W. Farnsworth Loomis, "Skin-Pigment Regulation of Vitamin-D Biosynthesis in Man," *Science,* CLVII (1967) , 501–506. See also Gabriel W. Lasker, "Human Biological Adaptability," *Science,* CLXVI (1969) , 1480–1486.

existence of a "cold screen" in the Bering Strait area whence they had entered the Americas, served to hold back the most virulent disease germs. As a result, Stewart observed, "A handful of Spaniards and one Negro with smallpox conquered Mexico."[74]

The effect of epidemics brought by the white man—smallpox was the worst—was catastrophic and nearly universal. New England's coastal areas were cleared "providentially" by such epidemics—probably introduced by early explorers or fishermen—prior to the arrival of the Plymouth settlers in 1620 and the Massachusetts Bay settlers in 1630. Bruce Trigger has estimated that both the Huron Confederacy and the Iroquois Confederacy lost over half their populations in the 1630s and 1640s as a result of epidemics. Both numbered, according to Trigger, approximately 18,000 to 20,000 prior to those epidemics. Interior populations as well as coastal populations, especially in the Southeast, were also decimated judging from the decline in cultural complexity evident in the archaeological records and judging from the accounts of De Soto's expeditions in the 1540s in comparison with those of later centuries.[75]

The effect of the smallpox epidemic of 1781 among the Piegan tribe of Blackfoot Indians was typical of such catastrophes. More than half the people died. The disease was caught in the course of a raid on a Shoshoni camp all of whose inhabitants were found dead or dying. The association of the plague with whites was frequently, as in this case, not made. During a later epidemic, that of 1837, several passengers on a keelboat bound for Fort McKenzie with supplies and goods for the Blackfoot trade came down with the disease. Alexander Culbertson, in charge of Fort McKenzie, when he learned of the situation, tried to forbid the further progress of the boat until the cold weather set in. His Blackfoot clients, however,

74. T. Dale Stewart, "A Physical Anthropologist's View of the Peopling of the New World," *Southwestern Journal of Anthropology*, XVI (1960) , 259–273; T. Dale Stewart, "Biological and Medical Conditions of Human Freedom," in *The Concept of Freedom in Anthropology*, ed. David Bidney (The Hague, 1963) , pp. 35–48, at 47; T. Dale Stewart, *The People of America* (New York, 1973) , pp. 19, 37. The reference is to an infected Negro who accompanied Pánfilo de Narváez (a rival of Cortés) from Cuba to the mainland in 1519. See also Alfred W. Crosby, Jr., *The Columbian Exchange: Biological and Cultural Consequences of 1492* (Westport, Conn., 1972) , pp. 35–63.

75. Trigger, *op. cit.*, pp. 12, 16; personal conversation with William C. Sturtevant, Smithsonian Institution, Washington, D.C.

refused to listen to his warnings and threatened to bring the boat to the fort themselves if he would not do so. He thereupon allowed the boat to come, trade ensued, and ten days after leaving the fort the Indians were decimated again. Two-thirds of the 6,000 Blackfeet succumbed. Unlike the Mandans farther down the Missouri River, who were hardest hit, the Blackfoot survivors did not blame the whites for the event.[76]

Anthropologist John Ewers has expressed his conviction that epidemics of white men's diseases "were more numerous and wreaked more havoc with Indian population and culture than scholars have demonstrated to date." His list of epidemics among the Blackfeet, who experienced smallpox in 1781, 1837–1838, 1849–1850, and 1869–1870, scarlet fever in 1837, and measles in 1864–1865, is not, he believes, complete. Yet the impact of those epidemics, in addition to reducing the population, very probably altered marriage taboos, affected the status of medicine men, and increased concern with health, magic, and the like.[77]

The cholera epidemic of 1849 rapidly communicated itself from the port cities of New York and New Orleans across the mountains and up the rivers to St. Louis, where thousands of gold seekers brought it to the Plains along the Oregon Trail. The Indians received the disease along the Platte River and passed it to others beyond them. Captain Howard Stansbury, surveying a new route to Salt Lake, came up the Platte River in July, 1849, and found dead and dying individuals in almost every Sioux village he encountered. The agent for the Pawnees estimated in June, 1849, that 1,200 Pawnees had died of the disease. Fear induced the Pawnees to scatter in all directions and to refuse to bury their dead. When smallpox ravaged the Sioux in 1850 they blamed the epidemic on white magic designed to further their extermination.[78]

American Indians, while well adjusted physically to the environment in which they had developed over thousands of years, became victims of the physical isolation to which they fell heir. European disease germs brought across the Atlantic decimated the Indian

76. Ewers, *The Blackfeet,* pp. 65–66.

77. Ewers, "Influence of the Fur Trade," in Bolus, *op. cit.,* p. 20.

78. Robert Anthony Trennert, "The Far Western Indian Frontier and the Beginnings of the Reservation System, 1846–1851" (Ph.D. diss., University of California, Santa Barbara, 1969) , pp. 370–371, 388–389.

1. "The Murder of Jane McCrea." Painting by John Vanderlyn (1775–1852).
The murder, committed on July 27, 1777, by Indians attached to British General
John Burgoyne's army, which was attempting to split the colonies in two,
stimulated patriot reaction to the British move.

2.   Silver Passport issued by authorities of the Colony of Virginia in 1661 to the King of the Potomac Indians. The passport, or medallion, served as a safe-conduct badge.

(Virginia Historical Society, Richmond)

3.   Indians of the New World eating human flesh and pouring gold down a Spaniard's throat. Engraving from 1594 edition of Theodor de Bry, *America*.

(Library of Congress)

AFFECTING

HISTORY

OF THE

DREADFUL DISTRESSES

OF

FREDERIC MANHEIM's

F A M I L Y:

TO WHICH ARE ADDED, THE

SUFFERINGS OF 'JOHN CORBLY's FAMILY.—AN ENCOUNTER
BETWEEN A WHITE MAN AND TWO SAVAGES—EXTRAOR-
DINARY BRAVERY OF A WOMAN—ADVENTURES OF
CAPT. ISAAC STEWART—DEPOSITION OF MASSY
HERBESON—ADVENTURES AND SUFFERINGS OF
PETER WILKINSON—REMARKABLE AD-
VENTURES OF JACKSON JOHONNOT.

WITH AN ACCOUNT

OF THE DESTRUCTION OF THE SETTLE-

MENTS AT WYOMING.

PHILADELPHIA:
PRINTED BY HENRY SWEITZER,
FOR MATHEW CAREY, No. 118, HIGH-STREET.

1800.

(PRICE A QUARTER DOLLAR.)

4. Title page and frontispiece of typical Indian captivity narrative.

(Smithsonian Institution)

5. "Escape of Israel Putnam from the Indians." An incident of the American Revolution. Painting by Asher Durand (1796–1886).

(New York State Historical Association, Cooperstown)

6. Silver Belt Medal bearing the Royal Mint mark, engraved with the arms of Great Britain and presented to Tecumseh by General Sir Isaac Brock, at Fort Malden, western Canada.

(Royal Ontario Museum, Toronto)

7. Silver gorget engraved with the royal arms of George III and inscribed to "Loyal Chief Outacite Cherokee Warrior."

(Royal Ontario Museum, Toronto)

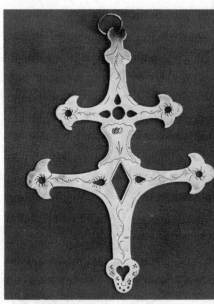

8. Northern Athapascan or Eskimo Mask from Anvik, Alaska.

(Smithsonian Institution)

9. Double-barred silver cross from the Six Nations Reserve, Brantford, Ontario, probably given originally by early Catholic missionaries to the Iroquois in New York State. Maker's initials "CA."

(Royal Ontario Museum, Toronto)

10. Powder Horn decorated with scenes and inscriptions commemorating the Indian Congress held at Fort Picolata, west of St. Augustine, at which Governor James Grant, the royal governor of East Florida, and the head men of the Creek Nation negotiated the treaty of November 18, 1765, which established a boundary line between the province of East Florida and the Creek Nation.

(Royal Ontario Museum, Toronto)

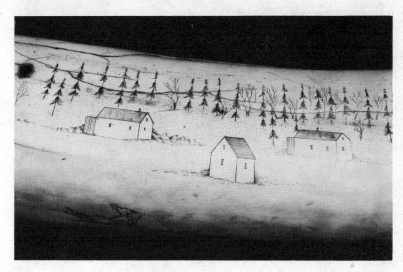

11. Mammoth Tusk from northwest Alaska decorated with scenes of the village of Unalakleet, an Eskimo community in Norton Sound, engraved in 1889 by Angokwazhuk (known as Happy Jack to miners and whalers), a crippled Eskimo ivory carver from Little Diomede Island.

(Royal Ontario Museum, Toronto)

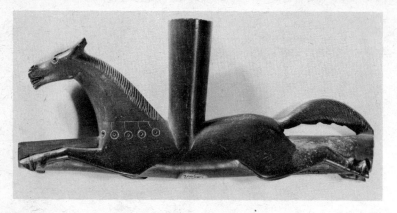

12. Sioux catlinite pipe and stem.

(Smithsonian Institution)

13. The Washington Covenant Belt (of 1775 or 1789, depending upon which of two possible events it could be associated with), the longest of the Iroquois wampum belts, shows a chain of men wearing hats and clasping hands, seven on the left and eight on the right, the interior pair holding firm to the Longhouse, symbol of the Iroquois Confederacy.

(New York State Museum and Science Service, Albany)

14. Brass tomahawk and peace pipe presented to Tecumseh by order of General Sir Isaac Brock, on the Detroit River at Fort Malden or Amherstburg in western Canada, on the occasion of Tecumseh and his warriors concluding to join forces with the British during the War of 1812. Tecumseh had this tomahawk in his belt behind his belt medal (see illustration 6) when he was killed at the battle of the River Thames in western Canada, October 5, 1813.

(Royal Ontario Museum, Toronto)

15. Iroquois "false face" wooden mask cut from solid piece of wood, painted red with eye sockets of tin and wig of horsehair, from the Six Nations Reserve, Grand River, Ontario.

(Smithsonian Institution)

16. Pottery, probably Zuñi, bought in Santa Fe, New Mexico, by President Rutherford B. Hayes during his Great Western Tour, October 28, 1880.

(Rutherford B. Hayes Library, Fremont, Ohio)

17. Tcha-kauks-o-ko-maugh, the Great Chief, a Menominee boy, painted by George Catlin in 1836.

(Smithsonian Institution)

18. Seneca Steel, described as a great libertine, a Seneca of New York State painted by George Catlin in 1829.

(Smithsonian Institution)

19. Seehk-hee-da, the Mouse-colored Feather, or "White Eyebrows," described as a very noted brave, a Mandan who was killed and scalped by the Sioux two years after this portrait was painted by George Catlin in 1832.

(Smithsonian Institution)

20. Osceola, the famous Seminole chief, painted by George Catlin on January 25, 1838, five days before Osceola's death.

(Smithsonian Institution)

22. Cunne Shote, one of several Cherokee chiefs who accompanied Henry Timberlake to England in 1762. Painting by F. Parsons, done in London in 1762.

(Smithsonian Institution)

21. Susquehannock Warrior, as depicted in engraving from Theodor de Bry, *America*, Pt. 13 (Frankfurt, 1634), derived from Captain John Smith's *Map of Virginia* (London, 1612).

(Library of Congress)

23. Chippewa Mother and Child. Lithograph from Thomas L. McKenny and James Hall, *The Indian Tribes of North America* (Philadelphia, 1838).

(Library of Congress)

24. Little Crow, Sioux chief and leader of the Indian Massacre of 1862 in Minnesota. Photograph by Whitney, 1862.

(Library of Congress)

25. Geronimo, Apache chief. Photograph © Gerhard Sisters 1904.

(Library of Congress)

26. Red Cloud and American Horse, Sioux chiefs. Photograph by Grabill, 1891.

(Library of Congress)

27. Young girl of mixed blood, of the Mattapony-Powhatan Confederacy, State Reservation, Mattapony River, King William County, Virginia. Photograph by James Mooney, Smithsonian ethnologist, 1900.

(Smithsonian Institution)

28. Ma-ka-tai-me-she-kia-kiah, or Black Hawk, a Sauk chief. Lithograph from Thomas L. McKenney and James Hall, *The Indian Tribes of North America* (Philadelphia, 1838).

(Library of Congress)

30. Red Jacket, a Seneca chief. Painting by Thomas Hicks, 1867, after portrait by R. W. Weir.

(Buffalo and Erie County Historical Society)

29. Joseph Brant (Thayendanegea), a Mohawk chief. Painting by Ezra Ames, 1806.

(New York State Historical Association, Cooperstown)

31. Seminole attack on block house during Second Seminole War, about 1836. Lithograph published by Gray and James, Charleston, South Carolina, about 1837.

(Library of Congress)

32. Execution of thirty-eight Sioux Indians at Mankato, Minnesota, December 26, 1862, in the aftermath of the Sioux Uprising. Lithograph (Milwaukee, 1863).

(Library of Congress)

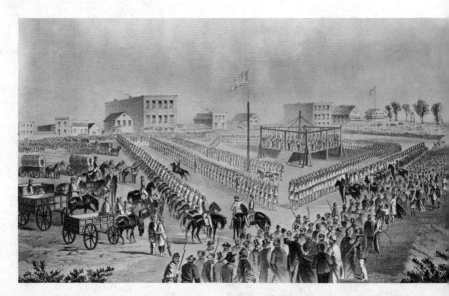

33. "Encampment of Crow Indians." Painting by Alfred Jacob Miller (1810-1874).

(Gilcrease Institute, Tulsa, Oklahoma)

34. "Snake and Sioux Indians on the Warpath." Painting by Alfred Jacob Miller (1810-1874).

(Gilcrease Institute, Tulsa, Oklahoma)

35.   United States Cavalry pursuing Indians, 1876. Lithograph (Akron, Ohio, 1899).

(Library of Congress)

36.   Artist's conception of the Battle of Little Big Horn, June 25, 1876: General George A. Custer's Death Struggle. Lithograph (San Francisco, 1878).

(Library of Congress)

37. William Penn's Treaty with the Indians, after the painting by Benjamin West. English copper-plate print on cotton textile, about 1800.

(Metropolitan Museum of Art, Bequest of Charles Allen Munn, 1924)

38. Indian Camp on the River Brule near Pine Ridge, South Dakota. Photograph by Grabill, 1891.

(Library of Congress)

39. Ship's figurehead in form of Indian squaw, about 1850.

(The Mariners' Museum, Newport News, Virginia)

40. Carved wooden cigar store Indian: a familiar advertising device of the mid-nineteenth century.

(Smithsonian Institution)

population because Indians had not developed resistance to them. Disease literally destroyed much of the native population of America and altered and shaped the customs of the survivors. Unwittingly, disease was the white man's strongest ally in the New World.

No evidence is more voluminous than that detailing Indian drunkenness. Whatever the area, whatever the time, report after report expressed the surprise of whites at the ardent desire of Indians to acquire "strong waters," and, having obtained them, their proclivity to total inebriation, often followed by injury or death to themselves or to their fellow tribesmen. A handful of examples will suffice to illustrate this fact.

Charles Stuart, the British Indian agent to the Choctaws during the American Revolution, reported that he saw "nothing but Rum Drinking and Women crying over the Dead bodies of their relations who have died by Rum." Stuart warned that "unless some Step is taken to put a Stop to this abuse we need not look for any assistance from this nation, for at the very time they may be wanted they may be all drunk and Rum flows into their land from all quarters and is in my Opinion the only source of all abuses and complaints." One chief estimated that more than a thousand people had died from excessive drinking in a period of about eighteen months.[79]

Little Turtle, chief of the Miamis, in a speech to Thomas Jefferson, President of the United States, in 1802, compared the happiness of his people prior to the introduction of the white man's liquor with their condition after the introduction of "this fatal poison." "Your children," Little Turtle told Jefferson, "have not that command over themselves, which you have, therefore, before anything can be done, this evil must be remedied."[80]

Cephas Washburn, a missionary and teacher among the western Cherokees in Oklahoma, complained in 1830 to Superintendent of Indian Affairs Thomas McKenney about the illicit sale of liquor to Indians near Fort Smith on the Arkansas River. The missionary

79. Charles Stuart to John Stuart, March 4, 1777, and April 8, 1777, quoted in O'Donnell, *op. cit.*, p. 150.

80. Quoted in Royal B. Hassrick, "Alcohol and Indians," *The American Indian*, published quarterly by the Association on American Indian Affairs, New York, IV (1947), 19.

claimed he knew of five Indians whose deaths within a ten-day period were the result of "intemperate use of whiskey."[81]

To what cause or causes can Indian drunkenness be attributed? Most explanations are cultural in nature, though they range from attributing Indian drunkenness to despair over the loss of Indian culture on the one hand, to an exultant affirmation of Indianness on the other.[82] A less popular explanation looks to genetics and physiology for an answer. Anthony Wallace's study of the Iroquois from the days of their power and glory to those of frustration and dependency lends some support to the cultural explanation of Indian drunkenness. Although occasionally given to brief, drunken orgies in the heyday of their power, the Iroquois in their decline in the 1790s raised drinking to the level of a steady, serious social problem. Many of the Iroquois leaders, including Red Jacket, Logan (the Great Mingo), and Handsome Lake, became great drunkards. Nor was the drinking merely quietly despairing. Rather, it resulted in what Wallace has called "explosive, indiscriminate hostility that vented itself in fighting even within the family."[83]

When spirituous liquors were introduced by traders among the Salish Indians of British Columbia they were quickly integrated into Salish culture by means of the potlatch, the gift-giving feast by which individuals gained recognition of their status by their generosity in sharing their possessions: in this case, their liquor. Drinking was always social, never solitary. The drinkers would drink until the supply was exhausted, usually sharing the same cup or dipper, which was passed from person to person. To get drunk as quickly as possible was almost universally desired. The whiskey potlatch, particularly in early times, was an occasion for singing, telling of stories, and occasionally sexual license. Later, particularly in response to the condemnation of drinking by the Catholic priests who converted many of the Salish in the late nineteenth century, it became somewhat more covert and removed from its traditional and social context. Indian behavior when drunk tended to be the

81. Ed Bearss and Arrell M. Gibson, *Fort Smith: Little Gibraltar on the Arkansas* (Norman, Okla., 1968), p. 110.

82. The latter theory is expressed in Nancy Oestreich Lurie, "The World's Oldest On-Going Protest Demonstration: North American Indian Drinking Patterns," *Pacific Historical Review*, XL (1971), 311–332.

83. Wallace, *Death and Rebirth of the Seneca*, pp. 199–200.

converse of Indian behavior when sober. The impassive, reserved, dignified sober Indian was quickly transformed into the reeling, boisterous, uncontrolled drunken Indian. The extent to which the desire to get drunk quickly was achieved through subjective rather than objective means was a subject for debate among white observers. No stigma was attached by fellow Indians to Indian drinking or to acts committed while under the influence of liquor, however much such acts might be condemned when committed sober.[84]

Although scholars have linked Indian drinking to its societal functions—for example, as a means of social integration, rather than a response to anxieties—recent research suggests that there may well be genetic differences between Indians and whites which help explain the phenomenon of Indian drunkenness. Certain metabolic mechanisms which evolved and were transmitted genetically in the pre-European-contact environment may well put Indians under a tremendous disadvantage when acculturated to European eating habits. Studies of the Tarahumara Indians of northwestern Mexico, closely related to the Pima Indians of Arizona, have sought to explain why these physically outstanding Indians, whose endurance was legendary, show signs of deterioration under the impact of refined sugar and distilled alcohol introduced by Western man. Their traditional diet—principally Indian corn and beans (their main source of protein)—is converted with amazing efficiency into energy in the bloodstream as glucose and glucose-6-phosphate and into a slow heartbeat. Acculturated Tarahumaras, on the other hand, are now subject to obesity, diabetes, and ischemic heart disease. The Tarahumara's genetic superiority in having evolved a very efficient metabolic mechanism for the retention and utilization of environmentally scarce glucose precursors has gone for naught; indeed, it "has produced a medical disaster," in the words of one authority, because of the inability of this mechanism to withstand exposure to high-concentrate energy sources—refined sugar, distilled spirits, and candy in quantity. The Tarahumaras, whose traditional social structure incorporated drinking bouts with a corn beer called *tesquina,* apparently with few ill

84. Edwin M. Lemert, "The Use of Alcohol in Three Salish Indian Tribes," *Quarterly Journal of Studies on Alcohol,* XIX (1958) , 90–107.

effects, have fallen victim to the white man's diet as they have to so many other aspects of the white man's culture. "Wouldn't it be ironic," one authority has written, "if something as innocuous as food and drink turns out to have been more damaging to native Americans than smallpox or firearms?"[85]

85. David G. Mandelbaum, "Alcohol and Culture," *Current Anthropology*, VI (1965), 281–292, especially 287; the Tarahumara study is discussed in William R. Hood, "A Bridge Over Troubled Waters: Ecology of Indian Biosocial Action," a paper presented at the annual meeting of the American Psychological Association, Sept. 6, 1971, mimeographed.

CHAPTER 5

Indian Response to Religious Persuasion

ONE of the great motivating forces underlying European expansion into the New World was the missionary spirit of Christianity. The belief that the heathen should be converted as a Christian duty was not limited to priests and ministers. Financial supporters of the earliest expeditions, ministers of state, and colonial officials sought genuinely to carry out what they regarded as a moral duty. Very rarely was the pious ideal of conversion realized. Typical was the experience of the Pilgrim colonists at Plymouth in 1620. John Robinson, their spiritual leader who remained in Holland when the *Mayflower* sailed for America, wrote sadly after learning of the first clash with the natives:

Oh how happy a thing had it been, if you had converted some before you had killed any! Besides, where blood is once begun to be shed, it is seldom staunched of a long time after.[1]

The missionary purpose was frustrated not only by contrary passions and hypocrisy among Europeans but also by the reluctance of many Indians to be converted. In most Indian societies no fine line of distinction was drawn between political and religious activities. Once an Indian became a professing Christian, therefore, he tended to reject more than the religious component of his former life. He rejected, to some degree or other, the political authority to

1. Letter of Dec. 19, 1623, in William Bradford, *Of Plymouth Plantation, 1620–1647*, ed. Samuel Eliot Morison (New York, 1952), pp. 374–375.

which he had previously been subject and the cultural values in which he had been nurtured. Thus it should not be surprising that conversions were not easily achieved and, when accomplished, that the Indian often felt deracinated.

The implications of conversion to Christianity threatened not alone the individual Indian's relationship to his tribe, but, in the eyes of some Indians, the tribe itself. Roger Williams of Rhode Island reported in 1654 that "At my last departure for England, I was importuned by the Narragansett Sachems, and especially by Ninigret, to present their petition to the high Sachems of England, that they might not be forced from their religion, and, for not changing their religion, be invaded by war; for they said they were daily visited with threatenings by Indians that came from about the Massachusetts, that if they would not pray, they should be destroyed by war." The colonial authorities, concerned about the possibility of Indian wars, avoided overt coercive measures and cautioned missionaries like John Eliot to "bee slow in With Drawing Indian proffessors from paying accustomed Tribute and performing other lawfull servises to theire Sagamores till you have seriously Considered and advised with the Majestrates and Elders of the Massachusetts least the passage and spreading of the Gosspell bee hindered thereby."[2]

The missionary effort in New England was aided by the resources provided by the Society for the Propagation of the Gospel in New England, which was authorized in 1649 by an act of Parliament and which received a royal charter in 1662 following the restoration of Charles II. With support from the New England Company, as the society was known, the Indian College at Harvard was built in the 1650s and the printing press, which published John Eliot's Algonquian translation of the Bible between 1660 and 1663, was established. But the missionary effort depended largely upon the dedication and skill of individual Puritan ministers whose responsibility lay first of all with their English parishioners. Despite the tendency of recent historians to speak disparagingly of the missionary work of seventeenth-century New England, the achievement, as Wesley Frank Craven has pointed out, was great. Although the provisions

2. Letter of Oct. 5, 1654 (Roger Williams to General Court of Massachusetts Bay); letter of Sept. 18, 1654 (Commissioners of the United Colonies to John Eliot), in *Letters of Roger Williams, 1632–1682*, 2 vols., ed. John Russell Bartlett (Providence, R.I., 1874), II, 270; *Records of the Colony of New Plymouth in New England*, X, ed. David Pulsifer (Boston, 1859), 123.

for the education of Indian youth and the translation of the Bible were important results in themselves, the creation of a string of "praying Indian" towns was perhaps even more significant. Prior to King Philip's War in 1675, there were fourteen such towns with over 1,000 Christian Indians. In all there were probably 4,000 Christians among the New England Indians before the racial suspicion engendered by King Philip's War erased much of the work of Eliot, Daniel Gookin, Thomas Mayhew, and other Englishmen concerned with the conversion of the Indians.[3]

However disappointing the New England record may seem, conversion was perhaps even less frequent in the other English colonies. Although conversion was a constantly reiterated goal of the Virginia settlement little was achieved there. The most spectacular conversion was that of Pocahontas by John Rolfe, but her conversion smacked more of political and carnal motives than of religious ones. Even the better-funded, better-organized Roman Catholic effort was frustrated by the cultural resistance of its Indian objects. The Jesuit missionary Father Biard, in 1611, remarked that the hundred Abenaki converts baptized by the priest Jesse Flèche in 1610 were indistinguishable from the unbaptized:

The same savagery and the same manners, or but little different, the same customs, ceremonies, usages, fashions, and vices remain, at least as far as can be learned; no attention being paid to any distinction of time, days, offices, exercises, prayers, duties, virtues or spiritual remedies.[4]

Nevertheless, the Catholic effort could count thousands of converts. In a census taken at the time of an episcopal visitation of converts made by Spanish Franciscans in Florida and southern Georgia in 1673–1674, 26,000 Christian Indians were identified. But the converts suffered under attacks by pagan Creeks under English leadership in the first decade of the eighteenth century and gradually declined in number. The efforts of dedicated Catholic missionaries in Maryland, Pennsylvania, and other English colonies were less effective in bringing converts into the church.[5]

3. John F. Freeman, "The Indian Convert: Theme and Variation," *Ethnohistory*, XII (1965), 113–128; Wesley Frank Craven, *The Colonies in Transition, 1660–1713* (New York, 1968), pp. 117–118.

4. Freeman, *op. cit.*, at 116.

5. Clifford M. Lewis, S. J., "Spanish Missions in Southeastern United States," draft of article for revision of *Handbook of North American Indians* now in preparation at the Smithsonian Institution.

The eighteenth century saw a continuing effort to convert the Indians, though without the high hopes of bringing whole nations into the fold, as some of the seventeenth-century Europeans had hoped. The Great Awakening of the 1740s in the English colonies provided examples of pious converts from Indians as well as from white communities. One of the most famous was Samson Occom (1723–1792), a Mohegan born near New London, Connecticut, who discovered "Salvation through Jesus Christ" when seventeen years old. After studying with Eleazar Wheelock, he played a leading role in obtaining support in England for the Indian Charity School which evolved into Dartmouth College.[6]

Among the most active missionaries in the eighteenth century were the United Brethren, or Moravians. Pietistic and pacifistic, the sect originated in Moravia in Austria, moved to Saxony in Germany where its members lived on the estates of Count Zinzendorf before moving to the New World. After a brief stay in Georgia, about 1741, the members settled in Pennsylvania, with Bethlehem as their center. The Moravians were active in missionary work on the frontier and in establishing schools. Their record of dedication to their Indian charges was impressive. "They did not make an assault upon the Indian's personality," the historian Paul A. W. Wallace has noted. Their sympathetic approach is perhaps best exemplified by the missionary career of John Heckewelder among the Delaware and Mahican Indians and by the establishment of the Gnaden-hütten mission on the Muskingum River in Ohio. Though ninety Christian Indians were, without justification, massacred there on March 8, 1782, by American forces, putting an inglorious end to the station, it was, in the view of Wallace, "the noblest experiment in race relations this continent has yet seen."[7]

One of the most famous converts of the Moravians was the Delaware warrior Teedyuscung, whose conversion experience provides a model of the process as experienced by individual Indians in the eighteenth century. Wavering and uncertain, caught between the onrushing, land-grabbing whites and his own culture, Teedyuscung

6. Leon Burr Richardson, *An Indian Preacher in England* (Hanover, N.H., 1933); see also *The Letters of Eleazar Wheelock's Indians*, ed. James Dow McCallum (Hanover, N.H., 1932).

7. Paul A. W. Wallace, ed., *Thirty Thousand Miles with John Heckewelder* (Pittsburgh, 1958), pp. 3, 31, 189–200; Louis B. Wright, *The Cultural Life of the Colonies, 1607–1763* (New York, 1957), p. 61.

came reluctantly to baptism at the mission station of the Moravians at Gnadenhütten on the Mahoning, at its junction with the Lehigh River. The event itself, which occurred on March 12, 1750, was of true significance for Teedyuscung, who was given a new name: Gideon. Teedyuscung was spiritually reborn on the occasion, confessing his manifold sins, weeping and trembling, begging to be saved from sin and cleansed in the blood of the lamb. As the anthropologist Anthony Wallace has suggested, Teedyuscung's conversion may have represented an attempt to identify with the powerful, prosperous whites by the adoption of the white man's manitou, Jesus Christ, the Lamb of God, as his guardian spirit. After his baptism, Teedyuscung moved from his former Delaware village to Gnadenhütten, bringing his family with him.[8]

Indian conversion, as the example of Teedyuscung suggests, followed the traditional pattern described by the philosopher and psychologist William James: uneasiness of soul, desire to be saved, perception of the depravity of mankind, sudden realization that salvation can come only through God's grace and not through man's efforts, and finally relief and peaceful assurance that, as a result of this perception, one is "saved." The outward effects of conversion were usually evident in a changed life: abandonment of strong drink and loose living, a sweet conviction of being saved or chosen by God, and usually, in the case of Indian converts, a life more in the image of white ideals: living in a European-style house, wearing European clothes, engaging in agriculture, observing the Sabbath, and marrying in a Christian ceremony.

While the outward changes in the converted Indian's habits of life suggest the assimilation of white values generally—not only religious values—conversion did not necessarily imply a complete acceptance of the practices of white secular society. Both the Indian convert and the white convert stood out from the prevailing behavioral norms of white Christian society. Both served as a rebuke to the nominal Christians who lied and stole and acted in an unchristian manner in their daily lives. The saintliness of the numerous individual Indian and white converts who led lives of purity and charity must be honored. But for the Indian convert the state was one of personal isolation from both the white world and the Indian

8. Anthony F. C. Wallace, *King of the Delawares: Teedyuscung, 1700–1763* (Philadelphia, 1949), pp. 39–44.

world in which he had been born. It was a private world whose sorrow—induced by alienation from both the real white world and the traditional Indian world—could be overcome only by the self-justification of a pure life. Despite the numbers of converts, and the apparent strength of the Christian movement among Indians, the effects of conversion were too often either peripheral, divisive, or narcotic. Christianity at best helped the Indian accept the poor place the white world offered him and helped him overcome the rage and despair he might otherwise have felt because of his inability to prosper in that world.

The persistence and optimism of the Christian missionaries with regard to the Indian seem remarkable to us in a nonreligious age. However much the temporal power saw the religious impulse as merely a support for its own ends, the religious orders of Catholic France and Spain and the missionary societies of Protestant England worked with dedication and sincerity toward the missionary goal. The religious orders had to measure success in some way, and the numerical "soul count" of baptisms—equivalent to the "body count" of a later missionary enterprise—was a handy measure, both for self-congratulation and for the satisfaction of superiors in the mother church and mother country. Too often the missionaries took a liberal if not casual view of the degree of comprehension of the mysteries of the faith required of successful converts. Chronicles of the early Spanish conquests are replete with reports of mass conversions, signifying little. Where European missionaries existed in some degree of dependence upon their native charges or where their security depended upon good relations with the Indians, the test of conversion was fairer. Thus it is of significance that in the case of both the French missionaries among the Hurons in the seventeenth century and the Spanish missionaries among the Indians of Texas in the eighteenth (both posts being at the "end of the line" from the centers of their colonial power), the number of conversions was minimal. Because most Huron baptisms were made on the death bed by the zealous French priests, baptism into the Christian faith and death were closely correlated in the minds of the Hurons. In the case of the Spanish mission of Nuestra Señora del Rosario de los Gujanes, established in November, 1754, on the San Antonio River four leagues from La Bahía presidio, only twelve adults and nine children were baptized in the first four years of existence and all were death-bed baptisms.[9]

Spanish missionary activity in the Southwest progressed under the covering arm of the Spanish military power centered in Mexico. In its earliest phases it was marked by scandalous scenes of plunder, slaughter, and rape. Coronado's 1540–1541 expedition failed to find the wealth of Mexico and Peru in the southwestern desert and the Spaniards expended their fury in sacking and looting, showing little inclination to propagate the Word of God. Both church and state subsequently sought ways in which Spanish power and Christian influence could be spread without scandal to the name of either.

In 1598 Juan de Oñate struck out from southern Chihuahua with a more restrained party of about 400 colonists, soldiers, Franciscan missionaries, and Indians. His purpose was to colonize New Mexico. Misfortune and dissension marked the expedition. Although not so crude a foray as Coronado's expedition, the Christianization and colonization of New Mexico was marked by bloodshed and cruelty. Grants of land (encomiendas) with the right to utilize the services of Indians living on the grants (repartimientos) were authorized to encourage settlement. Spanish presence was established in the midst of the populous eastern pueblos of the upper Rio Grande. The missionaries built churches, baptized the Indians, and introduced new agricultural methods. Sometimes the missionaries found themselves at odds with the civil governors whose interests often conflicted with those of the missionaries and of the Indians. Each side charged the other with exploiting the Indians and with immoral behavior.[10]

While Franciscans jointly with Spanish civil authorities penetrated the northern pueblo villages in the seventeenth century, Jesuits under the leadership of Father Eusebio Francisco Kino, an Italian Jesuit, spread the faith among the upper Pimas on Mexico's northwestern frontier, in the territory that eventually became part of the American Southwest. Kino's work spanned the period from 1686 until his death in 1711. Kino had obtained an exemption of

9. Thomas Wolff, "The Karankawa Indians: Their Conflict with the White Man in Texas," Ethnohistory, XVI (1969), 9.

10. Edward H. Spicer, Cycles of Conquest: The Impact of Spain, Mexico, and the United States on the Indians of the Southwest, 1533–1960 (Tucson, Ariz., 1962), pp. 156–159.

the targeted Indians from forced labor or demands for tribute during the missionary program. As he penetrated the desert as far as Bac near the present-day Tucson, Arizona, in the 1690s, Kino drove cattle ahead of him to create a food supply for the missions he later established. Although normally operating without the intimidating presence of Spanish soldiers, Kino was to suffer from the occasional conflicts that erupted between the Spanish soldiery and the Indian tribes of the area. But because of his instinctive tolerance, his love of ceremonial, and his willingness to listen to the Indian viewpoint, he was more successful than other missionaries among the Indians.[11]

The prevailing pattern of Spanish missionary activity in the Southwest was the establishment of fixed missions, as self-contained as possible, centered around the physical church, to which the Indians of the area were drawn—largely by voluntary means—to learn the worship of the true God and to practice the arts of civilized man. While the mission regime, which expanded up the California coast in the eighteenth century, was harsh and demanding, it provided some measure of protection from the onslaught of the Spanish government and colonists who were less interested in Indian souls than in Indian lands and bodies. Until the break-up of the mission system in the early nineteenth century, the Spanish missions held Indian bodies and souls precariously together in a school which sought not only to convert the Indians to Christianity but also to European concepts of gaining a livelihood.

As Spanish power in the borderlands grew, tolerance of Indian deviation from European norms grew less. Missionaries, bewildered by the continued existence of Indian ceremonials even after the adoption of Christian ones, sometimes sought to abolish and prohibit the continued practice of native rites, occasionally with a zeal not shared by the civil governors of the area.

Of the two orders, the Franciscans were less tolerant of native ceremonies. Thus, the Franciscan missionaries sought to destroy the kachina figures of the eastern pueblos, to raid the kivas where the sacred native ceremonies were held, and to root out the non-Christian ceremonies of the tribes. Jesuits were less given to destroying the sacred objects of the natives, although no less convinced of their error. Similarly, the Franciscans made it almost a point of honor not to learn the native languages but to force the Indians to

11. *Ibid.*, pp. 120–126, 315.

receive instruction in Spanish. The Jesuits, on the other hand, sought to instruct the Indians in their native tongues and attempted to enforce language proficiency among all their missionaries. Both orders sought to convert by peaceful means and by persuasion but both were willing to enforce church discipline by whipping—often severe and often brutal—and by various other forms of coercion up to and even including the support of punitive military expeditions against recalcitrant natives. When the Jesuits were expelled from the New World in 1767 the more arbitrary and less enlightened spirit of the Franciscans replaced the more tolerant and sophisticated manner of the Jesuits.[12]

The Spanish mission system is normally seen in spiritual terms as self-contained islands of godliness in a sea of heathen natives and exploitative whites. Yet the material aspects were perhaps even more important. Not only did the missions serve as outposts of Spanish empire, albeit not under direct Spanish civil rule, but they were agents of change among the peoples to whom they ministered. The Indian could there obtain Spanish goods, tools, medicines, and the like. He might find protection from his traditional enemies. His sincerity in receiving the religious instruction of the missionaries might be doubted, as it frequently was by the missionaries themselves, who nevertheless considered it a good bargain to have the Indians available to receive instruction, whatever their motives. The extent to which Indian ways were changed by the introduction of mission stations can be dramatically illustrated by the material remains of such stations. Of particular interest is the different effect upon Indian men and women. In his excavation of the 540-foot-long Indian barracks built in 1814 at La Purisima Mission in Lompoc, California, near Santa Barbara, the archaeologist James Deetz divided artifacts of male association from those of female association and compared them with inventories from contemporary aboriginal village sites in the same area. Deetz found the female-associated artifacts—bowls, mortars, pestles, baskets, manos, and metates—equally common in the barracks site and in the aboriginal village sites. On the other hand, only a few artifacts of male association—stone knives, points, and scrapers—were found in the barracks site in comparison with the abundance of such objects found in the villages. Since documentary evidence provided proof that

12. *Ibid.*, pp. 326–327.

adults of both sexes occupied the barracks (the only Indians excluded from the barracks were unmarried adolescent girls), the archaeological evidence provided convincing proof of the sudden shift in roles for Indian males at the mission in comparison with the virtually identical activities performed by women in the pre- and post-contact periods. The men became herders, farmers, and craftsmen, abandoning their earlier hunting and fishing roles. But the women continued to perform the tasks they had always performed.[13]

Protestant missionary activity burgeoned after the American Revolution with the creation of the Society for Propagating the Gospel among the Indians and Others in North America (1787), the Society of the United Brethren for Propagating the Gospel among the Heathen (1787), the New York (1796), the Northern (1797), the Connecticut (1798), the Massachusetts (1799), and the Western Missionary (1802) societies, which were soon followed by the American Board of Commissioners for Foreign Missions (1810), the United Foreign Missionary Society (1817), and the Missionary and Bible Society of the Methodist Episcopal Church in America (1820).

Increasingly, missionaries came to believe that "civilization" must go hand in hand with Christianization if either was to succeed. The cultural assumptions underlying each concept required support from the other, at least as perceived by the white agents of both. Missionaries found themselves, as one put it, "entirely unable to separate religion and civilization." What they brought to the Indian was "Christian civilization."[14] "In the school and in the field, as well as in the kitchen," one missionary wrote, "our aim was to teach the Indians to live like white people."[15] The effect of this limited cultural vision was to apply an arbitrary, external, and societal standard to an internal, moral, and individual problem. Little wonder that missionaries, like others, missed the real Indian in seeking to coerce him into an alien cultural mold.

Little wonder, too, that the Indian became increasingly suspi-

13. James Deetz, "Late Man in North America: Archaeology of European Americans," in *Anthropological Archeology in the Americas* (Washington, 1968), pp. 121–130, at 124.

14. J. Potter to S. B. Treat, July 14, 1849, quoted in Robert K. Berkhofer, Jr., *Salvation and the Savage: An Analysis of Protestant Missions and American Indian Response, 1787–1862* (Lexington, Ky., 1965), p. 10.

15. John H. Pitezel quoted in *ibid.*

cious of the white man's formulation of the problem. Why had not the Great Spirit given the Indians direct knowledge of the Bible if it had been meant for the Indians as well as the whites, the Seneca chief Red Jacket asked missionary Joseph Cram in 1805. "We only know what you tell us about it," he noted; "how shall we know when to believe, being so often deceived by the white people?" Red Jacket pointedly noted the inability of the white men to agree among themselves on how to worship the Great Spirit even though all could read the Bible. The Great Spirit, Red Jacket observed, had made his red and his white children different in their customs, their complexions, their arts: perhaps he had given Indians and whites different religions also. "Brother, we do not wish to destroy your religion, or take it from you," he told Cram; "we only want to enjoy our own. . . ." Red Jacket concluded his response to Cram in a passage of practical good humor. Since Cram was preaching to the white neighbors of the Iroquois, Red Jacket promised to see what effect his preaching had upon them. "If we find it does them good, makes them honest, and less disposed to cheat Indians, we will then consider what you have said."[16]

The powerful Cherokees proved similarly reluctant to cast aside their ancient beliefs. The Cherokee chiefs, in a response to the letter of Acting Agent Joseph McMinn, November 21, 1818, explained patiently that he should not expect to see the Cherokees quickly embrace the white man's religion.

Religion is certainly commendable [the chiefs noted]; but the force of our prejudices forbids that you should at once expect to see us embrace yours. We, like yourselves, found ours upon our prejudices, and follow the religion of our fathers. A different education would beget different prejudices, and, with your education, we should no doubt adopt your prejudices as well as religion.[17]

This course, the Cherokees pointed out, was not likely to occur if they were forced to go west of the Mississippi as the white negotiators were then attempting to persuade them to do.

Indian conversions were most successful where whites were fewest and least threatening and the message was introduced into the

16. Quoted in Anthony F. C. Wallace, *The Death and Rebirth of the Seneca* (New York, 1970), pp. 205–206.

17. *American State Papers . . . Indian Affairs*, 2 vols. (Washington, 1832–1834), II, 486–487.

tribes by the natives themselves. A startling example of this type of conversion occurred in the Oregon country in the first half of the nineteenth century. Two Indian boys from this area, a Kutenai named J. H. Pelly and a Spokan named Nicholas Garry, were taken by George Simpson of the Hudson's Bay Company over the Canadian Rockies to the Red River mission school in 1825. After four years at the school, the young men went back to their families and taught groups of Indians of different tribes about the white man's God. The resulting changes in Indian religious habits startled the American trappers and explorers when they arrived soon after 1830. They found many tribes observing the Sabbath, renouncing raids for revenge, charitably supplying strangers with food, and showing tenderness and pity to such a degree that the explorer Captain Benjamin Bonneville, when he met the Nez Perces, asserted, "Simply to call these people religious would convey but a faint idea of the deep hue of piety and devotion which pervades their whole conduct. . . . They are certainly more like a nation of saints than a horde of savages."[18]

The piety of many of the Indian tribes in the Northwest can be seen alternatively as a sincere conversion to Christian principles, as an expression of preexisting attitudes, or an attempt to add the white man's "medicine" to their own. The fact that Christian practices did not necessarily displace native beliefs or destroy the existence of native medicine men suggests, perhaps, that all three explanations are valid.

The Christian virtues and aspirations of the Nez Perce and Flathead Indians were dramatized by a well-publicized visit by four Nez Perce (mistakenly thought to be Flathead) Indians to St. Louis to visit Superintendent of Indian Affairs William Clark in the fall of 1831. Little communication was possible between the Indians and the whites, two of the Indians died while in St. Louis, and no mention of the visit is made in the official records. Nevertheless, a visitor to Clark's house while the Indians were there, William Walker, a white man married to a Wyandot Indian woman and a leader of the Wyandot tribe, reported their mission to a Methodist friend in New York, who in turn transmitted the story of the epic 3,000-mile walk of the "Flatheads" to St. Louis presumably to ask

18. Quoted in Alvin M. Josephy, Jr., *The Nez Perce Indians and the Opening of the Northwest* (New Haven, Conn., 1965) , pp. 81–91, at 91.

for missionaries to be sent them. The story was embellished as it was transmitted and was reprinted frequently after its first appearance in the *Christian Advocate and Journal and Zion's Herald* in New York on March 1, 1833. The publication of the story of the dramatic visit touched off a rush of Protestant missionaries to answer the call.[19]

The early work of missionaries, both Catholic and Protestant, in the Northwest was such that when white settlers began to arrive in the late 1840s and 1850s they found Indian tribes leading lives that combined the communal and nomadic ways of their ancestors with rules of Christian love and cooperation introduced by the Jesuits or New England Protestant missionaries. The Jesuits seem to have succeeded better than the Protestant missionaries in convincing the Indians of their good intentions and of their utility to the increasingly beleaguered natives. The Jesuits, heirs of a worldwide tradition of work with such sophisticated peoples as Chinese and such simple people as the Indians of Paraguay, believers in the "incarnational" conviction that all human good was potentially Christian, giving, moreover, examples of personal self-denial, succeeded in winning an influence over the Plateau tribes that baffled and sometimes enraged Protestant missionaries and United States administrators. Protestants, indeed, accused the Catholics of conspiring with the Indians to attack white Protestant settlers. The Jesuit conspiracy theory was also used to "explain" each of the wars with which the white settlers were plagued. Though the causes of these wars were sometimes complex, the explanation is easier to locate in white encroachment on Indian lands or abuse of Indian persons than in a Catholic conspiracy to seize the West for Rome.[20]

The leading missionary figure in the Northwest was the Belgian Jesuit Father Peter De Smet, who was sent to the Oregon country in 1840. De Smet worked assiduously to create a new Paraguay from St. Louis to Oregon within which the Indian tribes might be allowed to govern themselves under Jesuit advisers in protected "reductions." By gathering the Indians in compact settlements around missions, they could be encouraged to engage in agriculture, cattle

19. *Ibid.*, pp. 93–102; the story has more recently been told by Howard L. Harrod, *Mission Among the Blackfeet* (Norman, Okla., 1971), pp. 23–38.

20. Robert Ignatius Burns, S.J., *The Jesuits and the Indian Wars of the Northwest* (New Haven, Conn., 1966), pp. 31–116.

raising, and crafts or work in the sawmills, forges, and other centers established there. Though the life was communal in the native and early Christian sense, any Indian desiring his own farm could have one. Where tribes had formerly made hunting forays for buffalo onto the Great Plains, they tended to continue the activity, though discouraged by the Jesuits. Recognizing the threat of well-armed Blackfeet raiders, the Jesuits took pains to provide arms and ammunition for their charges that they might not only hunt success-fully, but also protect themselves from the feared Blackfeet. With the Indians concentrated to a greater degree than before, the Jesuits attempted to educate them in Christian and "civilized" ways, utiliz-ing songs, recitation, formal assemblies, division of the children into competing bands, and the like. Through the process of education, the Jesuits sought to change values such as the Indian predilection for revenge, for gambling, for intoxicating spirits, and for polyg-amy; and their aversion to manual labor. Though Protestant ob-servers often conceived of the relationship between Jesuit and Indian as one of absolute physical control by the former over the latter or as the result of deception, ignorance, or superstition, the Jesuits in fact labored to create a voluntary bond of mutual interest and shared obedience to Christian ethics. Often, to express their displeasure, or at the temporary request of the Indians themselves, the Jesuits would leave their charges to their own devices until (as often happened) the Indians asked them back again.[21]

The Jesuits' Northwest missions in the period 1840 to 1880 were scarcely reductions in the South American sense. Most of the tribes under Jesuit influence ranged over the country as they had in the past: hunting, gathering, and fishing. But the mission was always their center. A nucleus of tribesmen engaged in farming, lived in cabins and tipis around the mission, and attended Christian wor-ship in the mission chapel, confessing their sins to the priest. The "dream of an Oregon Paraguay," as the Jesuit historian of the experiment puts it, "was to be a failure."[22] The job was too big; the obstacles too great. The passion for war that motivated many of the Indians, their great numbers, the vast distances, and the con-stantly threatening incursions of white settlers forestalled what might conceivably have been a successful accommodation with the

21. *Ibid.*
22. *Ibid.*, p. 55.

future. The Jesuits labored mightily to prevent wars from breaking out and sought to end them when begun. They attempted to isolate the Indians from the onrush of white settlers and to mediate for them with the territorial government. They accepted the concept of reservations imposed on the Indians in 1855 but strove to insure that adequate amounts of land were left the Indians, that adequate and prompt compensation was paid, and that the Indians were respected in their persons and in their love of their land. Isaac Ingalls Stevens, appointed in 1853 as first territorial governor of Washington, found in his negotiations with the Indian tribes of the Northwest that he was dealing to a great extent with Christian Indians and with tribes who had already many of the accoutrements of civilization—sawmills, blacksmiths, and churches—which he had hoped to be able to offer the Indians as part of his plan to concentrate them on reservations. Jesuit priests often served as intermediaries in his negotiations, maintaining a delicate position of responsibility to their Indian friends on the one hand and respect for the law and power of the United States on the other. The Jesuits were unable to prevent the coercion of the Indians of the Northwest, however, despite their diligent efforts.

To sum up: When the Indian was confronted by the aggressive idealism of the Christian missionary, he always politely listened, often asked searching questions, sometimes rejected the alien teachings in favor of his own, and sometimes accepted the "good news" directly or indirectly. By nature given to thought about the supernatural and about proper behavior, the Indian found Christianity an import as significant as the more material aspects of Western civilization. Many observers considered the Indian in his untutored state to possess Christian virtues more fully than did professing white Christians. Yet, more often than not, whites were unconsciously critical when they saw that Indians seemed to "take no thought for the morrow" and lacked such civilized traits as selfishness. The interaction between Christianity and paganism had its ludicrous aspects, but, though the Indians were reluctant to accept the profession of Christians, they took seriously the message of Jesus Christ.

CHAPTER 6

Indian Wars in the Colonial Period

WHILE the wars that led to the destruction or subordination of the major Indian nations in the East were the product of the late colonial and early national period, the early colonial wars foreshadowed the outcome. These wars cleared the immediate coastal area of any independent Indian sovereignties, though often incorporating individual Indians within the colonial economy as servants, slaves, or hangers-on. In some cases, tribal or band organization was maintained although the Indians lived in subjection to the larger sovereignty and power of the colonial governments.

While the initial reception accorded the first English colonists in the New World was generally friendly, sufficient cause of conflict soon arose. The origins of each war provide subjects for detailed research and complex debate. Such wars were, of course, perceived differently by the two sides. Enough evidence exists to indicate the strongly felt grievances of the coastal Indians that led them occasionally to strike the first blow. Those grievances were not simply conflicts over land. While land—the urge to get land and the urge to keep it—underlay most Indian-white conflicts, the opportunity both to get and to keep land was available to Europeans without the necessity to resort to arms. The sparse native population of the colonies—made even sparser by the "providential" plagues which cleared many of the coastal areas simultaneously with the arrival of the whites—made the acquisition of land by the few early European settlers easy. There was land enough for all—a sentiment frequently expressed by the Indians—as long as appropriate procedures were followed in its acquisition. Often the Indians gave permission for the settlers to sit down on a piece of land without exacting any return. More often, in the manner of traditional native exchange, equivalent gifts—trade goods, for example—were expected and received. The early records, as Thomas Jefferson discovered when he began to look into the matter, are filled with accounts of such negotiated exchanges, usually for practical considerations. Such exchanges were not often noted in England, where the theoretical legal right of the king to grant by charter the land of the Indians, or the moral validity of exchanging the spiritual blessings of Christianity for the surplus land of the Indians, was assumed. Nevertheless, negotiation and purchase probably constituted the principal method by which the English acquired land in America.

The next most important method was by war. What most often precipitated war were the unreasonable demands made upon the Indians by the whites and the unwillingness of the English authorities to concede to the Indian nations with which they were dealing the same rights to honor, existence, and subsistence that the English settlers claimed for themselves. The early history of the Virginia settlement, for example, is replete with accounts of forced requisitions made upon the Indians for food to subsist the improvident settlers. In the hard school of the times, little consideration was given to formal right. If the Indians of North America could be browbeaten or coerced by fear to supply European wants (as all the world knew the Indians of Central and South America had been coerced by the Spanish), so much the better. One could find a theological justification without too much difficulty. Indians had been kidnapped by ship captains from the earliest period of exploration. Their graves and their food caches had been broken open and robbed by visible saints in Massachusetts, by "pilgrims" in Plymouth, as well as by outlaws and pirates elsewhere. Their lands were also, at times, occupied with less than adequate ceremony. Nevertheless, colonial governments normally attempted to formalize the relationship with their Indian neighbors and often did so, as the examples of Governor Bradford in Plymouth and Captain John Smith in Jamestown demonstrate.

The agreements hammered out by such leaders were, however,

increasingly unstable because of the rapidly changing power relationships and because of the elements of coercion and fear which informed some of the agreements. Peace rested uneasily on agreements which were too often misunderstood by the Indians or broken by the whites. When, in the course of the Indian's continuing relationship with the white man, the latter's arrogance or demands became excessive or his contempt for Indian sovereignty unbearable, violence erupted. This is the pattern that emerged in Virginia and New England as well as in the other colonies.

The great massacre of 1622 in Virginia, which nearly caught the colonists unaware, expressed the smoldering resentments that had been built up during the early years of the settlement. The comments of Powhatan and his successor, Opechancanough, as they were repeatedly forced against their will to succor the colonists and allow English settlement of the interior, leave no doubt that exasperation at the course of the colonists' unending demands precipitated the violent reaction of 1622, a reaction that could just as easily have been forestalled by a more moderate course of action by the Virginia colonists.

Three hundred and fifty Virginians (out of a total population of less than 2,000) were killed by the Indians in the massacre of 1622. The blow, powerful though it was, did not eradicate the colony. English reaction was stern and unyielding. Perpetual war was declared on the surrounding Indians and even good faith often yielded to the desire to destroy so "faithless" an enemy. All Indians within the range of English power were either driven from their homes, destroyed, or subordinated to English authority. The range of English power in 1622 had been limited to the coastal fringe of the Chesapeake Bay and a few miles inland. As English expansion continued after 1622, and as relations were renewed with the Indian tribes of Virginia, new tensions developed which exploded in violence in 1644 when another coordinated Indian attack was made on the settlements. Although the colony reeled under the blow (500 of the roughly 8,000 colonists were killed) the attackers were eventually put down by the skilled management of Governor Sir William Berkeley though not before the captured Emperor Opechancanough had been dishonorably shot by his guard while in English custody.

The victory over Opechancanough eliminated the last remaining Indian opposition to further expansion, which thereupon continued at an even more rapid pace in the 1650s, when English royal authority was replaced in Virginia by a more casual form of parliamentary control. The expansion of the fifties and sixties, and the influx of both colonists and slaves in the third quarter of the century, created the pressure that resulted in the third major Indian war of Virginia's colonial period. That explosion, which was intimately related to the internal conflict known as Bacon's Rebellion, is better documented than earlier struggles. The evidence enables us to attribute the cause of the outbreak to a series of bloody exchanges on Virginia's upper Potomac frontier in which English breach of faith in killing several chiefs under a flag of truce was the precipitating factor that brought death and destruction to the frontier, retaliatory but unauthorized strikes by Bacon and his volunteers, and eventually total chaos and rebellion in the colony. By 1677 the Indian tribes in the Tidewater area were no longer able to threaten the colony. To the extent that they were hostile they could wage guerrilla warfare; to the extent they were peaceful, they could only flee the indiscriminate blows of Bacon's followers, who sought to exterminate all Indians—friendly or enemy.[1]

The pattern of warfare in early New England followed the Virginia example. At first each side had something to gain from the other and each dealt cautiously with the other, establishing a logical basis for coexistence. As English demands and expectations mounted, the Indians were placed in an increasingly untenable position. Indian lands became objectives to be sought, usually with the aid of one group of Indians against their hereditary enemies. The controversies concerning New England's Indian wars are many and intense. Some historians give the Puritans a clean bill of health; others condemn their alleged greed. The first great New England Indian war, the Pequot War, is subject to these conflicting interpretations. The cause of the war—the colonial reaction to the killing in 1634 of an English ship captain, Captain Stone, by

1. This summary of Virginia's early Indian wars is based on numerous accounts, including Richard L. Morton, *Colonial Virginia*, 2 vols. (Chapel Hill, N.C., 1960) ; and Wilcomb E. Washburn, *The Governor and the Rebel: A History of Bacon's Rebellion in Virginia* (Chapel Hill, N.C., 1957). A fuller account of Indian wars in Virginia and New England by the author of the present volume will appear in Volume XV of the revision of the *Handbook of North American Indians,* now in preparation at the Smithsonian Institution, Washington, D.C.

western Niantics allied with the Pequots and of another ship captain by Narragansetts on Block Island in 1636—is illustrative of the harsh standards established by the English for Indian behavior.

Although Pequot guilt in the killing of Stone had been at least partially expiated, and although both captains had unsavory records of illegal activities, the Massachusetts Bay Colony authorized a punitive expedition against the Pequots and against the Indians on Block Island. The expedition against the Pequots of eastern Connecticut, commanded by Lieutenant Lion Gardiner, was an unsuccessful search and destroy mission that placed the young Connecticut colony in grave peril when the Massachusetts troops went home leaving the Connecticut settlers to face the wrath of the outraged Pequots, who rejected Puritan accusations of their culpability in the deaths the Massachusetts government sought to avenge. The Pequots at this time attempted to patch up their differences with the Narragansetts to the east, urging that the English would destroy each in turn if they failed to unite. The Pequot effort was frustrated by Puritan diplomacy and by the sweet taste of revenge to the Narragansetts. In 1637 Captain John Mason of Connecticut, with ninety Englishmen and hundreds of Indian allies, marched to the principal Pequot village on the Mystic River and succeeded in utterly destroying the inhabitants—most of whom were women and children—to the horror of his Indian auxiliaries. John Underhill, in his account of the battle, noted that the native allies of the English, while rejoicing in the victory, "cried Mach it, mach it; that is, It is naught, it is naught, because it is too furious, and slays too many men." Massachusetts troops also seized the Pequots who had voluntarily surrendered to the Narragansetts (whom the latter wished to integrate into their ranks after the Indian custom), executed the men, and enslaved the women and children, an action which shocked the Narragansetts' sense of fair play in war. The Pequot tribe was virtually erased as a factor in New England life.[2]

While Massachusetts continued to encroach—physically and cul-

2. This account of New England's early Indian wars is based on numerous primary and secondary sources, including Alden T. Vaughan, *New England Frontier: Puritans and Indians, 1620–1675* (Boston, 1965); and George D. Langdon, Jr., *Pilgrim Colony: A History of New Plymouth, 1620–1691* (New Haven, Conn., 1966). John Underhill's comment is quoted in James Axtell, "The Scholastic Philosophy of the Wilderness," *William and Mary Quarterly*, 3d ser., XXIX (1972), 335–366, at 342.

turally—upon the neighboring Indians, a major conflict was averted until 1675, when King Philip's War ravaged New England. In terms of the percentage of white casualties among the total population and in the extent of destruction of villages, homes, and property, it was the most costly war in American history. Although described by English historians of the time and since as a conspiracy of the Indians against the white settlements, it is more likely that each side stumbled into war believing it to be the victim of past unwarranted assaults or the intended object of future ones. The fighting broke out in the border town of Swansea lying between the Plymouth Colony and King Philip's Wampanoag tribe near Narragansett Bay. Relations between the colonists and King Philip had become strained through a series of claims and counterclaims as a consequence of which the Plymouth authorities had forced a number of humiliating concessions upon King Philip, much in derogation of his claimed independence and personally insulting to his honor and to his pride.

The immediate cause of the war may be said to have been the murder of a "praying Indian" named John Sassamon shortly after he had reported to Governor Winslow of Plymouth in 1675 that Philip was preparing for war. Three Indians were condemned to death by a Plymouth court for the murder, one of whom, according to the English, asserted Philip's complicity. Philip himself protested his innocence. The Plymouth Colony prepared for war. The Indians, too, prepared for the worst. Few historians have noted that the first blood in the contest was drawn by the English, who shot Indians pilfering articles from a house the English had abandoned. There followed a classic case of escalation of the conflict, with most of the English jurisdictions in New England and most of the Indian tribes of the area inexorably drawn into the vortex of raid and counterraid. The thirst of some of the colonies for the expected fruits of war—Indian land and plunder—did not go unnoted, particularly by the Quakers of Rhode Island. Chief victims were to be (beside Philip and his Wampanoags) the faithful Narragansett allies of the English against their earlier enemies, the Pequots. The Narragansetts were accused of harboring Wampanoag refugees (as, indeed, they could be expected to have done in the context of Indian hospitality and adoption policies), and after some hesitation they were invaded by Connecticut and Massachusetts forces. The war was thus once more widened and the circle of Indian allies fighting what seemed to them to be a desperate battle for survival expanded.

The vengeance of Wampanoags, Nipmucks, and Narragansetts against isolated colonial settlements was sharp, and the wide destruction throughout New England led even so perceptive an observer as Governor Sir William Berkeley of Virginia to suspect that a general Indian conspiracy from New England to Virginia might exist. Philip's attempt to enlist Mahican Indians of New York was frustrated when Governor Andros of New York pressured the powerful Mohawk Indians to attack Philip and his men. Philip, bloodied by the hostility of the Iroquois, returned to fight a desperate guerrilla war in New England. The Indian forces were gradually neutralized, almost invariably with the aid of Indians who remained allied to, and served as auxiliaries with, the English forces. Indeed, the fortunes of the English in the war were directly correlated to the number of Indians in the English expeditions. When the war was finally won in August, 1676 (King Philip was killed by an Indian—not an Englishman—when his small force was trapped in a swamp), the English could count losses of 600 men and £150,000. Making up that bill were 1,200 houses burned and 8,000 head of cattle destroyed. Probably 3,000 Indians were killed. The independent power of the Indians of New England (with the exception of the tribes of Maine) was terminated. Thereafter most Indian-white relations in the interior of southern New England were conducted on an individual rather than a tribal basis.[3]

English colonization in the lower South, as elsewhere, proceeded without undue native opposition in its earliest stages. As settlement continued and the interests of the two sides came into conflict, the few powerful coastal tribes were either destroyed, driven away, or incorporated into the colonial defense system. In the colony of South Carolina, the point of explosion was reached early in the eighteenth century. In 1711 and 1712 the Tuscarora Indians, residing within the charter limits of North Carolina, lashed out at English encroachments. South Carolina, more populous and powerful than its northern neighbor, sent out expeditions against the

3. Douglas E. Leach, *Flintlock and Tomahawk: New England in King Philip's War* (New York, 1958) ; Wilcomb E. Washburn, "Governor Berkeley and King Philip's War," *New England Quarterly*, XXX (1957) , 363–377.

Tuscaroras. The Tuscarora power was broken and many were killed. The survivors trekked northward to become the sixth nation of the Iroquois Confederacy.

In 1715 the Yamasee Indians attacked the South Carolina settlements and plunged the colony into its most costly war. Four hundred colonists were killed and £116,000 sterling expended in the first two years of the war. Hostilities commenced with a surprise attack on the frontier settlements near Port Royal on Good Friday, April 15, 1715. Most of the Indian nations bordering on South Carolina joined in the attack, which has been attributed by the most thorough student of the subject solely to the abuses practiced by the Indian traders upon the Indians, abuses which the colony failed to prevent. The involvement of the powerful Creek nation in the war led Governor Charles Craven of South Carolina desperately to seek the support of the still neutral Cherokees. While one expedition attacked the Yamasees and forced their retreat across the Savannah River into Florida, Craven with a force of 300 men marched north with the hope of overawing the Cherokees and establishing an alliance with them. The Cherokees, who were being courted simultaneously by the Creeks, were split into two factions. The killing of several of the visiting Creek chiefs by Cherokees favorable to the English precipitated an alliance between the Cherokees and the English in January, 1716, an alliance which enabled the English to neutralize and eventually to overcome the hostility of the Creeks.[4]

The Dutch colony of New Amsterdam found itself engaged in warfare with the neighboring Indians for many of the same reasons that bedeviled the English in New England and in the southern colonies. The Dutch were even more insensitive and uncompromising than the English. Thus, in 1639, the Dutch attempted to levy a contribution "in peltries, maize or wampum" on the Indians around Manhattan on the excuse that the Dutch had hitherto protected these tribes against their enemies, an excuse which Allen W. Trelease notes "was completely specious since that service was neither asked for nor rendered." Other incidents began to poison the relationship between the Dutch and their red neighbors. In

4. M. Eugene Sirmans, *Colonial South Carolina: A Political History, 1663–1763* (Chapel Hill, N.C., 1966), pp. 111–115. See also E. Lawrence Lee, *Indian Wars in North Carolina, 1663–1763* (Raleigh, N.C., 1963), pp. 21–45.

1640 the Raritan Indians were blamed, perhaps unfairly, for killing some pigs on Staten Island. A Dutch retaliatory force ignored its instructions to demand payment for the loss, and instead killed and tortured several Indians. Similar incidents with other Indian tribes embittered relations and led to occasional border warfare. In February, 1643, the Dutch massacred in cold blood between 80 and 120 Wecquaesgeek Indians who had fled from the attacks of Mahican or Mohawk Indians and had gathered under what they thought was the protection of the Europeans at Corlaer's Hook on Manhattan Island and at Pavonia in the territory of the Hackensack Indians. The massacre immediately set the countryside on fire and Governor William Kieft's unnecessary war wracked the colony. Although perhaps a thousand Indians lost their lives in the period 1640–1645, Kieft's policy of intimidation was, in the opinion of Trelease, a failure. The Indians were neither exterminated nor cowed into submission, but became a threat rather than a support to the tiny Dutch colony in the decade to come.

While Kieft's successor, Peter Stuyvesant, was off on an expedition to conquer New Sweden in September, 1655, New Amsterdam was assaulted by 500 armed Indians, seeking revenge for various affronts. The Peach War it was called, since it was alleged to have started because of Hendrick van Dyck's killing a squaw whom he caught stealing peaches from his orchard. Although the causes of the outbreak may have been varied, Governor Stuyvesant himself attributed the outbreak to Dutch rashness as much as to any Indian fault. The ensuing Esopus Wars, as they were denominated because of the role of the Esopus Indians, came to an end in 1664. Although leaving the Algonquian bands of the lower Hudson River satellites of the Dutch, the victory was won at a cost of unprovoked war with the natives and interrupted growth of the colony. The weakened colony fell readily into the hands of an invading English fleet in September, 1664.[5]

The ability of the Indians of the East Coast vigorously to contest the European invasion of their lands derived in part from their ability to modify their traditional tactics to meet the European

5. Allen W. Trelease, *Indian Affairs in Colonial New York: The Seventeenth Century* (Ithaca, N.Y., 1960), pp. 65–83, 139, 143, 173–174; see also Thomas J. Condon, *New York Beginnings: The Commercial Origins of New Netherland* (New York, 1968), pp. 154–156.

threat and in part from their readiness to adopt the new technological instruments brought by the European. Nowhere was their ability more clearly demonstrated than in the St. Lawrence valley down which the French began their expansion into the interior of North America. Prior to 1609, both the Mohawks, one of the Iroquois Confederacy, and their enemies wore body armor, carried shields, and fought with bows and arrows. Their traditional tactics, indeed, bore some resemblance to European field tactics, with the opposing forces forming two lines in the open and discharging their weapons at each other. With the introduction of European firearms by Champlain, these tactics broke down. Moreover, because Champlain took the side of the Algonquians against the Iroquois, the latter were, for some time, placed at a disadvantage in relation to their traditional foes. The Mohawks thereupon resorted to a greater use of ambushes and other stratagems which would reduce the advantage held by their foes should the confrontation take place in the open. From 1609 until 1641 the Iroquois developed guerrilla warfare tactics which helped to neutralize the advantages of the European matchlock. By the latter date, the Iroquois began to acquire European firearms from the Dutch at Albany. The Iroquois thereupon came once more out of the forest and utilized the new weapon for assault purposes, following up the discharge of their arquebuses with hand-to-hand fighting. At the same time, they retained their ambush tactics, utilizing their new firearms with deadly effect, particularly in laying ambushes along the banks of rivers to intercept Huron canoes laden with furs. Gradually, with the increased use of firearms, body armor was discarded and the Iroquois warrior went into battle with little more than a loincloth and moccasins. The Iroquois battle line became a skirmish line, with individuals spread out widely, maintaining contact by voice. Envelopment became a favorite tactic. A Frenchman, describing the tactics of Iroquois warriors, noted that "they approach like foxes, fight like lions and disappear like birds."[6]

Because the Iroquois were an agricultural people and could

6. The following discussion is derived from Keith F. Otterbein, "An Analysis of Iroquois Military Tactics," *Ethnohistory*, XI (1964), 56–63, reprinted in *Law and Warfare: Studies in the Anthropology of Conflict*, ed. Paul Bohannan (New York, 1967), 345–349. The quotation is from Ruth M. Underhill, *Red Man's America: A History of the Indians in the United States*, rev. ed. (Chicago, 1971), p. 96.

prepare food to carry with them on long forays, they had an advantage over some of their enemies who were more dependent upon hunting animals on the hoof. They were thus able to move large war parties over long distances. Combining their natural bravery, European arms, an interior geographical position, and a strong unity within the league, the Iroquois overcame the initial disadvantage to which they had been put by the arrival of the Europeans and gradually attained a position of dominance in the whole Northeast region.

The Iroquois, more so than other Indian nations, were able to modify the traditional blood feud and to turn their aggression outward. When a member of one's family was killed by an outsider, the Iroquois family was morally obliged to avenge the killing. A feud might be precipitated by almost any "cause" and, as it was avenged, an equivalent "cause" was established on the other side. Eventually each side had so many scores to settle that a state of chronic war was created. It was to eliminate just such feuds that the League of the Iroquois was established among the five (later six) members of the Iroquois Confederacy. The purpose is clearly stated in the so-called Dekanawidah myth describing the origin of the league, and in the condolence ceremonies which marked the death of any one of the forty-nine members of the council. Anthony Wallace has hypothesized that the success of the Iroquois in eliminating internal blood feuds intensified the zeal and ferocity with which league members settled external scores. "The *pax Iroquois*," he has asserted, "resulted in the displacement of revenge motivations outward, onto surrounding peoples, Indian and European alike." This displacement of aggression, however, created further problems as more and more warriors were involved in more distant and costly feuds. The manpower loss was replaced in part by captives or by nearby Indian nations who were coerced into a subordinate relationship to the league. Nevertheless, the pressures—both physical and psychological—created an almost Spartan preoccupation with death and combat.

The superstructure of coordinating authority represented by the league sachems could not peremptorily or authoritatively prevent individual warriors or groups of warriors, often acting at the instigation of the women whose men had been struck down by the enemy, from avenging their kinfolk's losses even while the league itself was committed to neutrality or peace. This lack of control often puzzled and outraged the European allies and enemies of the Iroquois, but the chiefs could honestly say that they could not control their young men, who were apt to listen to the women rather than to them.[7]

While it has been customary to interpret many of the Iroquois wars of the seventeenth century in economic terms—the Iroquois, according to this thesis, sought the beneficial position of middleman in the fur trade between the Indians and the Europeans—it is possible to interpret the hostilities of the Iroquois with the French and their Indian allies as the result of cross-cultural misunderstanding. A study of the causes of the Fourth Iroquois War (1657–1667) gives support to this thesis.[8]

When thirty Oneidas murdered three Frenchmen near Montreal in October, 1657, Louis d'Ailleboust, the acting governor of New France, ordered the arrest of all Iroquois to be found in the colony. Twelve were seized, a few of them Onondagas and the rest Mohawks. All were put in chains and imprisoned. The Mohawk leaders, in particular, were furious, disclaiming responsibility for the Oneida incident of which they knew nothing, and complaining, furthermore, of the murder of several of their men by the French. They asked for the release of their captives and offered to forgive their other injuries. The French response was one of disdain and rejection of the request. The war was now on and the familiar pattern of misunderstanding followed by escalation became operative. By 1663 the war was so severe that Louis XIV felt compelled to assume direct responsibility for the colony, until then governed by a trading company, the Company of One Hundred Associates. French pride as well as ignorance was now a principal mover of policy. Louis appointed Alexandre de Prouville, Marquis de Tracy, Lieutenant General of America with orders to chastise the Iroquois by carrying the war to their country killing man and woman, young and old. Four companies of regular troops from the West Indies were sent for the purpose along with a regiment direct from France.

7. Anthony F. C. Wallace, *The Death and Rebirth of the Seneca* (New York, 1970) , pp. 44–48.

8. George T. Hunt, *The Wars of the Iroquois: A Study in Intertribal Relations* (Madison, Wisc., 1940) ; Edward H. Spicer, *A Short History of the Indians of the United States* (New York, 1969) , pp. 25, 27; Raoul Naroll, "The Causes of the Fourth Iroquois War," *Ethnohistory,* XVI (1969) , 51–81.

The power of the Sun King, however, did not extinguish the independence of the Iroquois. Although French forces ravaged the Iroquois country, destroying crops and burning villages, they were not able to destroy the Iroquois population. Nevertheless, the Iroquois asked once more for a peaceful settlement and in 1667 it was granted.

What the French had overlooked was the intensity of the feeling that revenge, or reparations, must be obtained for violations of the rules governing interaction between peoples. The Indians' attempt to settle, in their customary fashion, violations of the peace existing between themselves and the French was rarely accepted or comprehended by the latter. Nor was the factor of prestige and status, which loomed large in Indian warfare, fully comprehended. Nor was the lack of arbitrary power of the Iroquois League to discipline individual nations or individual members. The French and Iroquois faced each other with startlingly different assumptions. For the Iroquois, gaining a livelihood was largely a communal affair while fighting was largely an individual one. For the French, fighting was largely a communal affair; gaining a livelihood largely an individual one. The Oneida party that killed the three Frenchmen were individuals probably acting in obedience to the dictates of prestige. In French eyes they represented a calculated policy of Iroquois insolence and contempt for the French.

That motives of prestige and revenge predominated over those related to the economic value to be gained by control of the fur trade routes is suggested by the low value placed by Iroquois chiefs on material wealth. Numerous observers noted that chiefs among the Iroquois (as Johannes Megapolensis, a Dutch missionary who visited them in 1644, put it), "are generally the poorest among them, for instead of receiving from the common people, as among Christians, they are obliged to give to the mob. . . ." Moreover, in the peace negotiations between the Iroquois and the French in this period, no mention was made of the fur trade. What was of concern to the Indians was the bad treatment received by their ambassadors and wrongs suffered in violation of earlier treaties.

Just as prestige and outrage at the violation of accepted norms of behavior motivated the Iroquois, so too did similar motives trigger French reaction. Neither the desire to increase her territorial holdings, nor to increase her trade, nor to propagate the faith seems to have weighed as heavily with the French as concern with upholding France's "honor" against the assumed "insults" of the Iroquois. French assumptions of the duplicity and untrustworthiness of the Iroquois can perhaps be explained as a misunderstanding of Indian behavior. By failing to respond generously to the generous Iroquois offers of accommodation and settlement of differences, the French foreclosed peaceful means of resolving those differences. By assuming a perfidy and contempt that very probably did not exist, the French forced upon themselves an exhausting and unrewarding relationship of permanent hostility.[9]

Indians were capable not only of adopting European military tactics in the colonial period but of more fully utilizing European military "hardware" than is realized. The traditional picture of the Indian as entirely dependent upon the white man for the repair of weapons and the manufacture of bullets needs to be modified. William Bradford, governor of Plymouth Colony in its formative years, complained that the Indians of New England, particularly those under the direful influence of Thomas Morton of Merrymount, in addition to having many fowling pieces, muskets, and pistols, "have also their moulds to make shot of all sorts, as musket bullets, pistol bullets, swan and goose shot, and smaller sorts." In addition they possessed "screw-plates to make screw-pins themselves when they want them, with sundry other implements, wherewith they are ordinarily better fitted and furnished than the English themselves." Bradford was afraid that Indians would soon learn to make gunpowder.[10]

When Massachusetts officials forbade the mending of Indian weapons by English blacksmiths in the 1640s, some Indians acquired the requisite skills to perform the task. The Narragansetts, who possessed their own forge and a skilled blacksmith, suffered a heavy blow when the English discovered and destroyed the Narra-

9. Naroll, *op. cit.*, especially 54, 56, 59.
10. Patrick M. Malone, "Indian and English Military Systems in New England in the Seventeenth Century" (Ph.D. diss., Brown University, 1971); paper prepared by Malone for annual meeting of the Organization of American Historians, Washington, D.C., April 5–8, 1972, entitled "Changing Military Technology Among the Indians of Southern New England, 1600–1677," printed with editorial revisions in *American Quarterly*, XXV (1973), 48–63.

gansett fort in the Great Swamp during King Philip's War in 1676. The English killed the blacksmith during the fight, demolished his forge, and took away his tools. In May, 1676, again during King Philip's War, an Indian camp on the Connecticut River was taken. The soldiers "demolished two forges they had to mend their arms; took away all their materials and tools . . . and threw two great pigs of lead of theirs (intended for making bullets) into the said river."[11]

Even the fortifications of the New England Indians during the seventeenth century were often constructed after European models. While the early Indian forts were often built by the English for their allies, their features were occasionally adapted by the Indians in the forts they later built for themselves. A particularly ingenious stone and boulder fort known as "the Queen's Fort," occupied by the Narragansetts after their wooden fort was destroyed in King Philip's War, was constructed by a Narragansett stonemason, Stone-wall John, and included a semicircular bastion and a sharp flanker, features derived from European forts of the period.[12]

By the end of the seventeenth century the coastal tribes along most of the Atlantic seaboard had been destroyed, dispersed, or subjected directly to European control. Yet the interior tribes—particularly those who had grouped themselves into confedera-tions—remained powers (and were usually styled "nations") who dealt with Europeans on a rough plane of equality. Throughout the eighteenth century, the Creeks, Choctaws, Chickasaws, Cherokees, and Iroquois, as well as the tribes of the Old Northwest, alternately made war and peace with the various European powers, entered into treaties of alliance and friendship, and sometimes made ces-sions of territory as a result of defeat in war. As the imperial power of France and Great Britain expanded into the interior, these powerful Indian nations were forced to seek new orientations in their policy. For each Indian nation the reorientation was different, yet each was powerfully affected by the growth of European settle-ments, population, and military power. The history of the reorien-tation of Iroquois policy toward the Europeans may serve as an

11. Malone, "Changing Military Technology," pp. 10, 12 (58 in printed version) .

12. *Ibid.*, pp. 13–14 (59–60 in printed version) .

example of the process that all the interior nations experienced in the eighteenth century.

The stability that had marked the Iroquois Confederacy's generally pro-British position was shattered with the overthrow of James II in 1688, the colonial uprisings that followed in Massachusetts, New York, and Maryland, and the commencement of King William's War (the War of the League of Augsburg) against Louis XIV of France. The increasing French threat to English hegemony in the interior of North America was signalized by French-led or French-inspired attacks on the Iroquois and on outlying colonial settlements in New York and New England. The high point of the Iroquois response was the spectacular raid of August 5, 1689, in which the Iroquois virtually wiped out the French village of Lachine, just outside Montreal. A counterraid by the French on the English village of Schenectady in March, 1690, instilled an appropriate measure of fear among the English and their Iroquois allies.

The Iroquois position at the end of the war, which was formalized by treaties made during the summer of 1701 in Albany and Montreal with the British and French, and which was maintained throughout most of the eighteenth century, was one of "aggressive neutrality" between the two competing European powers. Under the new system the Iroquois initiated a peace policy toward the "far Indians," tightened their control over the nearby tribes, and induced both English and French to support their neutrality toward the European powers by appropriate gifts and concessions.

By holding the balance of power in the sparsely settled borderlands between English and French settlements and by their willingness to use their power against one or the other nation if not appropriately treated, the Iroquois played the game of European power politics with effectiveness. The system broke down, however, after the French became convinced that the Iroquois were compromising the system in favor of the English and launched a full-scale attempt to establish French physical and juridical presence in the Ohio Valley, the heart of the borderlands long claimed by the Iroquois. As a consequence of the ensuing Great War for Empire, in which Iroquois neutrality was dissolved and European influence moved closer, the play-off system lost its efficacy and a system of direct bargaining supplanted it.[13]

13. Wallace, *Death and Rebirth of the Seneca*, pp. 111–114.

Relations with the powerful interior Cherokees, Creeks, Choctaws, and Chickasaws in the South in the eighteenth century were carried on by the southern colonies with the same diplomatic concern demonstrated by the northern colonies in their dealings with the Iroquois. Not only was diplomacy expensive in Indian presents, but it was time-consuming and difficult for colonial officials to make sure that private injuries committed by one side against the other did not lead to public war. Trade, often the source of disputes because of the temptations involved, was the subject of strict regulation by colonial governments in an attempt to minimize the threat of war.

The focal point of Indian relations in the southern colonies in the eighteenth century was South Carolina. After crushing the small coastal tribes, the colony sought to establish alliances with the powerful inland nations against the French and Spanish. The game of diplomacy-war-trade went on throughout the eighteenth century with the Indian nations being courted by all the European powers. When the Choctaws were weaned away from their French alliance in 1746 by the efforts of James Adair, the Indian trader who served also as the representative of the governor of South Carolina, the English seemed on the point of a major diplomatic triumph. Yet, the affair was botched through inefficiency and inaction on the part of the colonial government and the Choctaws reverted to their earlier comfortable relationship with the French. The English were more fortunate in maintaining the continuing support of the brave Chickasaws, far distant though they were in the Mississippi country, largely through the Chickasaws' inveterate hatred of the French, but also because of the effective policy of trade and support extended to them by the South Carolina government.[14]

Less effective were South Carolina's relations with the Cherokees. Although marked by many years of peace and friendship, during which time the Cherokees urged the Carolinians to build a fort in their country to aid against the inroads of French-supported Indians, poor handling of the periodic crises that arose resulted in a long and costly war in the period 1759–1761. Although the serious-

14. Wilcomb E. Washburn, introduction to James Adair's *History of the American Indians* (London, 1775) , in *The Colonial Legacy,* ed. Lawrence H. Leder, Vol. III (New York, 1973) , pp. 98–110.

ness of the war was emphasized by the sending of regular troops in 1760 and 1761 to aid the colonial forces, the results were disappointing. The war came "ingloriously" to an end, as one historian has put it, "having cost the province over a hundred thousand pounds sterling, between a hundred and fifty and two hundred lives, and the devastation and partial abandonment of a large part of its area." No compensating advantage was gained for either province or Crown.[15]

A less belligerent but more effective policy was established by the colony of Georgia with the neighboring Creek nation. That policy, formulated by Governor Henry Ellis in the period 1756–1760, relied on diplomacy rather than force to induce the powerful Creeks to turn away from their alliance with the French and to heighten their aversion for the Spanish in Florida. Ellis carefully regulated the Indian trade of the colony so that disputes and the cheating of the Indians were minimized. Ellis also sought to redress injustices committed by the English against the Creeks, and he was slow to interpret individual Creek depredations against outlying Georgia settlers as expressing the will of the Creek nation to go to war. Ellis always received Indian visitors with ceremony and politeness (in one year's time he entertained nearly 1,300). He was careful to distribute bountiful presents to Creek headmen to maintain the good relations that he had established with them. The success of Ellis's policy can be measured by the fact that, though the South Carolina border was laid waste by the Cherokees during Ellis's term as governor, Georgia itself was largely spared Indian attacks, and Creek neutrality was, to a large extent, maintained.[16]

The early years of Pennsylvania's history, after its founding in 1681, lack the bitterness and conflict with the local Indian population that marked the early history of the other colonies. As William Penn, the founder, put it in his *Further Account of the Province of Pennsylvania*, in 1685, despite the many stories that have been "prejudicially propagated, as if we were upon ill terms with the

15. Robert L. Meriwether, *The Expansion of South Carolina, 1729–1765* (Kingsport, Tenn., 1940) , p. 240.

16. William W. Abbot, *The Royal Governors of Georgia, 1754–1775* (Chapel Hill, N.C., 1959) , pp. 72–82.

Natives," the truth was otherwise, namely, "that we have liv'd in great friendship." Penn was scrupulous in paying for the land claimed by the Indians and in seeing that no affronts were offered them.[17]

Pennsylvania's generally peaceable relations with the Indians were increasingly eroded as France and England began to struggle for preeminence in the interior of the continent and on the "back sides" of the English coastal settlements. During King William's War, beginning in 1689, a growing conflict developed between the Quaker-dominated government, which could not be true to its beliefs and still support military measures, even in defense of the colony, and the growing body of non-Quakers who thought in terms more typical of the citizens of other colonies. Yet, as one scholar has pointed out, not until 1754, when Virginia sent George Washington to drive the French from the forks of the Ohio, did France and England fight a battle on Pennsylvania soil. Nor had there been a significant Indian raid or attack on frontier settlements in Pennsylvania prior to that time.[18]

When most of the Quakers elected to the Assembly of 1756, following the initiation of French-English hostilities, declined their seats, the end of Quaker Indian policy could truly be said to have been reached. Pennsylvania was no longer a "Quaker" province. An imperial government took charge of Indian affairs in the province.[19]

Pennsylvania now became the scene of the worst examples of unjustified violence against the Indians, just as it had earlier been the scene of the most generous examples of goodwill toward the natives. In December, 1763, one of the worst atrocities in American history occurred, committed by the "Christian white savages" (as Benjamin Franklin called them) of Peckstang and Donegall who, in cold blood and without justification, massacred a group of

17. Albert Cook Myers, ed., *Narratives of Early Pennsylvania, West New Jersey and Delaware, 1630–1707* (New York, 1912) , p. 276.

18. Edwin B. Bronner, *William Penn's 'Holy Experiment': The Founding of Pennsylvania, 1681–1701* (New York, 1962) , p. 181; Robert L. D. Davidson, *War Comes to Quaker Pennsylvania, 1682–1756* (New York, 1957) , Preface, vi. Gary B. Nash, *Quakers and Politics: Pennsylvania, 1681–1726* (Princeton, N.J., 1968) , p. 87, comments that though Quaker relations with the Indians were conducted "with unusual success," nevertheless, "historians have exaggerated the state of harmony between the two cultural groups."

19. Albert T. Volwiler, *George Croghan and the Westward Movement, 1741–1782* (Cleveland, 1926) , pp. 125, 187–193.

unoffending Christian Conestoga Indians. Pennsylvania's vast and
strategic frontier was marred by many such incidents of violence,
often of an individual or small group character, which quickly
altered the character of Penn's "peaceable kingdom."[20]

20. Benjamin Franklin, *A Narrative of the Late Massacres, in Lancaster
County, of a Number of Indians, Friends of This Province, by Persons Unknown. With Some Observations on the Same* (Philadelphia, 1764) .

CHAPTER 7

The American Revolution and Its Aftermath

T HE period of the American Revolution was one of those turning points in American Indian history that changed fundamentally the character of Indian-white relations on the continent. Like the period of removal in the 1830s, when most of the principal Indian nations east of the Mississippi were required to move west of that river, and the period of westward expansion in the 1840s and 1850s, when the great majority of tribes west of the Mississippi were defeated and shunted onto reservations west of that river, the forces unleashed by the American Revolution undermined the power and independence of Indian nations which had formerly dealt on a rough plane of equality with the white settlers and their governments.

The defeat of the French during the Great War for Empire in midcentury had left most of the Indian nations of the interior without a potential ally against the encroaching English colonists. Though temporarily restrained by the Proclamation of 1763 limiting white settlement to the area east of the Appalachians, the colonists showed increasing signs of breaking the bonds that limited them to the East Coast littoral. Formal treaties with the Indian nations of the interior attempted to establish English title to areas west of the mountains, in anticipation of future white settlement, but these treaties sometimes exacerbated tensions rather than relieved them.

By the Treaty of Fort Stanwix in 1768 the Iroquois surrendered their claim to the lands south of the Ohio and Susquehanna rivers. Although these lands were occupied by Indians—such as Mingos and Shawnees—acknowledging dependence upon the Iroquois, these Indians denied the right of the Iroquois to sell their lands since their dependency, they claimed, was based on a compact of mutual responsibilities rather than a unilateral surrender of their rights. The Six Nations, though embarrassed by the objections raised (and though inclined to support their former friends in the hostilities that soon ensued), attempted to justify and rationalize the sale by claims of unrestricted authority over the Indians of the area. With the "sale," white land jobbers began moving into the rich lands of Kentucky. One party of these frontiersmen committed unprovoked murders on the family of Logan, the Great Mingo, a Cayuga Indian born on the Susquehanna River who had emigrated to the Ohio River and married a Shawnee wife. In addition to evoking one of the finest Indian speeches ever recorded (made famous by Thomas Jefferson's investigation of the matter), the murders provoked what has been known as Lord Dunmore's War, after the name of the colonial governor of Virginia who prosecuted it, in 1774. The war was pursued by the Virginia militia until the defeat of the outnumbered Indians—Shawnee, Delaware, Mingo, Wyandot, Seneca, Cayuga, and others—at the Battle of Point Pleasant. Lord Dunmore's War was an anticipation of the larger and more serious struggle that burst forth in the following year and which engulfed the most powerful Indian nations from the St. Lawrence River to the peninsula of Florida.[1]

When the opening shots of the American Revolution were fired at Lexington and Concord the relationship of the powerful Iroquois Confederacy with the rebels on the one hand and the loyalists on the other assumed increasing importance. The Iroquois had traditionally played a vital role in conflicts between Europeans and had maintained their independence proudly and fiercely, however much European powers claimed a theoretical sovereignty over them. The strategic location of the Iroquois, close to the Hudson River axis dividing New England from the middle and southern colonies, with interior lines of communication to the backsides of all of the

1. Anthony F. C. Wallace, *The Death and Rebirth of the Seneca* (New York, 1970), pp. 121–125; Wilcomb E. Washburn, "Logan's Speech, 1774," in *An American Primer*, 2 vols., ed. Daniel J. Boorstin (Chicago, 1966), 1, 60–64.

northern and middle colonies, made Iroquois intentions of particular concern to both sides. Both loyalists and rebels had established
bonds of friendship and interest with the different league members
and each side sought to explain the causes of the conflict to the
uncomprehending tribesmen. Guy Johnson, who had replaced his
father-in-law and uncle, Sir William Johnson, as superintendent of
Indian affairs in the northern area, explained the quarrel simply:

This dispute was solely occasioned by some people, who notwithstanding a
law of the King and his wise Men, would not let some Tea land, but
destroyed it, on which he was angry, and sent some Troops with the
General, whom you have long known, to see the Laws executed and bring
the people to their senses, and as he is proceeding with great wisdom, to
shew them their great mistake, I expect it will soon be over.[2]

The Second Continental Congress, meeting in Philadelphia in
the summer of 1775, concerned lest the continuing influence of the
king's loyal superintendents of Indian affairs might work to the
colonists' disadvantage, organized an Indian Department of its own
and appointed commissioners to deal with the various Indian
nations. There followed a series of congresses with the Six Nations
called by each side in the revolutionary struggle to further its purposes. The Americans urged that the Six Nations sit the war out;
that they remain neutral in what was a family quarrel between
Englishmen on two sides of the ocean. "We don't wish you to take
up the hatchet against the King's troops," the Continental Congress
assured the Iroquois. "We desire you to remain at home, and not
join on either side."[3]
At a congress held in Albany in August, 1775, the Six Nations
solemnly pledged to remain neutral in the struggle. The Iroquois
for some time maintained a neutral stance despite the blandishments of the king's representatives, but soon cracks in the league
structure began to appear. Under the prodding of Colonel John
Butler, the British commander at Fort Niagara, the Senecas were
prevailed upon, at a council at Irondequoit in July, 1777 (after
being liberally entertained with feasts, rum, and gifts) to "take up
the hatchet" against the Americans. Shortly before this meeting, on
May 25, 1776, the Continental Congress had passed a resolution

2. Quoted in Barbara Graymont, *The Iroquois in the American Revolution*
(Syracuse, N.Y., 1972) , p. 57.
3. Quoted in *ibid.,* p. 72.

recommending a direct military alliance with the Indians and authorizing the enlistment of Indian allies. Although the Americans were less active than the British in urging the Six Nations to abandon their neutrality, they did seek and accept aid from those nations—notably the Oneida and Tuscarora—most inclined to their side.[4]

Soon brother was fighting brother and the great League of the Iroquois, founded to avert such a clash, lay shattered, never fully to recover its ancient power or glory. At Oriskany, on August 6, 1777, the American General Nicholas Herkimer, marching to the relief of Fort Stanwix with a force which included sixty Indians, mostly Oneidas, was ambushed and badly mauled (sustaining 500 casualties) by Sir John Johnson, Joseph Brant (the brilliant Mohawk chief), and a force of Seneca warriors under Sayenqueraghta. Although loyalist losses were small in comparison with those of the Americans, seventeen Senecas were killed and sixteen wounded. Five Seneca chiefs were among those killed. In Indian terms, the losses were great, and the resentment of the Senecas at the Oneida force supporting Herkimer was particularly intense. The blood drawn at Oriskany helped embitter and accentuate the divisions already existing among the Six Nations.

At a council held in Albany in September, 1777, those Iroquois favorably inclined to the American side—mostly Oneidas and Tuscaroras, but also a few warriors from the Onondaga and Mohawk nations—took hold of the war belt proffered by the American commissioners and, in effect, formally declared war on their brothers arrayed in the British camp. In the course of the council, news of the engagement between the forces of General John Burgoyne moving south from Canada toward Albany and an American army under General Horatio Gates at Freeman's Farm was received and 150 Oneida and Tuscarora warriors moved swiftly through the night to render important assistance to the rebels the following day. Burgoyne's thrust was stopped and his army forced to surrender.[5]

Although Britain's northern army had been frustrated in its attempt to cut the colonies in two, combined British and Indian forces operating in the Iroquois country were able to ravage the frontier with dozens of well-executed and destructive raids, mostly

4. *Ibid.*, pp. 100, 122–124.
5. *Ibid.*, pp. 148–150.

in the Wyoming Valley of Pennsylvania in July, 1778, and at Cherry Valley, New York, in November of the same year. The seriousness of the threat posed by the guerrilla warfare organized in the Iroquois country was sufficient to induce General George Washington to strike back with an all-out blow in August and September, 1779. A three-pronged attack was carefully planned utilizing four brigades under the command of Major General John Sullivan. Sullivan laid waste the houses and fields of the hitherto untouched enemy villages after defeating in a pitched battle the combined British-Indian force that attempted to prevent his advance. While Sullivan did not destroy the Indians he effectively chastised them. Many died of freezing or starvation in the extraordinarily cold winter of 1779–1780. In the retaliatory attacks that followed in 1780 the faithful Oneida and Tuscarora nations suffered greatly. They discovered, moreover, that their American allies seemed unable or unwilling to relieve their suffering and losses in a timely manner.

The advent of the American Revolution in the South placed the powerful Indian confederacies in that region in a dilemma similar to that which faced the Six Nations Confederacy in the North. Could the Cherokees, Creeks, Choctaws, and Chickasaws—who could bring 10,000 warriors into the field—stand aside from the conflict? If not, on whose side should they throw their weight? As the war began, the king's superintendent for Indian affairs in the South, John Stuart, was confident in the ability of his deputies—Alexander Cameron among the Cherokees, David Taitt among the Creeks, Charles Stuart among the Choctaws, and Farquhar Bethune among the Chickasaws—to keep these powerful Indian nations in the British interest. In the summer of 1775, Stuart, a long-time resident of Charlestown, was forced to flee, first to Georgia, and finally to St. Augustine, to avoid the wrath of the patriots who accused him of stirring up the Indians to attack the frontier settlements.[6]

6. James H. O'Donnell, III, "The Southern Indians in the War of Independence, 1775–1783" (Ph.D. diss., Duke University, 1963), pp. 9–10, 17, 102–103, 163. O'Donnell's dissertation, in substantially the same form, was published by the University of Tennessee Press, Knoxville, 1973, under the title *Southern Indians in the American Revolution*. The story of the Southern Indians during the American Revolution was earlier told by Helen Louise Shaw, *British Administration of the Southern Indians, 1756–1783* (Lancaster, Pa., 1931).

To handle their Indian affairs, the rebels appointed their own representatives to the Indians. South Carolina's Provincial Congress in July, 1775, created two committees of inquiry for Indian affairs. George Galphin and Edward Wilkinson, two traders of long standing, were appointed to the committee. Galphin, a friend of trader-historian James Adair and active in the Creek trade since the 1740s, informed the Creeks that he had been appointed to fill the place of John Stuart. The Continental Congress, meanwhile, in its plan for the management of Indian affairs adopted July 12, 1775, appointed commissioners for each of three departments—southern, northern, and middle—with authority to treat with the Indians and to apprehend anyone guilty of stirring them up. The Congress, as noted earlier, at this time urged the Indians to stay out of what was described as a "family quarrel."[7]

The English commander in North America, General Thomas Gage, proposed to Lord Dartmouth, Secretary of State for the Colonies, in June, 1775, that, because the rebels were allegedly seeking the services of the Indians, "we need not be tender of calling upon the Savages. . . ." Dartmouth agreed and sent instructions to Colonel Guy Johnson, the superintendent of the northern Indian department, to enlist Indians against the rebels. The same policy was commended to John Stuart by General Gage "when opportunity offers." Stuart chose to interpret the instructions from Gage to imply that the Indians could act most effectively in conjunction with troops, not independently in indiscriminate attacks on the frontiers. Late in 1775 Stuart decided that the time had come to enlist the Creeks and Cherokees in support of the loyalists who had taken arms to resist the rebels. Stuart promised to supply the tribes with provisions and war materials. But he still warned against indiscriminate attacks on the frontier.[8]

British agents journeyed to the Cherokees and sought to allay the distress caused them by American encroachments on their land and by the curtailment of trade relations. The British agents, Alexander Cameron and Henry Stuart (John's brother and deputy), at the request of the Cherokees, wrote letters to the American settlers encroaching on Indian land at Watauga and Nolichucky advising

7. *Ibid.*, pp. 33–34, 37.
8. *Ibid.*, pp. 13–15, 21–26; Gage to Dartmouth, June 12, 1772, in Thomas Gage, *The Correspondence of General Thomas Gage with the Secretaries of State, 1763–1775*, 2 vols., ed. Clarence E. Carter (New Haven, Conn., 1931) , I, 404.

them to withdraw within twenty days. The settlers were thereby both placed on their guard and given evidence documenting, in their eyes, the threat of Indian attack, instigated by the British, on their homes. Rumors were spread that loyalist houses were to be spared by a prior understanding to mark them in a distinctive way.[9]

The rebels, meanwhile, worked to neutralize the Indians. A conference was called with the Cherokees in April, 1776, and with the Creeks in May. The Indians voiced complaints about white encroachment on their lands, attacks on their persons, the building of forts near their lands, and the closing of trade. Little progress was made owing to the factionalism of the Indians and the inability of the rebel commissioners to resolve the complaints of the Indians.

Soon after this meeting, however, the Cherokees were swayed by a delegation of northern Indians—consisting of Shawnees, Delawares, and Mohawks—urging war. The resulting blows fell on the outlying settlements in Virginia, North Carolina, and South Carolina to whom warnings had previously been sent. Reports of pillage and death stirred the rebels. Retaliation followed swiftly. By the end of July Colonel Andrew Williamson of South Carolina had raised a force of over a thousand men and begun a campaign of destruction in the Cherokee lower towns. Every town was burned and all the corn that could be found was destroyed. North Carolina and Virginia put several thousand men under arms under the command of Colonel William Christian and General Griffith Rutherford. This force brought a taste of death and destruction to the middle and upper towns in September, 1776, and forced a negotiation which spared the northern Cherokees the destruction that had been dealt the southern Cherokees.[10]

On October 1, 1776, Colonel William Christian led his Virginians toward the Overhill Cherokee towns. Most of the Cherokees fled, leaving their horses, cattle, hogs, and fowls, as well as corn. Dragging Canoe, a leading chief, and some loyal followers moved down the Tennessee to build new towns in the vicinity of the present Chattanooga. The majority sought to avoid destruction by agreeing to give hostages, to seize the king's representatives, and to cede a

9. O'Donnell, *op. cit.*, pp. 21–26, 66–72.
10. *Ibid.*, pp. 23–25, 71–78.

portion of their land. Details were to be worked out in a formal peace treaty the following spring. The collapse of Cherokee resistance was disappointing and frustrating to the king's agents.

The fate of the Cherokees proved effective propaganda in the hands of rebel leaders. George Galphin spread the word among the Creeks and Choctaws of the fate of their northern neighbors. In spite of outrages committed against the Creeks by American frontiersmen, Galphin was able to keep the tribesmen from raiding the American settlements. The British Indian officials were discredited and the tribes discouraged from attempting action that might lead to similar retribution. The destruction of the Cherokees dampened the ardor of all the southern tribes and made John Stuart's task after 1777 virtually hopeless.[11]

Poor coordination and communications plagued the British. When a British force came to Georgia late in 1778, taking Savannah and striking toward Augusta, they found only a few hundred loyalists and no Indians. No one informed John Stuart in Pensacola of the move until late in January, by which time the king's army had withdrawn. Nevertheless, Stuart attempted to raise a Creek force to join the British troops. They met, instead, rebel troops, and retired in disgust. A few hundred Creeks under Alexander McGillivray did reach the British army in Savannah and served during the spring and summer of 1779 with the royal forces.[12]

When John Stuart died in Pensacola on March 21, 1779, Governor Peter Chester of West Florida asserted his authority over the Indian department until a new superintendent was commissioned. Lord George Germain, Secretary of State for the Colonies, eventually divided the department, appointing Alexander Cameron superintendent of the Mississippi District (which included the Choctaws and Chickasaws) and Lieutenant Colonel Thomas Browne of the East Florida Rangers to be head of the Atlantic District (Cherokees and Creeks), both men to be subordinate to the ranking military officer in their districts, with orders to supply auxiliaries for the army when requested. Germain also tightened up the financial authority formerly given to Stuart. Each district was authorized £1,955 for salaries, presents, rum, provisions, and other

11. *Ibid.*, pp. 91–100, 107–109.
12. *Ibid.*, pp. 190–194.

contingencies. The belt-tightening was in response to parliamentary criticism in the spring of 1779 of the rising costs of the war, particularly of the cost of supporting Indians in the South.[13]

The uncomprehending and niggardly behavior of General John Campbell, commander of the British forces at Pensacola in 1779 and 1780, in managing England's Indian allies helped to assure British failure in their struggle against the Americans. Constantly rejecting the advice and pleas of superintendent of Indian affairs Alexander Cameron, who had been placed under his operational control, Campbell was one of that fraternity of military commanders who are "hard-nosed" to the point of military failure. Even the gallant fighting of the Choctaws against the Spanish garrison at Mobile in 1780 did not cause Campbell to change his mind. The assault on the rebels' Spanish allies at Mobile, though it failed, according to Alexander Cameron, because of the cowardice of the provincial loyalists who accompanied the Choctaws, might still have succeeded if the assaulting forces had been properly constituted. General Campbell refused to pursue a different approach and dismissed the warriors with a pound of ammunition apiece and thanks. Campbell's lack of generosity did not go unnoticed by the Choctaws.[14]

While British hopes faded in 1780, Lieutenant Colonel John Sevier, with 300 North Carolina volunteers, and Colonel Arthur Campbell, with 400 Virginians, ravaged the Cherokee country in a punitive expedition designed to forestall possible Cherokee action in behalf of General Cornwallis. Over 1,000 houses, 50,000 bushels of corn, and other provisions and supplies were destroyed. Even the capital town of Choate was razed. Twenty-nine Cherokees were killed and seventeen captured. Only one American was lost.[15]

When a Spanish fleet appeared off Pensacola in March, 1781, with an army under Bernardo de Galvez, General Campbell's ungenerous and vacillating conduct toward Britain's Indian allies reaped its final reward. Only a few hundred Choctaws and Creeks were present to support 1,500 British soldiers. Even so, the brave Choctaws at one point broke through the Spanish lines, only to find no support from the British regulars. Furious, the Choctaw leader

13. *Ibid.*, pp. 194–195, 211–214.
14. *Ibid.*, pp. 243–248.
15. *Ibid.*, pp. 252–255.

affirmed that every major effort against the Spanish had been accomplished by the Indians without support and without reward. Galvez's army of 4,000 was soon boosted to 7,000 by reinforcements, and on May 8, 1781, General Campbell surrendered his garrison and Pensacola. Not only did the fall of Pensacola signal the loss of a key British military outpost, but it also destroyed the headquarters of the southern Indian department, transferred from Charleston by John Stuart on the fall of that city to the rebels in 1775.[16]

Alexander Cameron and other Indian officials made their way into the interior, most into the Creek country. From there Cameron hoped to proceed east to loyalist Georgia to join Thomas Browne, the deputy for Indian affairs whose headquarters was in Augusta. However, Augusta came under attack by rebels, encouraged by the appearance of General Nathanael Greene's army in the area. The town was placed under siege. Browne called for help from the Cherokees and Creeks, but little help was forthcoming. In June he surrendered. Browne, fearing summary action by patriot soldiers, demanded that the Indians within the post be treated as prisoners of war in the same manner that he and the king's troops were to be treated. His request was honored by General Greene, who intervened with the local rebel force to preserve the Indians from the slaughter that might otherwise have occurred.[17]

By the late spring of 1782 British control extended little beyond Savannah. Parties of Creeks and Choctaws attempting to reach the city were captured or turned back by the rebels. Finally, in early summer, Savannah was evacuated by the British. The Crown's southern Indian department now withdrew to east Florida and, eventually, to extinction. Increasingly remote from their British protectors, the Cherokees and Chickasaws chose to make peace with the Americans. The Creeks maintained their ties with the British. The Choctaws wavered.[18]

Some of the Indians loyal to the British cause who thronged the streets of St. Augustine, the remaining British base in the South as the war drew to a close, demanded space on the British evacuation vessels. "If the English mean to abandon the Land," one of their leaders informed the British, "we will accompany them—We can-

16. *Ibid.*, pp. 265–267.
17. *Ibid.*, pp. 267–269.
18. *Ibid.*, pp. 282–284.

not take a Virginian or Spaniard by the hand—We cannot look them in the face." The commandant of the St. Augustine garrison asserted, "The minds of these people appear as much agitated as those of the unhappy Loyalists on the eve of a third evacuation; and however chimerical it may appear to us, they have very seriously proposed to abandon their country and accompany us, having made all the world their enemies by their attachment to us."[19]

In the fall of 1782 General Andrew Pickens led a force of patriots into the Cherokee country in order to force a peace upon the embarrassed tribe. The dispirited Cherokees scattered at his approach. Induced to come in for negotiations on pain of a further destruction of their country, the Cherokees began the process of hammering out an agreement. Pickens demanded for South Carolina a tribal cession of all lands between the headwaters of the Savannah and Chattahoochee rivers. As British power evaporated and the intent to withdraw became evident similar demands were made on the Creeks. Georgia demanded all the Creek lands east of the Oconee River as compensation for Creek injuries done the patriot side.[20]

The full extent of the tragedy of the American Revolution from the Indian standpoint became evident with the signing in Paris on November 30, 1782, of the preliminary articles of peace. No mention of Indians was made in the articles although the British ceded their claim to the lands the Indians occupied—as far west as the Mississippi River—to the Americans. The loyalist Indians were outraged when the news of the preliminary articles leaked out. The British officers concerned with their management were embarrassed by the abandonment of the king's faithful allies. The British Indian agent for the Six Nations in Canada, Daniel Claus, could not understand why Richard Oswald, England's negotiator with the American commissioners at Paris, had not been informed of the boundaries of the Indian country and the treaty line made at Fort Stanwix in 1768. "It might have been easily reserved and inserted," Claus wrote with annoyance, "that those lands the Crown relinquished to all the Indn. Nations as their Right and property were

19. *Ibid.*, pp. 303–307.
20. *Ibid.*, pp. 294–298, 305, 311–312, 313–316, 323–324.

out of its power to treat for, which would have saved the Honor of Government with respect to that Treaty."[21]

In the extended discussions leading to the Peace of Paris ending the Revolutionary War, the sovereignty of the Indian nations was largely ignored in favor of the assumption that their possessory rights—such as they were—must exist under the banner of one or the other competing non-Indian claimants. When Pedro Pablo Abarca de Bolea, Conde de Aranda, the Spanish negotiator at Paris, sought to reject the American claim to territory extending west to the Mississippi River, he asserted, "That territory belongs to free and independent nations of Indians, and you have no right to it." John Jay, one of the American negotiators, rejected the Spanish assertion, asserting in turn, "With respect to the Indians we claim the right of preemption; with respect to all other nations, we claim the sovereignty over the territory." Aranda's outburst did not stem from a tender consideration for a truly independent Indian sovereignty. Spain, equally with Great Britain, France, and the United States in their dealings with one other, recognized Indian independence as sometimes existing in fact but as ultimately qualified by a theoretical subordination to a non-Indian sovereignty. Opponents of the articles of peace in England, including the loyalist Governor William Franklin (Benjamin Franklin's son), denounced England's breaking of faith with the Indians in conceding their lands without their knowledge, but this was not the first or last peace in which the rights of peoples not present at the negotiations were sacrificed to the interests of more powerful participants. General Frederick Haldiman, British commander in Canada, did what he could to succor his loyal but abused allies, providing land in Canada for Joseph Brant and his Mohawks and for any other friendly Indians who wished to leave the United States and settle in Canada.[22]

Had the Iroquois Confederacy and the confederacies of the South maintained a neutral stance during the American Revolution, could they have maintained their independence and their lands following the Revolution? A neutral stance might have enabled the

21. Letter of June 14, 1783, in Graymont, *op. cit.*, pp. 262–263.
22. Richard B. Morris, *The Peacemakers: The Great Powers and American Independence* (New York, 1965), pp. 321–322, 419–420.

Indian nations to forestall American encroachments for a short time, but not for long. As the inheritor of the claims of Great Britain based on royal charters, Indian treaties, and the Peace of 1763, the United States would surely have extended its jurisdiction and sovereignty over the Indian nations of the East whenever its power was sufficient to effect it.[23]

In the hard bargaining that followed the Revolution, the Iroquois were humbled, forced to cede much of their land, and soon lost the independent status they had possessed up until that time. By the Treaty of Fort Stanwix of October 22, 1784 (one of several held at the fort) they were browbeaten into ceding land in western New York and Pennsylvania against their own interests and against the interests of the western Indians for whom they presumed to speak. Even the two Iroquois nations who fought with the Americans—the Oneidas and the Tuscaroras—while guaranteed in the treaty security in the possession of the lands on which they were then settled, were soon induced to sell their lands and move west. The commissioners who negotiated the postwar treaties with the Iroquois insisted that the Indians (the Oneidas and Tuscaroras excepted) were a conquered people and that their territories were forfeit to the Americans, even though the latter chose not to deprive them entirely of their lands. Painfully aware of their humiliation at the hands of the American negotiators, and conscious of their own breach of faith with the western Indians, the Iroquois repudiated the treaty two years later but, unwilling to take up the hatchet again against the Americans, they allowed the treaty tacitly to stand by default.

The failure of the Iroquois to protect the interests of their western brothers, plus the growing demonstration of Iroquois inability to resist the continued pressure of white land speculators, settlers, and official negotiators, caused the western Indians—the Shawnee, Delaware, Wyandot, Ottawa, Potawatomi, Chippewa, Miami, and other tribes—to form their own confederacy and to develop their own policies vis-à-vis the encroaching white settlements. In 1785 and 1786 the confederacy attempted to prevent any of its individual member tribes from selling lands to the Americans and demanded that the latter deal only with the confederacy in any negotiations. The confederacy also rejected the conquest theory of the Americans and declared invalid the earlier post-Revolutionary War treaties which asserted the right. The Ohio River was declared to be the boundary between whites and Indians. The United States ignored the confederacy and the Ohio boundary. Land grants to military veterans, speculation by land companies, and squatter settlements across the Ohio led to frontier clashes. Despite the attempt, by the Northwest Ordinance of 1787 and other legislative enactments, to regularize and control settlement in the area, a confrontation with the western Indians was unavoidable. A general council with the western Indians was held at Fort Harmar, where in January, 1789, a small group of Indians signed a document confirming the earlier disputed treaties and renewing the land cessions made at Fort Stanwix. The treaty was repudiated by the elements not in attendance and war soon broke out.[24]

It was increasingly evident that the Indians needed the support of a European power if they expected to resist the American advance successfully. Although the Indians recognized no right of the English to give away their lands, and were bitter at the failure of the English to provide for them in the treaty ending the war, yet they were conscious of their dependence upon English support against the new American state. The boundary worked out by the English and American commissioners at Paris thrust much farther north than the Indians would have allowed. Great Britain was bound under Article VII to hand over the nine forts she controlled in the Old Northwest "with all convenient speed." After some hesitation, both the British commanders in Canada and the home government decided to hold the forts not only to compel the Americans to fulfill other sections of the treaty, such as the payment of debts to loyalists, but, more important, to reassure the Indians that they had not been abandoned by the British and that they would be supported, at least defensively, against the American rush into the frontier areas. That the support was to be defensive and not offensive was made clear by the English government. Rifles and ammunition sufficient for hunting and self-defense would continue to be provided, but nothing more. The English, fearing Indian resentment for what could be interpreted as their "sellout" to the

24. Wallace, *op. cit.*, pp. 151–152, 157–158.

Americans, thus blunted the criticism, and in the opinion of one student of the period averted the outbreak of a full-scale frontier war with the Americans.[25]

The increasing impatience of the Americans at the failure of the British to turn over the forts caused the American government to adopt a more aggressive attitude in its dealings with the Indians whom they assumed to be willing partners with the British. In 1790 General James Harmar led an expedition to attack the Indians of the Maumee Valley. The result was an embarrassing failure. The following year, General Arthur St. Clair suffered an even more humiliating defeat at the hands of a numerically inferior enemy near the present Fort Wayne, Indiana. Evidently the Indians could, by themselves, successfully resist the greatest force the new American republic could bring to bear on them and did so, a fact which the new nation refused to acknowledge. Not only did the defeats spur additional American efforts, but the British and their continued possession of the forts came increasingly to serve as an excuse for American failure.[26]

In the southern states following the American Revolution a situation similar to that in the northern regions existed. The powerful southern tribes—Cherokees, Choctaws, Chickasaws, and Creeks—like their brethren in the North, possessed a degree of independence recognized by all of the European powers with whom they had dealings. Occupying the physical area between the Americans on the east and the Spanish and English (formerly the French) on the west, the southern Indian nations played power politics with skill. They possessed military force which commanded the respect, and often fear, of all the powers. To maintain the Indian position required, however, constant support, both in terms of political alliances and European trade goods. The Indians now faced aggressive frontiersmen freed from the restrictions a more concerned imperial government had placed upon them. The constant land hunger of the Americans combined with the inability of the new federal and state governments to exercise effective control over their white inhabitants enraged the Indians. Under capable chiefs—often

25. Charles R. Ritcheson, *Aftermath of Revolution: British Policy Toward the United States, 1783–1795* (Dallas, Tex., 1969), pp. 75, 168–169.

26. John C. Miller, *The Federalist Era, 1789–1801* (New York, 1960), pp. 146–147.

half-breeds like McGillivray of the Creeks—the Indians sought to reorient their trading and diplomatic relations away from the Americans and to the Spanish in Florida or New Orleans. Thus, by 1786, the Creeks could scorn the efforts of the Georgia commissioners to negotiate a settlement of a land dispute and in the following year could carry war to the Georgia and Cumberland settlers. Yet the Spanish, like the British in Canada, hesitated to embroil themselves too fully in a conflict with the United States by total support of their Indian allies. The Spanish governor and intendant of Louisiana and Florida, Miró, in 1788 informed McGillivray that Spanish aid would thenceforth be decreased.

McGillivray, in the spring of 1790, suddenly agreed to treat with the United States government in New York. The discussions were of advantage to both sides. The weak new federal government wished to assert its own authority against that of Georgia in Indian matters, and the Creeks saw, among other advantages, an opportunity to make favorable trade arrangements with the United States and thereby to end their dependence upon their increasingly fragile (particularly in the event of a war between Great Britain and Spain) supply sources in Florida. A treaty, signed on August 7, 1791, emerged from the New York deliberations, which found McGillivray at the height of his powers, honored and courted by officials of Great Britain, Spain, and the United States.

McGillivray's position with the Creeks was challenged by a former British soldier, trader, and gambler, William Augustus Bowles, who managed to pass himself off in England and elsewhere as the leader of a mighty Indian confederacy for whose favor and support he petitioned the English government. By 1792, however, Bowles had run out of luck with Creeks, Americans, and Europeans. He was packed off to Spain by the Spanish governor of New Orleans. The ability of the adventurer Bowles to cut a swath in affairs of state in an area of interest to American, Spanish, and English governments demonstrates the fluid character of power there. The leaders of numerous well-armed Indian confederacies at this time could and did exert a power difficult for Americans of a later date to conceive. The power of the Indian leaders and the independence of the Indian nations of the area were real, qualified only by a potential and theoretical limitation on their sovereignty that would eventually be exercised by their increasingly powerful American neighbor.[27]

In the spring of 1792, a year following the disastrous defeat of General St. Clair, President Washington dispatched a peace mission to the Indian tribes of the Ohio Valley. The President assured the Indians that the United States did not wish to deprive them of their lands and drive them out of the country. On the contrary, he asserted, "We should be gratified with the opportunity of imparting to you all the blessings of civilized life, of teaching you to cultivate the earth, and raise corn; to raise oxen, sheep, and other domestic animals; to build comfortable houses, and to educate your children, so as ever to dwell upon the land." General James Wilkinson, commanding officer of U.S. troops in the western department, reiterated Washington's desire that the white people and the red people live in harmony together, but, though he disclaimed the desire to "conquer or extirpate the Indian Nations," he warned the Miami, Shawnee, Delaware, Ottawa, Wyandot, Potawatomi, Huron, and Chippewa tribes that the United States could destroy them. "The warriors of the United States number like the Trees in the woods," he told them, "their meat & their bread grow in the fields and upon their farms, and they make arms and ammunition for their own use." He contrasted American power with that of the Indians, "who are scattered over a Country many hundred miles in extent, who depend on the forests and the casualties of the hunt for their subsistence and procure their arms and ammunition from a distant nation." Despite St. Clair's defeat in 1791, he asserted, the whites had numerous armies which could be sent to do successfully what St. Clair had failed to do. Wilkinson's speech was carried by Isaac Freeman, one of a mission which proved abortive when most of its members were killed or captured.[28]

The American government, perturbed lest the southern Indians should be induced by the northern Indians to join them in a continuation of the campaigns which had seen American armies routed, dispatched agents to the southern Indians to assert the

27. Ritcheson, *op. cit.*, pp. 174–175, 179–181.
28. *American State Papers . . . Indian Affairs*, 2 vols. (Washington, 1832–1834), I, 229–230; Paul C. Wilson, Jr., *A Forgotten Mission to the Indians: William Smalley's Adventures Among the Delaware Indians of Ohio in 1792* (Galveston, Tex., 1965), pp. 3, 5–6.

justice of the American cause and to enlist their support. American determination was finally rewarded with a major victory over the western Indians achieved by General Anthony Wayne at Fallen Timbers in August, 1794. In the negotiations that followed, at the Treaty of Greeneville in 1795, the United States obtained, in addition to peace, the cession of the southeastern quarter of the Northwest Territory in exchange for a small monetary consideration.[29]

Despite their defeat at Fallen Timbers, the Indians had achieved something in the complex round of negotiations and battles in the decade following the close of the American Revolution. Specifically, the Americans abandoned claims based upon conquest alone, the principle they had asserted in negotiations with the Indians following the Revolution. Instead, the government recognized the right of the Indians to the lands they occupied within the territorial limits of the United States, even while reserving the ultimate sovereignty to the new nation. Practical steps were also taken to remove the worst of the grievances over land cessions, to overcome legal disabilities faced by Indians, and to help meet their educational needs. The concessions, as they applied to the Iroquois, were far-reaching in their effect. They kept the Iroquois from supporting their western brethren in reaction to the advance of the Americans. They afforded the Iroquois a head start in adapting themselves to the situation of forced acculturation to which they would soon be subject. And, finally, the abandonment of the conquest theory asserted against the Iroquois, by extension to other Indian tribes, "affected the future of the continent."[30]

The persistent white pressure—both official and unofficial—on the lands of the Indians of the Old Northwest following the battle of Fallen Timbers led to the movement of Indian nationalism and Indian reform that is associated with the name of Tecumseh and his brother, known as the Prophet, of Shawnee-Creek parentage. The message of the brothers was that the sad plight of the Indians was caused by drunkenness, abandonment of old customs, internal divisions, and the loss of tribal hunting grounds through cessions to the whites. They cited the wearing of textile clothing as one of the corruptions that should be halted; the Indian was urged to return

29. *American State Papers . . . Indian Affairs*, I, 247; Miller, op. cit., p. 183.
30. Wallace, *op. cit.*, pp. 177–178.

to his skin clothing of the past. More important, they urged Indians to reject the white-imposed concept that they owned the lands upon which they hunted and could sell those lands to the white man. Rather, Tecumseh asserted, the Great Spirit had provided the land in common to his children. No single tribe could claim proprietorship to a given area and therefore no tribe or faction of a tribe could transfer title of land to the United States without the agreement of all Indians. So successful were Tecumseh and the Prophet in promoting their ideas that a new Indian nationalism arose with its center at the old Indian town of Kithtippecanoe, which became known as Prophetstown and to which more and more Indians of various tribes came to hear the brothers and in many cases to settle down to live. By 1811 the community contained 1,000 warriors from various tribes.[31]

The consolidation of Indian tribes under the banner of Tecumseh provided a major challenge to Governor William Henry Harrison, charged with the task of extinguishing Indian title to the lands of the Northwest. Various conferences whittled down the area remaining to the tribes. A crucial conference in August, 1810, between Tecumseh and Harrison at Vincennes led to a heated exchange. Harrison was, in effect, warned to go no farther. With British support and encouragement Tecumseh maintained his adamant position and in the summer of 1811 went to recruit support from the Cherokees, Creeks, Choctaws, and Chickasaws. Learning of his departure, Harrison moved toward Prophetstown with 1,000 men, where on November 7, 1811, he suffered heavy casualties but forced the Indians to abandon the village, which he then burned to the ground. Though destroying the headquarters of the dissidents, Harrison stirred up further attacks by Kickapoo, Potawatomi, and Shawnee bands who had rallied around Tecumseh. The battle of Tippecanoe, as well as being a prelude to a political career for Harrison, was also one of the preliminaries to the War of 1812, during which Great Britain and the United States once more argued over points at issue between the two nations. Indian support, as might be imagined, went largely to the British in this war. But with the slaying of Tecumseh at the battle of the Thames, on October 5, 1813, Indian nationalism, as well as the

31. Arrell M. Gibson, *The Kickapoos: Lords of the Middle Border* (Norman, Okla., 1963), pp. 58–59.

British cause with which Tecumseh was allied, suffered an irrepa-
rable loss. After Tecumseh's death, bands of Wyandots, Chippewas,
Delawares, and Miamis left the British side and made their peace
with General Harrison. If Americans were not significant winners
in the War of 1812, the Indians were losers. The threat of continuing European support for those Indian nations resisting the
advance of American settlement was once more removed.[32]

The advantages obtained by the Americans over the powerful
Indian tribes east of the Mississippi River in the first quarter of the
nineteenth century—whether obtained by force of arms or by
negotiation—were quickly exploited by the American government.
No individual is more closely identified with the policy that was
devised to exploit that advantage—the policy of removal of the
Indians east of the Mississippi to lands west of the river—than
President Andrew Jackson. A feared Indian fighter as well as
negotiator, contemptuous of Indian claims to sovereign status,
anxious to promote the welfare of the white citizens of the West,
President Jackson reversed the earlier philanthropic thrust of Indian policy formed in the image of Thomas Jefferson by which the
Indian nations, at their own pace, were to be brought by education
and religious persuasion to form an integrated part of the American
nation. Jackson's solution involved a cold-blooded removal of the
problem from the concern and consciousness of white Americans.[33]

The story of the removal of the eastern Indians during the 1830s
to lands west of the Mississippi River has frequently been told in all
its cruel detail. The picture of once proud nations, who had maintained centuries-long intercourse with colonial, federal, and state
governments, prodded by forced marches to forlorn lands across the
Mississippi, is one not easily forgotten or forgiven. Because of its
dramatic and pathetic qualities, it has obscured the genuineness of
the debate that lay behind it. Removal was not a simple exercise in
white greed. As in the case of the American Revolution, funda-

32. *Ibid.*, pp. 60–72; Henry Adams, *History of the United States of America
during the First Administration of James Madison,* 2 vols. (New York, 1909), II,
67–112.

33. Bernard W. Sheehan, *Seeds of Extinction: Jeffersonian Philanthropy and
the American Indian* (Chapel Hill, N.C., 1973); Francis Paul Prucha, *American
Indian Policy in the Formative Years: The Indian Trade and Intercourse Acts,
1790–1834* (Cambridge, Mass., 1962).

mental constitutional arguments were at issue. The Indian nations interpreted their treaties and compacts with the United States as recognizing their independence and investing them with authority sufficient to repel the extension of any alien authority over them except with their agreement. That independence continued, in the eyes of the Indians and their supporters, despite their decline in power vis-à-vis the United States, because it was incorporated in sacred legal and diplomatic instruments that could not, or should not, be violated.

The position of President Andrew Jackson, on the other hand, influenced by demands of the states of Georgia and Alabama for greater control over the lands and the persons of the Indians residing within their state boundaries, was that the Indian legal position was not valid against the legal claims of the states, and that Indian weakness and smallness of numbers made it expedient that they concede the point or be crushed militarily.

John Quincy Adams, who, as one of the negotiators of the treaty ending the War of 1812, had firmly rejected the British effort to create an independent Indian state in the upper Ohio Valley and, indeed, rejected any settlement that did not recognize total American control over the natives, and who, as President Monroe's Secretary of State in 1818 had defended General Andrew Jackson's expedition against the Seminoles in Spanish Florida as justified by the principle of self-defense, in the 1830s bitterly opposed the removal policy of President Jackson. Adams still did not believe that the Indians owned any "primitive abstract right of soil" when the European settlers first came to America, as he put it in 1830, but he perceived that Jackson's assault on the Indians, as on the Bank, the Public Lands, and the Public Debt, were threats to the Union which he sought to strengthen. "Better to let the Indians remain, than to allow the once-free lands to be tilled by the slave, or to fall under the land speculator's auction hammer" is the way one historian has interpreted Adams's position.[34]

The important legal questions at issue became the focus of nationwide debate. The halls of Congress rang to the oratory of partisans of both sides. Finally the Supreme Court was called upon

34. Lynn Hudson Parsons, " 'A Perpetual Harrow Upon My Feelings': John Quincy Adams and the American Indian," *New England Quarterly*, XLVI (1973) , 339–379, especially 363, 368, 378.

to make a determination about the validity of the legal argument, which it did in two famous cases. Those decisions, while declaring the Cherokee nation to have significant rights that could not be violated by the state of Georgia, reduced the Cherokee claim of sovereignty to that of a "domestic, dependent, nation." What solace the Cherokees obtained was destroyed by President Jackson's refusal to enforce the court's order barring the exercise of Georgia's authority against the Cherokees.

While the removal chapter is a sorry one in American history, sometimes ignored (as in Arthur Schlesinger, Jr.'s biography of Jackson) but more often violently condemned, it is important to recognize that in its refusal to accept the Indians' view of their sovereign rights the Jackson administration was doing no more and no less than virtually every succeeding administration. It is, moreover, possible to argue, as Paul Prucha does, that those advocating removal were concerned with the Indian's good rather than his harm. Most scholars, while accepting the good intentions of individuals, and even of the government, toward the Indians, prefer to judge the motives of the one and the policies of the other by the results achieved. By this measure, admittedly one of hindsight, neither individuals nor the government merit much praise.[35] Considering the practical alternatives faced by those concerned with Indian policy at the time, however, and accepting the limitations imposed by those alternatives, it is possible to understand, and possibly sympathize with, the policy that emerged. Thus, Thomas L. McKenney, the superintendent of Indian trade in the early years of the nineteenth century and a good friend of the Indian, recognizing the determination of President Jackson to remove the Indians at all costs, and aware of the inability of the American legal system to prevent it, urged their removal as the only practical way by which they could be saved. McKenney, writing on May 21, 1829, to the Reverend Eli Baldwin in support of a proposed organization of New York clergymen which became known as "The Indian Board, for the Emigration, Preservation, and Improvement of the Abo-

35. Francis Paul Prucha, "Andrew Jackson's Indian Policy: A Reassessment," *Journal of American History*, LVI (1969), 527–539; Wilcomb E. Washburn, "Indian Removal Policy: Administrative, Historical and Moral Criteria for Judging its Success or Failure," *Ethnohistory*, XII (1965), 274–278; Wilcomb E. Washburn, "Philanthropy and the American Indian: The Need for a Model," *Ethnohistory*, XV (1968), 43–56.

rigines of America," asserted that if the Indian tribes then within the boundaries of the states did not remove, they "must perish." Beyond the Mississippi, President Jackson had told the Creeks two months earlier,

Your father has provided a country large enough for all of you, and he advises you to remove to it. There your white brothers will not trouble you; they will have no claim to the land, and you can live upon it, you and all your children, as long as the grass grows or the water runs, in peace and plenty. It will be yours for ever.[36]

Jackson's words seem hollow now, but it is difficult to argue that they were meant to be hollow. More probably neither opponents nor proponents of the removal policy foresaw the explosive character of white expansion that would make a mockery of Jackson's words as they would of many another speech and treaty which rashly utilized the evocative Indian phrase for a permanent future.

The assumption that proponents of the removal policy acted, in most instances, in good faith is buttressed not only by their honest belief that the Indians would be able to maintain their independence and authority in another place and another time, but also by the serious negotiations carried on over payment for the lands taken in the East, the provisions providing individual allotments to those who preferred to stay rather than to remove, and the attempts to provide education to the Indians to fit them better to deal with whites. Although such factors are important considerations, it is clear that political advantage, cultural blindness, and economic greed provided the principal impetus to removal. That such powerful engines *should* have been stopped before they destroyed a helpless people cannot be denied. But that they *could* have been stopped, given the nature of the system and the people involved, is difficult to assert.

The 1830s saw the removal—voluntary, induced, and forced—of most of the four great southern tribes—Choctaw, Cherokee, Creek, and Chickasaw—as well as of the evasive Seminoles of Florida. Some bands avoided the fate of their nations and remained to form presently existing enclaves in their old homelands. But the bulk of

36. McKenney's letter and Jackson's talk of March 23, 1829, are printed in *Documents and Proceedings relating to the Formation and Progress of a Board in the City of New York, for the Emigration, Preservation, and Improvement of the Aborigines of America* (New York, 1829) , pp. 3, 5.

these once powerful, once prosperous nations was removed to the Indian Territory, there to await a partial repetition of the act by which they came. Removal became the goal—not always realized—of policy with regard to many other populous Indian nations east of the Mississippi. Only the smallest, least offensive, and most thoroughly integrated Indian tribes escaped the pressure to clear the eastern half of the continent of its original inhabitants.

In his study of federal Indian policy to 1850, George Dewey Harmon concluded that

After weighing the evidence for and against the federal Indian policy, it is difficult to determine whether that policy as a whole is worthy of praise or condemnation. Probably the truth of the matter is that the federal practice is to be praised and at the same time denounced.[37]

Harmon's point is well taken. Good intentions are fully in evidence; just as obvious has been the failure in practice. If one measures performance in comparison with other nations, one can similarly hand down a mixed verdict. In sum, the Indian policy of the United States, including the removal policy, cannot readily be dismissed either as a failure or a success, as malevolent or benevolent. It partakes of both.

37. George Dewey Harmon, *Sixty Years of Indian Affairs: Political, Economic, and Diplomatic, 1789–1850* (Chapel Hill, N.C., 1941) , pp. 369–370.

CHAPTER 8

The Coercion of the Western Indians

PRIOR to the expansionist policy of the 1840s the concept of a permanent (or at least a potential) separation between white Americans and red Indians informed American policy. Particularly was this the case when the Great Plains area west of the Mississippi was felt, on the basis of the early army surveys, to be less than ideal for white settlement. Whether the "Great American Desert," as it was sometimes called, was considered uninhabitable by whites and fit only for Indians is a question upon which scholars disagree.[1] There can be little doubt, however, that at least some statesmen thought the Indian problem in the East could be solved by moving the Indians beyond a line separating them from the areas into which white settlement was expected to flow. The removal policy of the 1830s was based on such an assumption. In fact the hope vanished almost as soon as it was expressed. Movements through the Plains to Santa Fe, to California, to Oregon—particularly in the 1840s—destroyed the sanctity of the reserve and the validity of the concept. That white Americans never fully accepted the idea that the western Plains were uninhabitable, however, is suggested by the failure of Congress to authorize by legislation a permanent Indian state or territory, though the idea was proposed and debated more than once.[2]

1. Francis Paul Prucha, "Indian Removal and the Great American Desert," *Indiana Magazine of History*, LIX (1963), 299–322.
2. Richard N. Ellis, *General Pope and U.S. Indian Policy* (Albuquerque, N.M., 1970), p. 40. See also Annie H. Abel, "Proposals for an Indian State, 1778–

By 1846 the United States government's responsibilities in the field of Indian relations had dramatically increased. The entry of Texas into the Union brought many Indian tribes with it; the defeat of Mexico in the Mexican War brought the populous tribes of the Southwest under U.S. control. In the Northwest, the establishment of the Oregon Trail through thousands of miles of Indian country emphasized the need for protection and control. Moreover, the Indians facing the United States in the late 1840s were, for the first time, predominantly mounted on horseback, unlike the "foot soldiers" of the Eastern Woodlands. Their military capabilities were thus enormously enhanced.

As the westward movement of whites and the extermination of the buffalo increased apace, hunger influenced the activities of the Plains Indians. The Catholic priest, Father P. J. De Smet, in 1848, noted that subsistence needs forced the Plains Indians into small bands who, "like hungry wolves," sought to poach on the game of their neighbors. "The Sioux," De Smet wrote, "must necessarily encroach on the lands of the Arickaras, Crows, Assiniboins, Sheyennes and Pawnees—the Crows and Assiniboins on the Blackfeet and vice versa, and thus endless struggles, and murderous and cruel wars daily perpetrated and multiplied."[3]

Though the responsibilities thrust upon the United States with the formal acquisition of most of the territory west of the Louisiana Purchase were staggering, those responsible for administering Indian affairs were slow to comprehend them. William Medill, who was appointed Commissioner of Indian Affairs under William L. Marcy, Polk's Secretary of War, controlled fewer than twenty-five agents and subagents in the field. Yet, instead of urging an enlargement of his department to take care of the new responsibilities the United States was inheriting, Medill, in his report to Congress in December, 1846, recommended a reduction in the number of agents. Medill imagined that eight agents and four subagents could

1878," American Historical Association, *Annual Report*, 2 vols. (Washington, 1908) , I, 89–104.

3. De Smet to Thomas H. Harvey, Dec. 4, 1848, quoted in Robert Anthony Trennert, "The Far Western Indian Frontier and the Beginnings of the Reservation System, 1846–1851" (Ph.D. diss., University of California, Santa Barbara, 1969), p. 12. The story of western expansion as it affected Indians is also told in Alban W. Hoopes, *Indian Affairs and their Administration, with Special Reference to the Far West, 1849–1860* (Philadelphia, 1932) .

handle the Indians, whom he thought could be grouped together in three superintendencies, two of them west of the Mississippi. Fortunately, the Congress, early in 1847, rejected Medill's recommendation for a reduction in the number of agents and, in the Indian Intercourse Act of March 3, 1847, tightened the regulations concerning the granting of annuities, the sale of alcohol, and similar dealings with the Indians.[4]

Criticism of the government's policy in 1847 led to the collapse of the "permanent Indian barrier" assumptions inherited from the past and inaugurated the belief that the tribes must be concentrated in smaller areas and closely supervised by the government. The policy of separation of the races gave way to segregation of the Indian.

In Commissioner Medill's report to Congress in 1848 the government's proposed solution was to concentrate the Indian tribes into two great reservations: one in the North and the other in the South. Between the two, in the Kansas and Platte valleys, would be a huge corridor through which the white population of the United States could move west on the railroads being planned. Of course, the proposal was asserted to work to the advantage of the Indian who, in his confinement, would gradually adopt white agricultural and labor practices and start on the route to Christianization and "civilization." The economy-minded Medill continued to assert the possibility of reducing the number of agents necessary to exercise control over the Indians.[5]

Medill's assumptions about the ease of controlling the Indians were increasingly challenged by representatives of the border states. Representative R. W. Johnson, Democrat of Arkansas, in a speech on July 6, 1848, noted the increasing contact between United States citizens and Indians and criticized the proposal to reduce the number of agencies from twenty-nine to fifteen. Fewer agents probably meant more hostilities, Johnson asserted, and flew in the face of the evidence that peaceful rather than warlike exchange between the two races was beneficial for both.[6]

4. Trennert, *op. cit.*, pp. 30, 38–40.
5. *Ibid.*, pp. 47, 49–51.
6. *Ibid.*, pp. 53–54.

The entry of Texas into the Union in December, 1845, brought with it Indian problems of great significance. An estimated 25,000 Indians inhabited the borders of the former republic, of whom 15,000 were southern Comanches, the fiercest horsemen of the Plains. Their power and skill, combined with Spanish and Mexican weakness in their periods of occupation, had allowed the Comanches to raid and plunder the Spanish settlements with relative impunity. Indeed, raiding border settlements had become a way of life. Other Indians, notably the Kiowas and Lipans, though smaller in numbers, were similarly inclined to raiding and warfare.[7]

When Texas revolted from Mexico in 1835 and established a republic, Sam Houston, the first president, attempted to establish a peaceful relationship with the Indians of the western portions of Texas. A treaty was concluded with the Prairie tribes in 1837 and efforts made to keep whites out of the Indian country. But the inevitable tide of white movement brought warfare to the frontier. Houston's conciliatory policy was a factor in his defeat by Mirabeau B. Lamar, Texas's second president, who promised a war to exterminate the Indians.[8]

Lamar, after his election in 1838, embarked on a war of extermination but succeeded merely in stirring up a deadly warfare between whites and Indians all along the frontier. The settlers were allowed to believe that it was "open season" on the Indians. The conflict was punctuated by the usual breaches of faith on the part of the whites. After having invited the Comanches to peace talks in 1840, the Texans attempted to seize the chiefs as hostages. The Comanches resisted and all were slaughtered. The consequences can well be imagined.[9]

With full-scale war ensuing, Houston was reelected in 1842 and attempted to institute a policy of reconciliation. To the Comanches he repudiated the Lamar policy and attempted, in peace talks, to create a boundary line, marked by a series of trading posts, to separate white man and Indian. The attempt, like other similar efforts to create a permanent line of separation between the races, failed. Texans penetrated the Indian territory and refused to

7. *Ibid.*, pp. 113–115.
8. *Ibid.*, p. 117.
9. *Ibid.*, p. 118.

recognize any Indian rights in the land. The policy of the republic
was to follow that of its citizens. All land was assumed to belong to
the state. The policy continued to be asserted by the state even after
it entered the Union in 1845. Though the United States recognized
in theory, at least, Indian possessory rights in the soil, Texas
adamantly refused to concede such rights to "its" Indians. As a
result, confusion reigned when Texas joined the Union. Under the
terms of entry, Texas retained the right to her public lands, and
came in directly as a state. Commissioner of Indian Affairs Medill
conceded his uncertainty as to whether the federal regulations
governing Indians could challenge or modify those already exercised by the state. The first Texas state legislature, in April, 1846,
was in no doubt. It asserted that

we recognize no title in the Indian tribes resident within the limits of the
state to any portion of the soil thereof; and that we recognize no right of
the Government of the United States to make any treaty of limits with the
said Indian tribes without the consent of the Government of this state.[10]

Congress hesitated to confront the Texas claim directly but, in
the face of continuing border warfare and the capture of numerous
women and children, appointed two commissioners to conclude
peace with the tribes and to obtain the release of the prisoners. The
two commissioners conferred with representatives of eleven tribes in
May, 1846. With war having already broken out with Mexico, the
importance of keeping the Texas tribes from taking the warpath
was particularly important. In their eagerness to achieve a lasting
settlement the commissioners wrote into the treaty, held at Council
Springs on the Brazos River, promises to the tribes of protection by
the national government, promises of liberal presents, and the
authority to establish agencies, trading houses, and regulations for
trade and intercourse with the Indians. The tribes willingly agreed
to "perpetual amity and friendship" with the United States, relieved to be free of the unremitting aggression of the Texans and
hopeful of the quick arrival of the presents promised.

When news of the treaty arrived in Washington, the Texas
delegation to the Congress exploded in outrage and challenged the

10. *Ibid.*, pp. 120–122.

right of the federal commissioners to usurp Texas's right to deal
with the Indian tribes within her borders. Congress, taken aback,
refused to ratify the treaty. The Indians soon sensed that the
United States did not intend to live up to the treaty and recommenced hostilities.[11]

At this juncture, President Polk appointed a thirty-year-old
Texan, Robert Simpson Neighbors, as special agent to explain the
delay of the United States in honoring the terms of the agreement
and to ask the Indians to remain at peace until Congress could
resolve the differences between Texas and the United States. Neighbors had knowledge of the Indians and compassion for them.
Though lacking any authority except messages from Commissioner
Medill and Sam Houston, Neighbors, in 1847, was able to convince
the tribes to remain at peace on condition that the promised
presents would be delivered the following spring. In the meantime
Congress, concerned by the threat of Indian hostilities, ratified the
treaty of Council Springs, but only after striking from the treaty the
articles defining the federal jurisdiction over the Texas Indians.
The Congress did not wish to challenge Texas. Only the provision
to honor the promise of presents was, in effect, granted.[12]

Neighbors's appointment was extended for another year. He was
directed by the Commissioner of Indian Affairs to keep in touch
with the tribes and to persuade them to stay away from white
settlements. But he had no authority to keep whites from poaching
on the Indians' preserves. In the opinion of Commissioner Medill,
the federal laws restricting white encroachment upon lands claimed
by the Indians were inoperative in Texas. Neighbors's only recourse
to prevent white aggression against the Indians was to appeal to the
Texas authorities. This was of little use since Texas recognized no
Indian right to the soil, even to lands they occupied.

The Comanches quickly recognized their position. They pro-
tested the omission of Article III of the treaty by which the United
States promised to keep whites out of their lands. As one chief told
Neighbors:

For a long time a great many people have been passing through my
country; they kill all the game, and burn the country, and trouble me

11. *Ibid.*, pp. 124–125.
12. *Ibid.*, pp. 126–127.

very much. The commissioners of our great father promised to keep these people out of our country. I believe our white brothers do not wish to run a line between us, because they wish to settle in this country. I object to any more settlements.[13]

Trouble came quickly. Large grants of land were made by Texas to individual speculators, much of it in territories claimed by the Indians. When the Indians reacted by killing four members of a surveying party trespassing on what they regarded as their lands, the familiar pattern of reprisal and escalation went into operation. Texans demanded action, a rejection of the policy of conciliation, and removal or extermination of the Indians. Neighbors's attempt to maintain peace was denounced as weakness. As surveying parties continued to encroach upon the Indians, Neighbors requested Texas's Governor J. Pinckney Henderson to prevent any more surveyors from entering Indian lands. On Henderson's protestation of inability to order such action, Neighbors concluded that friendly relations with the Indians could not be maintained until the United States assumed jurisdiction over the Texas Indians.

Presents authorized under the Council Springs treaty were finally received and distributed to eleven tribes gathered on the Brazos at a great council meeting called for September 25, 1847. But the Indians were only temporarily mollified. The universal fear that the Texans were intent upon taking their lands and massacring them caused their restraint to be limited.

The growing danger of an Indian war finally induced Governor Henderson to establish a temporary line beyond which no white person might go except for legal purposes. This action resurrected Sam Houston's proposal of a line of separation between white man and red in Texas. The Indians, as well as the whites, were to stay on their side of the line. Eight companies of Texas Rangers were to patrol the border keeping whites and Indians apart. Yet even the authority of the state was not enough to enforce the decision. Individual Texans violated the line and occupied homesteads in the Indian territory, threatening to "shoot the first Indian that came on the land." Indeed, in February, 1848, the Texas Emigration and Land Company threatened to send an armed force into the Indian country to survey lands it expected to occupy. Texas newspapers, in the tradition of frontier journalism, exploited rumors of Indian

13. *Ibid.*, p. 129.

attacks to give a picture of a frontier in flames. The corollary to this picture was the demand that the Texas Rangers wipe out the presumably offending Indians. The one-sided partisanship of the Rangers, who overlooked white encroachment above the line but prevented Indians from exercising even agreed-upon hunting rights below the line, exacerbated the situation. The Rangers, in the opinion of many, hoped deliberately to provoke the Comanches to respond so that further excuses for destroying them could be obtained.[14]

Under such provocation and deceit it is little wonder that the Indian chiefs could not prevent their young men from retaliating against white settlers who, however innocent they might individually be, represented the white thrust into their homeland. The Texans wanted war. The federal government and, indeed, the state of Texas could not prevent it. Although Congress once more considered the possibility of establishing some form of federal control over the Texas Indians, the attempt again failed under the attacks of Texas representatives. Even the authority of Neighbors as agent expired but his services as special agent were continued as the only alternative to immediate hostilities.

An incident soon triggered violence. A Ranger company, acting on the rumored murder of a settler, came upon a band of Wichitas, who probably had nothing to do with whatever violence may have occurred, gave chase when the Indians fled on sight, and massacred twenty-five. Neighbors, who pointed out that no evidence of a hostile action by the Wichitas had been reported, suggested that an investigation into the Rangers' action be undertaken. The Wichitas retaliated, killing three surveyors. Another Ranger company murdered a sixteen-year-old Caddo boy riding alone, and the Caddos were brought to the boiling point, though the government later paid a $500 indemnity to the boy's family.[15]

Soon the frontier was the scene of attacks on outlying Ranger stations by Wichitas, Comanches, and Wacos. Horses were stolen, crops destroyed. The Rangers struck out at any Indians they met. One company succeeded in stimulating the Lipans to war by an attack on a band mistakenly thought to have stolen some horses. Neighbors logically pointed out that peace was impossible so long as

14. *Ibid.*, pp. 137–139.
15. *Ibid.*, p. 147.

friendly tribes were attacked and their property stolen. But the war had gone beyond logic. The antagonists were locked in blind rage and hate.

The Treaty of Guadalupe Hidalgo, effective July 6, 1848, provided that the United States would prevent incursions into Mexico by Indians coming from U.S. territory. Regular troops and several Ranger companies were provided to patrol the border. The Comanches, whose treaty of 1846 had provided for peace with the Americans but not with the Mexicans, were outraged to be attacked by the Americans for following their wonted custom of raiding in Mexico. Moreover, the lack of discipline of the Rangers, nominally under federal control, guaranteed continued warfare. As Neighbors put it,

Under the present system the Treaty is forgotten and if a horse is stolen by an Indian there is no demand made through the agent for his recovery, but the first party of Indians that is fallen in with, is attacked and massacred.[16]

The continuing inability of the federal government to extend its authority over the Indians of Texas, combined with the continued efforts of the Texas authorities to displace or exterminate them, led Neighbors, on the accession of President Zachary Taylor to office in 1849, to recommend to Major General William J. Worth, U.S. military commander in Texas, the policy of removing the tribes from the territory which the Texans were likely to require in the near future to reservations acquired by the federal government from the state, there to be ministered to by federal agents under the trade and intercourse laws of the United States.[17]

Neighbors had expected to be retained as agent in Texas with the new administration in 1849, but was, instead, dropped and replaced by John Rollins. Rollins delayed in Washington until November and as a result the Indian affairs of the region during the spring and summer were left without management, let alone capable management. Because of the continuing invasion of their land by Texans, and the casual massacres of several Indian bands by Texas Rangers, the Comanches, Lipan Apaches, and others attacked along

16. *Ibid.*, p. 151.
17. *Ibid.*, p. 154.

the southern frontier, killing 171 Americans and capturing 25. The U.S. Army was called upon to restore order. Brigadier General George M. Brooke assumed command of the military forces in the area in June and, with the help of Texas Rangers, drove the raiders back across the dividing line established by Neighbors. General Brooke was soon convinced that Texas laws denying Indians any title to their land were responsible for the outbreaks. What was needed was assurance of their right, and recognition by whites of the bounds within which they might hunt and cultivate. Texans, Brooke predicted, would take every foot of Indian land if left to themselves. "As a humane and just people," he noted to General Winfield Scott, "are we to deprive the aboriginal proprietors of their whole country?"[18]

The army hoped to serve as a buffer between the Texans and the Indians, protecting each against the other. Texans still refused to concede any rights to the natives. They urged the removal of the Indians from the state, a policy Secretary of the Interior Thomas Ewing, and the Whig administration generally, rejected, preferring instead to establish reservations for the native tribes within the boundaries of the state. General Brooke reestablished and strengthened the forts running on an axis from Fort Worth to the Rio Grande, and others along the Mexican boundary, to keep the Indians out of Mexican territory. The line of forts was sparsely held by regular troops. Brooke was reluctant to accept Texas Rangers to support his operation for fear that "from their general and natural hostility to the Indians, that they would be very apt to bring about what we wish to avoid—a general war." Still, the huge gaps between the forts could not prevent the Indians from penetrating into the coastal settlements, or prevent the whites, including newly arriving German immigrants, from pushing out into the fertile Indian lands.[19]

Agent Rollins, in December, 1850, brought together 600 Indians at the San Saba and renegotiated the treaty of 1846, extending, on his own authority, the trade and intercourse laws of the United States over the Texas Indians. The Indians pledged peace, and Rollins promised them protection from the whites. Meanwhile,

18. *Ibid.*, pp. 324, 328.
19. *Ibid.*, pp. 332–333.

Congress, in the Compromise of 1850, while refusing to extend the trade and intercourse laws against the will of the state of Texas, appointed two special Indian agents for the state and authorized a three-man commission to go among the Texas Indians, collect information, and negotiate treaties. The commissioners, on arrival in Texas, realized the need for reservations to secure the Indians from the continuing white aggression. If Texas would not give lands for the purpose, they suggested that the federal government buy lands from Texas. Although Governor Bell of Texas agreed that reservations were the only means of restoring peace on the frontier and that removal would result in renewed warfare, he knew the unyielding temper of the Texans and was reluctant even to ask the legislature for authority to sell land for the purpose. Although the life of the commission was cut off by Congress before any agreement with either the Indians or with Texas could be made, its strong recommendation of reservations in the northwest portion of the state strongly influenced those that were established in 1854. The southern portion of the state was to be cleared of Indians, who would be concentrated in the north, above the main routes of communication to El Paso and New Mexico.[20]

When, on February 6, 1854, the Texas legislature finally authorized reservations, and the federal government gained sole jurisdiction over the Texas Indians, the problem seemed to be solved. But the implacable hatred of the whites prevented the Indians from enjoying even this brief respite. Local citizens invaded the reservations and slaughtered the tribesmen, destroying the work of the agents who sought to integrate them into the "superior" civilization that had engulfed them. In desperation, the government, in 1859, authorized the complete removal of all Texas tribes north of the Red River.[21]

When General Stephen Watts Kearny arrived in New Mexico with his Army of the West after the outbreak of war with Mexico in May, 1846, he found a situation in which the sedentary Pueblo villages were surrounded by a hostile group of nomadic and semi-nomadic tribes—notably the Navajos, Apaches, and Comanches—who were able not only to commit depredations against the Pueblos

20. *Ibid.*, pp. 347–348, 351–356.
21. *Ibid.*, pp. 358–361.

but to keep their Mexican rulers at bay. Mutual hostilities and cruelties had caused Mexicans and Indians to be bitterly opposed to each other. Relations between the Indians and the Americans coming into the territory were marked by similar hostilities. The American military authorities entering the new territories were thus faced with the task of establishing a greater degree of authority than had previously existed and a greater degree of security for Indian and white alike. Kearny's army assumed, as other American armies have assumed, that the problems others had failed to solve would soon disappear before American skill. One of Kearny's first acts on entering New Mexico was to promise the white inhabitants protection from the Apaches and Navajos—something he noted the Mexican government had failed to provide. Similar pledges were made in all the Spanish-speaking towns visited. The Mexican governor offered no opposition, the Mexican settlers put up no resistance, and New Mexico passed quickly to the Americans. The Pueblo Indians, impressed, sought assurances of amity and support from the Americans, which were immediately forthcoming.[22]

Kearny next sought to bring the raiding tribes into a conference to require them to stop their violence against the inhabitants of the Mexican and Pueblo villages. With some difficulty, Kearny rounded up some Utes and Apaches and impressed upon them the need to cease their raiding activities. But the Navajos avoided the conference and, when Kearny moved onward to California, resumed their attacks on New Mexican villages. Kearny thereupon instructed Colonel Alexander W. Doniphan, who had been left in New Mexico with a regiment, to chastise the Navajos. He also authorized the inhabitants of the Rio Abajo area, both Mexican and Pueblo, to form "war parties, to march into the country of their enemies, the Navajos, to recover their property, to make reprisals." The Navajos found it difficult to comprehend why they should be criticized for waging war upon the same people against whom the Americans were fighting. Colonel Doniphan could only assert that it was an American custom to treat those who surrendered as friends. However, the larger implications of American policy reflect the unconscious bias in favor of the sedentary versus the nomadic way of life and of the white over the red race. Temporary treaties were entered

22. *Ibid.*, p. 73. See also Ray Allen Billington, *The Far Western Frontier, 1830–1860* (New York, 1956), pp. 179–180.

into with the Navajos and other marauding Indians but a combination of Mexican intrigue, American overconfidence, and Indian persistence led to the Taos Revolt of January, 1847, in which Governor Charles Bent, appointed territorial governor under the military, and a number of other officials were killed. Although the revolt was quickly suppressed, depredations by the Navajos, Apaches, Utes, and Comanches soon left the territory in a condition of insecurity, a condition aggravated by the ineptness of the American response.[23]

The first Indian agent assigned to the New Mexico territory was James S. Calhoun, a South Carolina Whig politician, who arrived in the summer of 1849. Calhoun worked closely with the local military commander, and particularly with Lieutenant Colonel John Macrae Washington, who was appointed military commander in the last days of the Polk administration and who assumed the role of governor until Congress could provide a civilian governor. Finding constant raiding by the mobile hostile tribes, Colonel Washington led an expedition into the heart of the Navajo country in the fall of 1849. Meeting three Navajo chiefs in council, Washington and Calhoun attempted to impress upon them the power of the United States, its jurisdiction in the area, and its right to establish military posts in the Navajo country if necessary. The council broke up in violence when Washington attempted to seize a Navajo horse which one of his men, a Mexican volunteer, claimed had been stolen.[24]

After another show of force, Washington succeeded in obtaining the signatures of several minor Navajo leaders to a treaty which recognized United States jurisdiction, gave a promise to remain at peace, undertook to return all captives, and authorized the United States to determine the boundary of Navajo lands. The treaty meant little to the main body of the Navajo tribe and depredations continued. Calhoun felt that only the application of overwhelming force and the strict separation of the Navajos, Apaches, Comanches, and Utes into closely controlled reservations where they could be taught pastoral pursuits would prevent continued outrages against the white community. The cost of supporting such a reordering of Indian values and economy would be high, Calhoun admitted to

23. Trennert, *op. cit.*, pp. 81–82.
24. *Ibid.*, p. 285.

Commissioner of Indian Affairs Brown. But, he pointed out, "To establish order in this territory you must either submit to these heavy expenditures or exterminate the mass of these Indians."[25]

Agent Calhoun considered the sedentary Pueblos in quite a different class from the raiding Navajos, Apaches, Comanches, and Utes. Their substantial agricultural and pastoral life was apparent to all and contrasted sharply with the habits of their more warlike neighbors. Calhoun believed they should immediately become citizens and participate in local affairs. Because of their intelligence and probity, Calhoun suggested that they should select their own agents, or representatives, as the other residents of New Mexico would be entitled to do when Congress established a civil government there. Indeed, Calhoun thought that the Pueblos should be organized to keep the nomadic tribes in check. "Allow me to organize a force from the Pueblo Indians," he asserted, "with the means to subsist them, and to pay them, and my life for it, in less than six months I will so tame the Navajos and Utahs that you will scarcely hear of them again." Calhoun's ideas were too radical for the army. And they were too generous for the civilians. Were a state government to be set up in New Mexico before the federal Indian trade and intercourse laws were extended there, the white population saw the possibility of depriving the Indians of the rights they possessed under the Mexican government and which had been maintained by American military rule.[26]

The factions desiring statehood and those desiring territorial status debated over the proposed state constitution in the summer of 1850. When the residents voted for the state constitution and attempted to institute local government, the Pueblos, who had been urged to stand apart from the debate, feared their interests had been compromised. Though the vote had no effect unless and until Congress authorized a new status, the inhabitants went ahead to choose their own governor and legislature. Although the Constitution of 1850 did not exclude Pueblos as citizens, the legislature restricted the suffrage to males twenty-one years and older, "Africans or the descendants of Africans and uncivilized Indians excepted," thus raising fears of possible exclusion of any Indian. Congress later in 1850 denied statehood to New Mexico and in 1851

25. *Ibid.*, pp. 286, 289.
26. *Ibid.*, pp. 293, 300.

extended the trade and intercourse laws there. The Pueblos were temporarily relieved.[27]

By the Compromise of 1850, New Mexico was made a territory, and Agent Calhoun was appointed governor. By virtue of his position, he also assumed the office of Superintendent of Indian Affairs. Four agents were authorized to work under the superintendent. A new commander, Colonel Edward V. Sumner, also arrived in New Mexico in 1851 determined to remove the troops from the towns, where they had remained in previous years—largely ineffective against Indian raids—and put them on the frontier, where they might intercept the hostiles. Governor Calhoun, in the meantime, reluctantly authorized volunteer military forces, on March 18, 1851, to protect families, homes, and property. Such groups might go on the offensive against the Indians, dividing the booty and spoils among the participants. Calhoun authorized the Pueblos the same privilege. But, because of army suspicion that civilian groups were more interested in plunder than in providing protection to the settlements, little help, in the way of arms and ammunition, was given by the military.[28]

Governor Calhoun, besieged by Pueblos pleading for protection from whites attempting to appropriate their lands, referred the matter to the Territorial Legislature in his first message, on June 2, 1851. He failed to recommend Pueblo participation in political affairs and asked the legislature to decide among three alternative statuses for the natives: "slaves (dependents), equals, or an early removal to a better location for them and our own people." Though the Treaty of Guadalupe Hidalgo bound the United States to grant all political rights to Mexican citizens in the ceded territory, and though the Pueblos were Mexican citizens, the legislature failed to protect them in this right. Governor Calhoun, nevertheless, attempted to secure the Pueblos in their basic rights by the appointment of federal agents who, he hoped, would serve as a buffer between the white settlers and themselves. In this hope he was, to a large degree, sustained.[29]

With the arrival of Colonel Sumner, the troops were relocated from the villages to new forts. One, Fort Union, was built on the

27. *Ibid.*, p. 304.
28. *Ibid.*, pp. 307–309.
29. *Ibid.*, p. 311.

Santa Fe trail near Moro late in 1851. Another, Fort Defiance, was built at the same time in the heart of the Navajo country near the present Arizona-New Mexico border. The fort was literally an attempt on the part of the American authorities to convince the raiding tribes that the United States fully intended to stop their raiding and to confine them to closely supervised reservations. Additional forts, such as Fort Fillmore on the Rio Grande near El Paso and Fort Conrad near Valverde south of Santa Fe, were established and manned by troops formerly occupying the towns of the territory. Agents were next moved into the area, with headquarters at the army forts. They brought seed and farm implements to encourage the pursuit of agriculture among the chastened tribes.[30]

The border tribes along the Missouri River who found themselves directly in the route of the westward-moving Americans felt pressed both by the whites on the east and by the powerful Plains tribes to their north and west. Their plight worsened as the game decreased on the Plains and the more warlike tribes raided their villages and ran off their livestock. Typical of the border tribes were the Pawnees, a powerful group who agreed in 1833 to settle on an area near the Platte River in return for a promise of government aid in their civilization and education. Yet the Pawnee experiment in education proved difficult to maintain in the face of increasing attacks by Sioux, Cheyennes, and Arapahos.[31] The Otos, Missouris, and Omahas, inhabiting the area where the Platte enters the Missouri in the present state of Nebraska, were also exposed to the attacks of Sioux raiding parties. Similar fates were faced by tribes— many of whom had previously moved or been moved from the East —such as the Potawatomis, Ottawas, Chippewas, and Winnebagos in the area around Council Bluffs in western Iowa, and the Kansas, Delawares, and some Sac and Fox Indians in the Kansas area. Whether the fury of their red brethren was more destructive than the whiskey merchants and land grabbers coming from the East is hard to determine. Most possessed treaties with the United States and received annuities in return for the lands they had previously given up. But all tended to be sunk in despair.

30. *Ibid.*, pp. 313–316.
31. *Ibid.*, p. 157. The treaty of 1833 with the Pawnees is printed in Charles J. Kappler, ed., *Indian Affairs: Laws and Treaties*, Vol. II (*Treaties*) (Washington, 1903), 308–309.

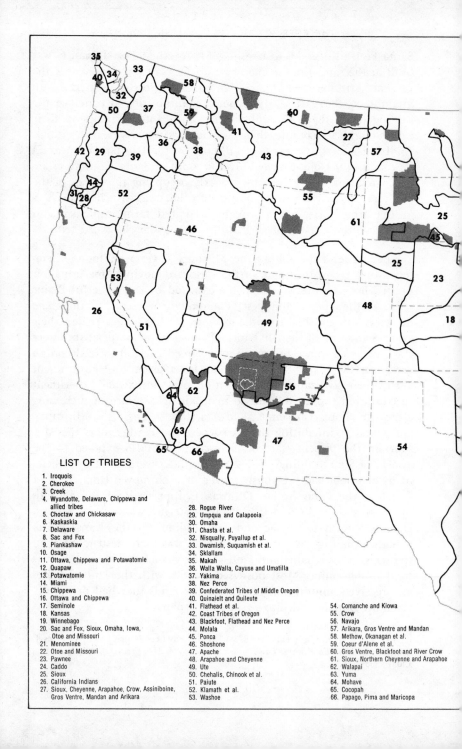

LIST OF TRIBES

1. Iroquois
2. Cherokee
3. Creek
4. Wyandotte, Delaware, Chippewa and allied tribes
5. Choctaw and Chickasaw
6. Kaskaskia
7. Delaware
8. Sac and Fox
9. Piankashaw
10. Osage
11. Ottawa, Chippewa and Potawatomie
12. Quapaw
13. Potawatomie
14. Miami
15. Chippewa
16. Ottawa and Chippewa
17. Seminole
18. Kansas
19. Winnebago
20. Sac and Fox, Sioux, Omaha, Iowa, Otoe and Missouri
21. Menominee
22. Otoe and Missouri
23. Pawnee
24. Caddo
25. Sioux
26. California Indians
27. Sioux, Cheyenne, Arapahoe, Crow, Assiniboine, Gros Ventre, Mandan and Arikara

28. Rogue River
29. Umpqua and Calapooia
30. Omaha
31. Chasta et al.
32. Nisqually, Puyallup et al.
33. Dwamish, Suquamish et al.
34. Sklallam
35. Makah
36. Walla Walla, Cayuse and Umatilla
37. Yakima
38. Nez Perce
39. Confederated Tribes of Middle Oregon
40. Quinaielt and Quileute
41. Flathead et al.
42. Coast Tribes of Oregon
43. Blackfoot, Flathead and Nez Perce
44. Molala
45. Ponca
46. Shoshone
47. Apache
48. Arapahoe and Cheyenne
49. Ute
50. Chehalis, Chinook et al.
51. Paiute
52. Klamath et al.
53. Washoe

54. Comanche and Kiowa
55. Crow
56. Navajo
57. Arikara, Gros Ventre and Mandan
58. Methow, Okanagan et al.
59. Coeur d'Alene et al.
60. Gros Ventre, Blackfoot and River Crow
61. Sioux, Northern Cheyenne and Arapahoe
62. Walapai
63. Yuma
64. Mohave
65. Cocopah
66. Papago, Pima and Maricopa

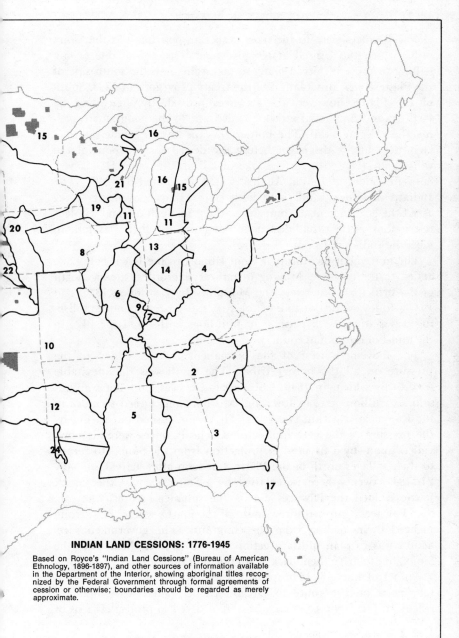

INDIAN LAND CESSIONS: 1776-1945

Based on Royce's "Indian Land Cessions" (Bureau of American Ethnology, 1896-1897), and other sources of information available in the Department of the Interior, showing aboriginal titles recognized by the Federal Government through formal agreements of cession or otherwise; boundaries should be regarded as merely approximate.

The foregoing tribes are listed in the order in which land cessions were effected. Tribes which made no cessions to the Federal Government are not included. The principal areas reserved from cession or receded to Indian tribes and commonly referred to as Indian reservations are shown thus.

Source: The HANDBOOK OF FEDERAL INDIAN LAW compiled by Felix S. Cohen (Washington, 1945)

The Pawnees were in the most desperate position and the Sioux raids, which the United States government seemed unable or unwilling to prevent, forced many to take refuge on the south side of the Platte River, in violation of the treaty provisions of 1833. South of the Platte, however, the Pawnees proved, by their begging, stealing, and occasional attacks, an irritant to the emigrants traveling the Oregon Trail. The border Indians saw the game, particularly the buffalo, disappear before the destructive weapons of the white man ("He kills for the sake of killing," Thomas H. Harvey, Superintendent of Indian Affairs at St. Louis noted in 1846). The Indians saw their lands used as a channel for movement. They asked the government to compensate them for such use and to place restrictions on the casual destruction of game. But little was done to meet the Indian objections.[32]

The movement of Mormons from Illinois to the Great Salt Lake added to the pressure. Moving in militarylike order, staying north of the principal route west, the Mormons, by December, 1846, had 15,000 followers in the Indian country, raising crops and establishing way stations with permanent buildings, mills, and the like, in the midst of the Indian country.

The movement west of the permanent frontier added to the pressure on all the border tribes. The result was the inevitable treaties by which, in 1846, Chippewas, Ottawas, and Potawatomis sold six million acres in Iowa and Missouri and agreed to move to the Kansas area within two years. They were rushed out earlier by the pressure of the voracious settlers. The Pawnees were also prevailed upon—by a promise of protection from the Sioux—to return to their villages north of the Platte, but soon after arrival, on May 21, 1847, twenty-three were killed by a Sioux party. Other Sioux parties raided the Pawnees during the summer to finish the job. The Pawnees again withdrew south of the Platte, where they recommenced their stealing from the emigrants. The government's reaction was to plan military action, not to protect them from the Sioux, but to drive them back again north of the Platte.[33]

An act of May 13, 1846, provided for the establishment of military posts on the route to Oregon to be staffed with mounted riflemen. The troop commanders were ordered to protect citizens of

32. Trennert, *op. cit.*, pp. 162–169.
33. *Ibid.*, pp. 172–175.

the United States lawfully within the territories of Indian tribes and also to maintain peace among the tribes. The Pawnee villages south of the Platte were to be destroyed and the Indians driven north once again. The proposal indiscriminately to attack the Pawnees appalled Superintendent Thomas Harvey, who pointed out to Commissioner of Indian Affairs Medill that the innocent would suffer with the guilty. The government similarly put pressure on the Mormons to move from the territory of the Omaha Indians and, after some resistance, the Mormons, in 1848, pulled back across the Missouri or proceeded west to Salt Lake.[34]

In the central area between the upper Platte and the Arkansas—roughly the area between the Oregon Trail and the Santa Fe Road—numerous smaller but warlike tribes lived. These Indians—Cheyennes, Arapahos, Teton Sioux—had no official relations with the Americans in 1846 when the Upper Platte agency under Agent Thomas Fitzpatrick, nicknamed "Broken Hand" because of a crippled left hand, began operations. These Indians had been in touch with American trappers and mountain men. The influence of the latter was to be seen in the addiction to whiskey of many of the tribesmen and in the movement of some tribes in response to the demands of the fur trade. For example, the Oglala Sioux in 1834 moved from the upper Missouri to the upper Platte in the vicinity of Fort Laramie attracting other Sioux until, by 1846, 7,000 lived along the Platte. The Cheyennes and Arapahos, some 2,500 each, ranged over a wide area of the Plains, but traded animal skins at Bent's Fort on the Arkansas.[35]

The fur traders were soon followed by the emigrants and the United States cavalry, neither group understanding or appreciating the position of the Indian as the traders had done. The cavalry could overawe the Indians when they were in evidence, but the Plains were vast and they could not be everywhere. Meanwhile, incidents between emigrants and Indians multiplied as the game utilized by both decreased. The Indians were perfectly well aware that their resources of game, wood, and water were being diminished or usurped by the emigrants and they occasionally formally complained of the fact. But the emigrants tended to ignore any Indian claim to what seemed to be the blessings of nature, and the

34. *Ibid.*, pp. 180, 182, 190–191.
35. *Ibid.*, pp. 202–204.

government was, as usual, even less effective in correcting abuses than in recognizing them. Typical of the bureaucratic reaction to such a complaint, forwarded by the Sioux to Commissioner Medill through Superintendent Thomas Harvey at St. Louis, was the commissioner's reply:

It is the nature of the Buffalo & all other kinds of game to recede before the approach of civilization, and the injury complained of, is but one of those inconveniences to which every people are subjected by the changing & constantly progressive spirit of the age.

Medill refused to consider reparations or compensation to the Sioux for such deleterious use.[36]

Denied government compensation, the Sioux demanded tribute of the emigrant parties for the privilege of passing through their land. Such presents were usually forthcoming, but through fear rather than from a sense of owed compensation. The emigrants' complaints filled the columns of frontier newspapers and reached the halls of Congress. The U. S. government's reaction, on the recommendation of the agents on the frontier, was to consider establishing forts along the trails and to chastise the Indians by military action.[37]

Expeditions against the natives, however, tended to be counter-productive because of poor intelligence of Indian capabilities and culture. "It is want of this knowledge," Agent Thomas Fitzpatrick wrote in August, 1848, "that has been the cause for the past few years of the total failure of all the expeditions made against the Indians; and which failures have a great tendency to make the Indians much more hostile, bold & daring than they were before any attempts were made to chastise them."[38]

The concept of reservations for the Plains Indian tribes derives from 1849, following the creation, in March of that year, of a Department of the Interior, to which the Indian Office was moved from its former spot in the War Department. Though strong opposition existed to the move—John C. Calhoun asked, "Who does not see that the Indian affairs are immediately connected with the War Department?"—the move was made, and incoming Presi-

36. *Ibid.*, p. 213.
37. *Ibid.*, pp. 214–215.
38. *Ibid.*, pp. 231–232.

dent Zachary Taylor appointed Thomas Ewing, a former Whig Senator from Ohio, as the first secretary. Ewing saw to it that deserving Whigs replaced no longer deserving Democrats in the offices available. In addition, Secretary Ewing moved the Upper Missouri agency to Salt Lake and the Council Bluffs agency to Santa Fe. Orlando Brown, a political friend of General Taylor, soon replaced William Medill as Commissioner of Indian Affairs. One of Brown's first recommendations was that clear and definite boundaries of what constituted Indian areas of residence and hunting be established and that no trespassing in these areas be allowed without the approval of the occupant tribes or the proper agents of government. Brown also suggested a common hunting ground be set aside for all tribes to use. One scholar has asserted that Brown's suggestion was the "first concrete proposal on the federal level for establishing a permanent reservation for the wild tribes of the prairies—for restricting them to well-defined lands instead of a vague general area."[39]

Brown and Ewing sought to establish a comprehensive solution to the problem which would concentrate and remove many of the Indian tribes from their customary locations athwart the emigration routes. A large increase in the number of Indian superintendencies and agencies was recommended by Brown. The proposals to negotiate a comprehensive treaty with the tribes of the Central Plains and to extend and expand the Indian administration of the United States were presented to the Thirty-first Congress, meeting in December, 1849, for consideration. The proposals were intimately related to other proposals to build a railroad to the Pacific.[40]

In his annual report for 1850, Commissioner of Indian Affairs Orlando Brown renewed his recommendation that reservations should be assigned to each tribe, which should consist of "a country adapted to agriculture, of limited extent and well-defined boundaries; within which all, with occasional exceptions, should be compelled constantly to remain until such time as their general improvement and good conduct may supersede the necessity of such restrictions." Brown urged that the government supply the tribes "with stock, agricultural implements, and useful materials for clothing; encourage and assist them in the erection of comfortable

39. *Ibid.*, pp. 242, 245, 248, 250.
40. *Ibid.*, pp. 251–255.

dwellings, and secure to them the means and facilities of education, intellectual, moral, and religious."[41]

A new commissioner, Luke Lea of Mississippi, and a new Secretary of the Interior, Alexander H. H. Stuart, of Virginia, replaced Brown and Ewing in 1850. Both supported the concept of reservations and the need to increase the number of agents to deal with the Indians. After a long, hard fight with opponents of too much government spending, an Indian Appropriation Act of February 27, 1851, provided funds to expand the Indian Department to meet the demands of the vast new territories acquired by the United States after 1846. The Congress also provided $100,000 to negotiate treaties with the mountain and prairie tribes so that peace could be secured and the paths to the Pacific cleared. The tribes were to be grouped on reservations and encouraged to resort to agriculture. The freedom of the Indian to move and interact with his neighbors as he saw fit, beyond the continuous line of the old Indian frontier, was a thing of the past. The government recognized that the new policy implied greater responsibilities on the part of the government. But it failed to recognize just how extensive those responsibilities would be.[42]

As whites streamed west, particularly in the central area, the hunting territories of the Plains and border Indians were literally overrun. The economy and ecology of the Plains were altered. Particularly along the Platte River, the animals, and the Indians who depended upon them, could not exist as they had before. As the federal government sought a way to reconcile the needs of the white emigrants, the demands of the railroad builders, and the plight of the Indians in the way, the plan of gathering up the natives and concentrating them off the path of the white movement came to seem a necessity. Accordingly, a great council of the tribes affected was called for the fall of 1851. Perhaps 10,000 Teton Sioux, Cheyennes, Arapahos, Crows, Gros Ventres, Assiniboins, and Arickaras gathered near Fort Laramie for the purpose. Intertribal conflicts were narrowly averted, particularly when the Snakes, ancient foes of the Sioux, arrived after the others. The Indians were told by Superintendent David Dawson Mitchell, of the St. Louis superin-

41. *Ibid.*, p. 267.
42. *Ibid.*, pp. 272–273.

tendency, a former fur trapper, that the United States would compensate the tribes for the grass and timber destroyed and the buffalo and game driven off by the emigrants, but that they in turn must allow unmolested passage and keep the peace. To facilitate this, military posts would have to be established in the Indian country and definite boundaries marked off for each tribe. Mitchell asserted that the U.S. was not thereby taking the Indians' lands from them but the restrictions on free movement and the conduct of war were necessary to meet the changed conditions. No longer was the game sufficient for all. No longer could Indian warfare be of no consequence to the white man. The Indian must recognize that his life had changed and would change. But to facilitate the transition, the federal government, Mitchell promised, was prepared to pay an annuity of $50,000 a year for fifty years.[43]

When the process of drawing the boundaries began, trouble arose. Sioux, Cheyenne, and Arapaho claims overlapped. The federal commissioners decided that the Platte should be the dividing line between the Sioux and the others. The Sioux, who hunted south of the Platte, protested. One of their leaders, Black Hawk, an Oglala Sioux, noted, "These lands once belonged to the Kiowas and the Crows, but we whipped these nations out of them, and in this we did what the white men do when they want the lands of the Indians." Mitchell conceded that they could continue to hunt south of the Platte if they remained at peace. The Cheyennes and Arapahos were assigned to the area between the Arkansas and North Platte, the Mandans and Gros Ventres along the Yellowstone, the Crows near the Powder River, and the Blackfeet their traditional lands at the headwaters of the Missouri. For the first time the great Indian nations of the Central Plains were restricted by an outside power to particular areas. Though the reservations were not precise, and the Indians retained the right to hunt elsewhere on the Plains, the United States had achieved its purpose in establishing some form of control over the native inhabitants of the interior.[44]

With the Plains tribes moved aside and contained, the weaker border tribes, including the Otos, Omahas, Iowas, Sac, and Foxes, were removed from their homes in eastern Nebraska and Kansas.

43. *Ibid.*, pp. 396–399.
44. *Ibid.*, pp. 399–400. The treaty is printed in Kappler, *op. cit.*, II, 440–442.

Most were sent to Oklahoma, others north to the Minnesota Territory.

The United States Senate refused to confirm the promise of Mitchell that annuities should be paid for fifty years and reduced the period to ten years. Only a few of the tribes accepted this amendment to the treaty, though the United States forced the others to comply. Similarly, other reasons were found to chip away at the land reserved to the Indians, and a sorry chapter of continued warfare ensued.[45]

The last of the Indian tribes living on the Great Plains south of the forty-ninth parallel to make a treaty with the United States was "the Blackfoot nation," consisting of the Piegans, Bloods, northern Blackfeet, and their allies, the Gros Ventres. The Blackfeet were not a party to the treaty of Fort Laramie, 1851, held by David D. Mitchell, Superintendent of Indian Affairs in St. Louis, with many of the other tribes of the Plains. Nevertheless, the territory of the Blackfoot nation was mentioned and respected in the treaty. However, shortly afterward, in 1853, with increasing interest in the development of new routes, particularly a railroad route, to the West Coast, Isaac I. Stevens, the governor of Washington Territory and ex-officio Superintendent of Indian Affairs there, as well as a military engineer, was assigned the responsibility of making a railroad survey, governing the new territory, and inaugurating negotiations with the affected tribes.

Stevens obtained the services of Alexander Culbertson as special agent to introduce him to the feared Blackfeet. Culbertson's wife, a Blackfoot woman, served as the indispensable link between the two cultures. Governor Stevens established friendly contact with the Blackfeet and achieved a desired conference at Fort Benton on September 21, 1853. Stevens addressed the Indians and said:

Your Great Father. . . wishes you to live at peace with each other and the whites. He desires that you should be under his protection, and partake equally with the Crows and Assiniboines of his bounty. Live in peace with all the neighboring Indians, protect all the whites passing through your country, and the Great Father will be your fast friend.

Chief Low Horn, answering for the Piegans, welcomed the sentiments expressed by Stevens but sounded the traditional note that the chiefs

45. Trennert, op. cit., p. 404.

could not restrain their young men, but their young men were wild, and ambitious, in their turn to be braves and chiefs. They wanted by some brave act to win the favor of their young women, and bring scalps and horses to show their prowess.[46]

In October, 1855, a great treaty council was held with the Black-feet tribes and a treaty signed. The expressed purpose of the whites was to convert the Blackfeet from a "warlike and nomadic to a peaceable and agricultural nation." Though experts like Culbert-son predicted that the Blackfeet would not think of agriculture so long as game was abundant—"it is beneath their dignity"—Gover-nor Stevens pushed forward with the basic plan. He urged the Blackfeet to grow crops and keep cattle and promised that the United States would build schools and mills to serve them. "You know the buffalo will not continue forever," he warned. "Get farms and cattle in time."[47]

The treaty, written by the commissioners and explained to the Indians, set aside certain common hunting grounds for all nations of Indians, established an exclusive territory for the Blackfoot nation, permitted United States citizens to live in and pass un-molested through their territories, and authorized the establishment of telegraph lines, military posts, missions, and schools in their terri-tory. In return for these concessions the United States agreed to spend $20,000 annually for ten years for goods and provisions for the four tribes of the Blackfoot nation and to spend an additional $15,000 annually during the same period to promote the education and Christianization of the Blackfeet. When the treaty was signed on October 17, 1855, the mountain of trade goods that had been piled high on the council ground was distributed.[48]

The Blackfeet looked upon the yearly gift by the whites as an indication of their friendship and worried less about the concession of portions of their sovereignty to the United States than about the injunction to cease the intertribal warfare which played so impor-tant a part in the life of the young Blackfoot male.

The California Indians, though numerous, were scattered in small tribes and bands, and were no match for the white miners and fortune hunters who swarmed into the state on the discovery of gold

46. John C. Ewers, *The Blackfeet: Raiders on the Northwestern Plains* (Norman, Okla., 1958), pp. 209–210.
47. *Ibid.*, pp. 214–216.
48. *Ibid.*, pp. 219–221.

in the late 1840s. The destruction and degradation of the California Indians is one of the sorriest blotches on the honor and intelligence of a nation. It was less a matter of war than of "sport." If the Indians were not shot or enslaved by private individuals, they were shunted onto hastily organized reservations by federal commissioners and soon despoiled even of these refuges when the Congress refused to ratify the treaties establishing the reservations.[49]

In little more than a decade, from the middle of the 1840s to the middle of the 1850s, the United States burst through the bounds—both of territory and policy—that formerly limited its sway among the Indians west of the Mississippi. In the wake of a successful war with Mexico, the admission of Texas to the Union, and the movement of thousands of its citizens across the plains, mountains, and deserts to the Pacific Ocean, the concept of a permanent boundary separating whites and Indians was dissolved. Once invincible Indian nations were humbled and reduced from independent powers acknowledging no external constraints to dependent communities acknowledging the right and power of the United States to set limits to their freedom of action. While not shorn by their conquerors of all their physical power or all their legal rights, the Indian nations were deprived in practice of many of these powers and rights. The greatest real estate transaction in history, effected through wars, treaties, and a mass population movement, had been accomplished.

49. Robert F. Heizer and Alan J. Almquist, *The Other Californians: Prejudice and Discrimination under Spain, Mexico, and the United States to 1920* (Berkeley, 1971) , pp. 23–91.

CHAPTER 9

The Civil War and Its Aftermath

WHEN the Civil War broke out in 1861 the Indians of the Indian Territory—primarily the Five Civilized Tribes (Cherokees, Choctaws, Chickasaws, Creeks, and Seminoles) who had been removed there shortly before—were in the same uncomfortable situation in which the Iroquois had found themselves during the American Revolution. Although the treaties by which the tribes—the Cherokees, Choctaws, Chickasaws, Creeks, and Seminoles—had moved to the area, and the treaties that had preceded the move, pledged the protection of the United States against all enemies, the Indian Territory was in fact left without protection with the evacuation of U. S. forces from Texas and Arkansas, and the adherence of those states to the Confederacy on the outbreak of war.[1]

On May 17, 1861, the Congress of the Confederacy passed an act annexing the Indian Territory to the Confederacy and placing all its tribes under the new government. At the same time Albert Pike was sent as commissioner to the Indian Territory to draw up new treaties with the Indians there and to enlist their aid on behalf of

---

1. S. David Buice, "The Civil War and the Five Civilized Tribes: A Study in Federal Indian Relations" (Ph.D. diss., University of Oklahoma, 1970), p. 25. The most complete account of the impact of the Civil War on the Indians of the Indian Territory is still Annie Heloise Abel's three-volume study of *The Slaveholding Indians,* separately titled and published as *The American Indian as Slaveholder and Secessionist: An Omitted Chapter in the Diplomatic History of the Southern Confederacy* (Cleveland, 1915), *The American Indian as Participant in the Civil War* (Cleveland, 1919), and *The American Indian under Reconstruction* (Cleveland, 1925).

the South. Pike's skillful and rapid mission was successful. The Indian nations had been thrown into confusion by the outbreak of war. Strongest of their leaders was John Ross of the Cherokees who urged a firm adherence to existing treaties and a cautious neutrality. But neutrality was a luxury not to be allowed the tribesmen. Pike, although instructed to inform the Indians that it was the intention of the Confederacy to advance the tribes toward a system of landholding in severalty and to create a territorial government, carefully suppressed these instructions, which were the very intentions the Indian nations feared most and which they attributed to the North rather than to the South.

Rather, Pike played on the Indians' fear of the loss of their lands and of their tribal governments at the hands of the Northerners. The Indians were acutely sensitive to this possibility since such sentiments had been bruited about for many years. Robert J. Walker, governor of Kansas Territory, had stated in 1857, for example, that the Indian Territory would soon become a state of the Union and that Indian treaties would pose no obstacle. During the 1860 presidential campaign, William H. Seward, soon to be Secretary of State, declared, "The Indian Territory . . . south of Kansas, must be vacated by the Indians" to make room for the settlers.[2]

Pike also played upon the Indians' fear that Southern power might be exerted over them if they failed to cooperate. He tempted them instead with promises that slavery would be recognized, their tribal lands would be guaranteed to them in fee simple in perpetuity, and that no attempt would be made to establish a territorial government over them except upon their voluntary application. Pike even promised to meet the annuity payments the Indians derived from their treaties with the United States. Pike's tactics were persuasive and he was able to sign treaties with the Five Civilized Tribes, despite the opposition of portions of the tribes, and to enlist Indian units in the Confederate forces. In addition, Pike managed to negotiate treaties with the Quapaws, Senecas, and Shawnees as well as with the Great Osages. These latter tribes also agreed to furnish troops to the Confederacy but did not receive the

2. Arrell M. Gibson, *The Chickasaws* (Norman, Okla., 1971), p. 261. The original of one of Pike's treaties, that of August 12, 1861, with bands of the Comanche, Wichita, Caddo, and Waco Indians, is in the Newberry Library, Chicago, Ayer MS. 438.

privilege promised the Five Civilized Tribes of sending delegates to the Confederate Congress. As it turned out, the representation provision was deleted when the treaties were ratified in Richmond between November, 1861, and January, 1862.

Northern efforts to secure the loyalty of the tribes of the Indian Territory were belated and failed to forestall Pike's moves. Over the protests of Commissioner of Indian Affairs William P. Dole (when he finally heard about it) United States military forces were withdrawn from the Indian Territory, as they were from Texas and Arkansas at the beginning of the war. Nevertheless, plans were soon afoot to send a military force into the territory to reestablish Union authority. The plans for the expedition were, however, subject to hopeless confusion. Senator James Henry Lane of Kansas, after securing a brigadier's commission from the War Department, attempted to raise two regiments of Kansas volunteers for the purpose. He was blocked by his political rival, Kansas Governor Charles Robinson, and by the regular army commander in the district, who preferred to command any such invasion himself. In the meantime Confederate forces inflicted a severe defeat on loyal Indians in the Indian Territory and sent thousands of refugees scurrying northward into Kansas. The presence of these refugees heightened the desire of Commissioner Dole to mount an invasion, both as a means of getting the refugees back—since he lacked relief supplies to sustain them in Kansas—and as a way of creating defections among the Confederate Indians. A federal force under Colonel William Weer of Kansas eventually moved into the Indian Territory in July, 1862, and inflicted a defeat on Missouri rebels under Colonel J. J. Clarkson. Fifteen hundred Cherokees deserted the Confederacy after the victory and joined the federal forces. Suddenly, however, the imperious Colonel Weer was placed under arrest by one of his fellow officers and the entire command ordered to retreat northward over the protest of Bureau of Indian Affairs agents accompanying them. The expedition was thus aborted and those Indians who had defected on the arrival of the federal force, including John Ross, the Cherokee chief, traveled north with the withdrawing column to avoid the retaliation that would have been in store for them had they stayed.

The succeeding war years in the Indian Territory present a confused picture of raid and counterraid, unified only by the suffering of the Indian inhabitants, both those who remained at home and those who escaped to the North as refugees. But the war facilitated the eventual destruction of the territory as an exclusively Indian home. Bills were introduced in Congress to clear Kansas of Indians and send them to the Indian Territory. Other bills were submitted to establish a territorial government in Oklahoma and eventually to open the territory to white men. Bills to facilitate the construction of railroads both north and south and east and west across the territory were similarly pushed in Congress. Because of the peculiar juridical condition of the tribes in the Indian Territory, particularly in the light of their partial defection to the Confederacy, the task of wringing concessions from them was facilitated.

When John Ross went to Washington and consulted with President Lincoln over the status of the Cherokee nation and the other Civilized Tribes, the matter was so complicated by the difficult legal questions at issue and by the intense pressure of legislators from surrounding states for concessions that no resolution was effected. Lincoln drafted a Proclamation to the People of the Cherokee, Chickasaw, Creek, Seminole, and Choctaw Nations late in 1862, in a tone of "stern and understanding reproach," in which he warned the Indian nations that if they allied themselves with the South and lost they could not expect the United States to uphold the treaties they had despised and abandoned. But the proclamation was never issued, perhaps because of the pressures of those who wished to take the occasion of the war to destroy all preexisting treaty relationships with the Indian nations of the Indian Territory. Those pressures were heightened in October, 1862, when Governor Alexander Ramsey of Minnesota asked Lincoln to remove the Sioux, Winnebagos, and Chippewas from Minnesota following the great Sioux uprising. Lincoln passed the problem on to Congress in his State of the Union message of December 1, 1862, urging a remodeling of the Indian system.[3]

The process of rewriting the agreements between the United States and the Five Civilized Tribes began in 1863. A treaty with the loyal Creeks made in September, 1863, was so modified by the Senate that it was not acceptable to the Creeks. The Senate eliminated a guarantee of past treaty stipulations and added a requirement for the tribe to cede additional territory to the United States.

3. Buice, *op. cit.*, pp. 122–123 and *passim*.

The new treaty asserted that those Creeks—one-half of the nation—who had joined with the Confederacy had absolutely forfeited all their rights and claims to land of the Creek tribe. Their portion was to be ceded to the United States, which would hold the land in trust for the use of those hostile Creeks who reestablished friendly relations with the federal government as well as for the use of other friendly tribes and persons. Although abortive, the Creek Treaty of 1863 was a guide to the negotiations that were to follow in 1865 and 1866 when the United States, first at a council at Fort Smith and then by means of negotiations in Washington between delegates of the different tribes, reestablished the relationship between the once potent nations of the Southeast and the federal government. The United States was able to use the defection of the tribal governments to the South as a club to reduce the power and independence of each nation. The federal negotiators also made skillful use of the controversies between loyal and disloyal factions of the tribes over the terms of the new treaties to minimize further the extent to which earlier treaty rights were carried over into the postwar period.

The Seminole Treaty of March 21, 1866, the first concluded, granted amnesty to all Seminoles, abolished slavery, and required the Seminole nation to cede for 15 cents an acre the two million acres it had acquired under the Treaty of 1856. In return the Seminoles were resettled on a 200,000-acre tract for which the tribe paid 50 cents an acre. Fifty thousand dollars of the tribe's own money, obtained through the surplus acquired in the sale, was to be used to compensate loyal Seminoles for their losses. A right of way for railroad construction was also granted. The treaties with the other civilized tribes followed suit. The treaty made jointly with the Choctaws and Chickasaws, whose support of the Confederate government had been most pronounced, was generous in not demanding surrender of all tribal rights and privileges. Nevertheless, these tribes were required to cede the Leased District, an area west of the ninety-eighth meridian leased to the United States (for the settlement of other Indian tribes) by the terms of an 1855 treaty. Railway concessions were also extracted from the Choctaws and Chickasaws.[4]

4. *Ibid.*, pp. 323–327. See also M. Thomas Bailey, *Reconstruction in Indian Territory: A Story of Avarice, Discrimination, and Opportunism* (Port Washington, N.Y., 1972), pp. 12, 71–73, 131–135.

In sum, the Civil War, while it did not extinguish the reserved rights of the Five Civilized Tribes in the Indian Territory, severely restricted them. The tribes, as were the Iroquois in the American Revolution, were caught in a maelstrom from which there was no easy exit. They attempted to maintain their neutrality and their ancient rights. Under the pressure of both sides in the great struggle that wracked the Union, they were torn apart. As one authority commented, even though many stood by the Union, "in the end all were treated as traitors, and, faced with the prospect of Federal forfeiture of their traditional rights and privileges, all were forced to yield to the demands of the United States."[5]

The Sioux Indians of Minnesota and the Dakotas occupied the last area and lived in the last time when Indians of North America dealt on a plane of political and military equality with the United States. Yet they were crushed militarily during the Civil War and the years immediately following, forced onto increasingly restricted reservations, and coerced into the unnatural life of agriculturalists and dependents on annuities grudgingly doled out to them by their conquerors. Although resistance and bloodshed continued spasmodically even into the 1890s, the fatal blow was struck during the Civil War. The agent of change was Union General John Pope, fresh from service as commander of the Army of Virginia. When Sioux attacks on the frontier town of New Ulm and other settlements in Minnesota in 1862 spread panic throughout Minnesota and Wisconsin, appeals for help came urgently to Washington. Governor Ramsey of Minnesota declared that the Sioux outbreak was not a local matter but a "national war."[6]

Commissioner of Indian Affairs William P. Dole, who had himself been negotiating with the Chippewas of Red Lake and the Red River of the North at the time of the Sioux attacks on various Minnesota towns, reported meeting the Sioux agent in flight from his station in a hysterical state. The agent believed that there was a "general and preconcerted rising of all the Indians of the country," including such traditional enemies as the Chippewas and Sioux.

5. Buice, *op. cit.*, p. 346.
6. Richard N. Ellis, *General Pope and U.S. Indian Policy* (Albuquerque, N.M., 1970) , p. 12.

Fully persuaded that we were surrounded by Indians, he started from St. Cloud for St. Paul, warning the people along his route to flee from the country; and a few days afterwards was found dead some distance from the road. He had evidently become deranged and committed suicide.[7]

Following the defeat of the Union forces at the second battle of Bull Run on August 30, 1862, General George McClellan had replaced Pope, leaving Lincoln with an unemployed major general. Pope was almost immediately, on September 6, assigned to command the new Department of the Northwest—covering the states of Wisconsin, Iowa, and Minnesota and the territories of Nebraska and Dakota—with headquarters at St. Paul, Minnesota. Declaring a war of extermination on the Sioux—a purpose he later modified—Pope vigorously organized the forces available to him and earnestly pressed for more from Washington. Although denied the numbers he wished, Pope was able to bring into the field sufficient troops to destroy the power of the several thousand hostile Sioux warriors. His instructions to Colonel Henry H. Sibley, Minnesota's first governor and commander of her militia, were explicit. No treaties were to be made with the Minnesota Sioux. "They are to be treated as maniacs or wild beasts, and by no means as people with whom treaties or compromises can be made." Sibley defeated the Sioux and captured approximately 1,800 in September. Three hundred and three were condemned to death, though President Lincoln authorized the hanging of only thirty-eight, much to the irritation of local Minnesotans who talked of total extermination or total removal of the Sioux from the state.[8]

A spring campaign was mounted in 1863 against other Sioux, particularly the Teton Sioux, who had announced that they would not allow the whites to pass through their country, either by land or by river. Again Pope ordered an aggressive campaign, declaring that, unless overruled by higher authority, his troops would pursue the hostiles across the international boundary should they attempt to escape in that direction. Again U.S. arms were successful.[9]

The Santee Sioux and the Winnebagos, who had had no hand in

7. *Annual Report of the Commissioner of Indian Affairs for 1862*, p. 15.
8. Ellis, *op. cit.*, p. 12.
9. *Ibid.*, p. 17.

the outbreak of 1862, were, in 1863, exiled to a forbidding reservation at Crow Creek on the Missouri River eighty miles above Fort Randall. Inadequate supplies and crop failures led to actual starvation in 1864.[10]

The 1864 campaign saw continued successes, though it never achieved the complete destruction of the Sioux forces. Nevertheless, the attrition was beginning to have its effect.

General Pope was made commander of a new Division of the Missouri, combining the departments of the Northwest, Missouri, and Kansas, in 1865, thus giving him control of all forces on the Plains. With the increased responsibilities went increased difficulties. While Pope was away from his command conferring with General Ulysses S. Grant about the new military organization in the West, Colonel John M. Chivington of the Colorado Volunteers, on November 29, 1864, attacked a band of friendly Cheyennes gathered under military protection at Sand Creek in eastern Colorado. The vicious attack not only destroyed the peaceful posture of the Cheyennes but exacerbated relations with many of the Plains tribes. The Sand Creek massacre, the My Lai of the day, poisoned relations between whites and Indians and provided ammunition for members of Congress, humanitarians, and others who accused the army of carrying on an unjust war in the West. General Pope, to his credit, did not countenance such behavior. Both civilians and soldiers, however, suffered the consequences of this outrage as Indian resistance doubled. The entire Plains area was soon turned into a battlefield. Not only the Cheyennes and the Sioux but virtually all the tribes of the Plains went to war.[11]

The report of the commission appointed in 1867 to make peace with the hostile tribes pulled no punches in its assertion of United States responsibility for the warfare that had swept the Plains in the years previous.

Among civilized men [the commission noted] war usually springs from a sense of injustice. The best possible way then to avoid war is to do no act of injustice. When we learn that the same rule holds good with Indians, the chief difficulty is removed. But it is said our wars with them have been almost constant. Have we been uniformly unjust? We answer

10. *Ibid.*, pp. 34, 74–81.
11. Report of Peace Commission to President Andrew Johnson, Jan. 7, 1868, in *Annual Report of the Commissioner of Indian Affairs for 1868*, pp. 26–50.

unhesitatingly, yes. We are aware that the masses of our people have felt kindly toward them, and the legislation of Congress has always been conceived in the best intentions, but it has been erroneous in fact or perverted in execution. Nobody pays any attention to Indian matters. This is a deplorable fact. Members of Congress understand the negro question, and talk learnedly of finance and other problems of political economy, but when the progress of settlement reaches the Indian's home, the only question considered is, "how best to get his lands." When they are obtained, the Indian is lost sight of.[12]

The commission criticized Congress and the executive department for failing even to communicate word of solemn treaties made with Cheyennes, Arapahos, and Apaches to military commanders in the field. Lieutenant General William T. Sherman's proposed plan of November, 1866, to restrict the Sioux north of the Platte and east and west of certain lines, and in a like manner to restrict the Arapahos, Cheyennes, Comanches, Kiowas, Apaches, and Navajos south of the Arkansas and east of Fort Union, dealing summarily with all found outside those lines without a military pass, was, the commission noted, in direct violation of such treaties.

Army generals, given the thankless task of carrying out a hopeless policy, complained that the reservations were often regarded as sanctuaries from which Indians could issue forth to raid the settlements and to which they could return to avoid the risk of retaliation by settlers or soldiers. The army authorities complained also that the treaty system gave the Indians privileges which need not have been granted and which they did not deserve, while the annuity system served as mere "bribes" for good behavior or, seen in another way, "rewards" for bad behavior. General Pope and others also pointed out that the friendly Indians who refused to go out on the warpath were often allowed to starve by the government, while the hostile Indians who exacted a deadly toll of blood from the white settlers were "rewarded" with rations and care.

To the army generals waging hard-fought campaigns in the Plains West during and following the Civil War the inadequacy of government Indian policy was patent. The government made no attempt to restrain the advance of settlement and yet guaranteed in solemn treaties that the lands reserved to the Indian tribes would remain inviolate. Indian agents of the Department of the Interior

12. *Ibid.*, pp. 40, 42.

were chosen to represent the United States in its dealings with the Indians, and yet were unable to keep the tribes from committing depredations upon white travelers and settlements. The United States Army, cut to the bone after the conclusion of the Civil War, was called upon to provide protection to every white man—deserving or not—in the Indian country. The military was condemned by Eastern humanitarians when it took harsh measures against any Indians and was condemned by Western settlers when it failed to take such measures. The prevalence of warfare in the period, and the predominant role of the army, led to suggestions and demands, many of them emanating from the army, that the Indian Bureau be transferred to the War Department and its operations coordinated with the military policy of the United States. The suggestion failed of adoption by the Congress of the United States, which continued to maintain the system of divided responsibility.

Despite the reputation many military men acquired of being exterminationists, in fact the military provided many examples of sympathy, understanding, and support for the needs and aspirations of the red men. Too often the reputation of the professional military was besmirched by the doings of hastily assembled volunteers such as Colonel Chivington's Colorado militiamen who perpetrated the Sand Creek massacre. Indians respected leaders like George Crook and General Oliver Otis Howard. Such generals were men of their word whom the Indians honored as such. In addition they tried, sometimes unsuccessfully, to educate their Washington superiors about the injustices and sufferings experienced by the Indians they were charged with controlling or fighting. General John Pope, commanding the Department of the Missouri between 1870 and 1883, repeatedly advised Washington that the nomadic tribes should not be forced to become farmers, not only because of the character of the geographic areas they inhabited, but because of their cultural backgrounds. Pope recommended that Plains hunters be encouraged instead to become stock raisers and cattlemen. While caught in the unenviable position of being the agent of an aggressive policy, the army demonstrated both understanding and concern for the Indian as a human being to a much greater degree than is commonly recognized.[13]

13. Richard N. Ellis, "The Humanitarian Generals," *Western Historical Quarterly*, III (1972), 169–178.

The history of warfare on the Plains in this period is one of the familiar stories of American history: the classic tale of which a hundred Westerns have been fashioned. Although often chastened by the U.S. Cavalry, although periodically suffering from hunger and near starvation as the buffalo, which provided their staple food source, diminished, the warlike tribes of the Plains gave tit for tat, sometimes destroying army units entire—like Captain William J. Fetterman's eighty soldiers on the Bozeman Trail in 1866 or Custer's regiment in 1876. In addition they raided the frontier, killing men, women, and children and carrying off horses and booty from terrified and vindictive frontiersmen. Although often thought to be on the receiving end of a policy of extermination, in fact, according to a recent study, it is improbable that more than 4,000 Indians were killed during the period 1789–1898 while in the same period Indians killed some 7,000 soldiers and civilians.[14]

As suggested by the unfavorable kill ratio, the United States Army did not successfully meet the challenge posed by the Indian warriors of the West. Indeed, Robert M. Utley, perhaps the leading authority on the army in the West, has spoken of the "impressive record of failures" of the military which, however, managed to score "enough successes to discourage serious analysis" of the "validity of possible alternatives." The army continued to be bogged down by heavy supply trains and inflexible logistical requirements. It rarely was capable of fighting a guerrilla war of surprise and movement against a guerrilla enemy. And it almost never was capable of distinguishing between the guilty and the innocent among the Indian population. Although its greatest successes were achieved by commanders who used friendly Indian auxiliaries to fight against hostile ones, the lesson seems never to have been fully learned.[15]

The "final solution" of the Indian problem came neither as a result of direct military action nor of enlightened government policy toward the Indian. It derived, rather, from the effect on the Indian of the extension of railway lines across the country. That

14. Don Russell, "How Many Indians Were Killed? White Man versus Red Man: The Facts and the Legend," *The American West*, X, No. 4 (July, 1973), 42–47, 61–63, at 62. Russell's figures tend to ignore the indirect casualties of war caused by starvation, dislocation, and the like.
15. Robert M. Utley, "A Chained Dog: The Indian-Fighting Army: Military Strategy on the Western Frontier," *The American West*, X, No. 4 (July, 1973), 18–24, 61.

effect was, however, clearly foreseen by federal authorities. As Francis A. Walker, Commissioner of Indian Affairs, wrote in his annual report of November 1, 1872, "The progress of two years more, if not of another summer, on the Northern Pacific Railroad will of itself completely solve the great Sioux problem, and leave the ninety thousand Indians ranging between the two transcontinental lines as incapable of resisting the Government as are the Indians of New York or Massachusetts." Similarly, Walker estimated that "three summers of peaceful progress" of railroads in the Southwest "will forever put it out of the power of the tribes and bands which at present disturb Colorado, Utah, Arizona, and New Mexico to claim consideration of the country in any other attitude than as pensioners upon the national bounty."[16]

Walker's prediction was overly optimistic. Nevertheless, it was basically accurate. No less an authority than General William T. Sherman noted, in 1883, that peace in the West was achieved by three things: the presence of the army, the growth of settlements, and the completion of the transcontinental railroad, and that of the three factors the last was the most important.[17]

16. *Annual Report of the Commissioner of Indian Affairs for 1872*, p. 9.
17. Quoted in Roger L. Nichols, "The Army and the Indians, 1800–1830–A Reappraisal: The Missouri Valley Example," *Pacific Historical Review*, XLI (1972) , 167–168.

CHAPTER 10

The Reservation Indian

WHEN the white man determined the boundaries of various Indian homelands, called them reservations, and began to control the lives of the Indians within their borders, the era of Indian-white equality was over. The loss of equality came at different times to different Indian groups and had different effects on Indian life.

Whatever else the reservation system may represent it does mark an acceptance of the Indians' right to live and to retain land and resources for their support. While such a concession may not seem exceptional, on balance it ran against a persistent current of thought—not solely in America—that cared little whether aborigines disappeared from the face of the earth. Initiated as a way of establishing a boundary between the white man and red so that responsibility for the actions of each against the other could be determined, the reservation, in the mid-nineteenth century, frequently took on the character of a concentration camp, onto which the Indians could be herded as the lands they formerly occupied came increasingly under the control of the immigrant white man. The power of white administrators on Indian reservations grew until a white agent appointed by the federal government became the central authority figure in place of the Indian chief formerly looked to by the tribe for leadership. In more recent times, the reservation has acquired the status of a home with a permanently secure land base for Indians who may try their luck in the outside white world but always know they can go back to their reservation home. The new concept of the reservation was developed fully only in the 1960s and 1970s when the Bureau of Indian Affairs gradually became more Indian-run as well as Indian-oriented, as the threat of "termination" of the federal trust relationship subsided, and as the enormous pressure of population growth on the available land resources convinced tribal members of the value of these enclaves of tax-exempt land held in trust by the United States for the benefit of their owners, the Indian tribes who inhabited them.

In the public mind, the concept of the reservation as a concentration camp is perhaps the most prevalent one today. Even the fact that the Indian is free to come and go on and off the reservation is unknown to many Americans, as is the fact that by 1970 probably more Indians lived off reservations than lived on them. However shrunken in acreage from the total once claimed, the lands reserved to the American Indian—the reservations—despite the drive to break up and destroy such units—remain significant. Of the 50 million acres owned and occupied by Indians today for which the federal government acts as trustee, nearly three-fourths are owned tribally—the balance being owned by Indian individuals.[1]

The earliest contact between the English colonials and the Indians they met was to a large degree based on a recognition that Indian "nations" occupied quite specific areas which were acknowledged as "theirs" despite the king's grandiose claims to sovereignty from sea to sea. Because of the sparseness of white settlement and the vast areas involved, there was at first no need to set forth specific boundaries between the territories of the two sides. Broad buffer zones surrounded each side's towns, fields, and hunting territories. Diplomatic missions from one side to the other normally traveled long distances into the wilderness to negotiate over trade, war, and peace.

In Virginia, the massacre of more than 350 colonists in 1622 by

1. *American Indians and the Federal Government,* Bureau of Indian Affairs booklet (Washington, 1966) , p. 6. Kirke Kickingbird and Karen Ducheneaux, in *One Hundred Million Acres* (New York, 1973) , p. 224, suggest a program by which the "national Indian land base" can be expanded to one hundred million acres. The principal addition to the existing fifty million acres of tribal lands and individual Indian allotments would be the forty million acres authorized the Alaskan natives under the Alaska Native Claims Settlement Act of December 18, 1971 (85 Stat. 688) .

the Indians of Powhatan's Confederacy shortly after the great leader's death led to a period of total war and nonrecognition of Indian rights by the colonists. After a second great massacre in 1644, in which an even greater number of Virginians were killed, the colonists carried on an equally bitter campaign against Opechancanough, Powhatan's successor, who was eventually captured and killed. By a treaty made with Necotowance, Opechancanough's successor, in October, 1646, that ruler acknowledged his subjection to the king of England, agreed to pay a tribute of twenty beaver skins a year, ceded to the English the peninsula between the York and James rivers from the falls of the James to Hampton Roads, and was restricted in his own territory to land north of the York.[2] "One of the most significant features of this treaty," one authority has pointed out, "was the recognition of the Indians' need and enjoyment of their own lands."[3]

In the following decade, as English settlement began to pass through the weakened tribes of Tidewater Indians, reservations were for the first time established by laws of the Assembly. In July, 1653, the Assembly set aside reservations for Chief Totopotomoi and the Pamunkey Indians in York County and required justices of the peace to remove whites who had settled on lands authorized the Pamunkey and the Chickahominy Indians. The Assembly also provided for reservations in Gloucester and Lancaster counties. This was the formal beginning of Virginia's reservation system.[4]

New England went through a similar evolution in its policy toward the local Indians, passing through the stages of recognition *de facto* of Indian tribal sovereignty, then to all-out war and nonrecognition of Indian territorial rights, and finally to the creation of reservations of land for towns of "praying Indians" living under the spiritual and juridical control of the Bay Colony government. Reservations in the colonial period affected only those weaker tribes who found themselves increasingly pressed by neighboring white settlers and who chose to make the best of their new situation by pledging friendship to, and accepting protection from, the colonists.

2. Richard L. Morton, *Colonial Virginia*, 2 vols. (Chapel Hill, N.C., 1960), I, 156.

3. Ben C. McCary, *Indians in Seventeenth-Century Virginia*, Jamestown 350th Anniversary Historical Booklets, Number 18 (Williamsburg, 1957), p. 81.

4. Morton, *op. cit.*, I, 177.

Such "friendly" Indians played a significant role—as spies, pickets, and auxiliaries—in the evolving English relationship with the "foreign" or "hostile" Indians outside the bounds of effective colonial control.[5]

One person who saw the reservation system as a means of preserving the Indians' rights to life, liberty, and property was Judge Samuel Sewall of Salem, in the colony of Massachusetts Bay. Himself the personal benefactor of many Indians, some of whom he sent to Harvard College, Sewall also served as treasurer of the Society for the Propagation of the Gospel, an organization with headquarters in London whose purpose was the Christianization of the Indians. Sewall worked to convince the magistrates of the Bay Colony to accept fixed boundary limitations between the Indians and the English, in the same manner that boundaries between townships were required by colonial law to be renewed every three years as a guarantee of honesty and peace among those who bordered one upon the other. When the eastern (Maine) Indians in conference with the governor of the Massachusetts Bay Colony at Georgetown on Arrowsick Island, August 9, 1717, proposed such a boundary, the English rejected it without any counteroffer, to the great displeasure of Sewall. In the absence of such fixed boundaries, Sewall foresaw only the continuation of the round of Indian raid-English punitive expedition, each party convinced that justice was on its side. With fixed boundaries, or reservations, for those Indians living on lands the English regarded as ultimately under the king's dominion, war would be avoided, costs reduced, and the Indians brought closer to the English life style and the Christian faith.[6]

While numerous small local tribes were overrun, exterminated, bought out, or established on small reservations by the encroaching European settlers in the seventeenth and eighteenth centuries, the larger nations of Indians, such as the Iroquois Confederacy in the North and the Creek Confederacy in the South, maintained their lands and their independent roles throughout the eighteenth century. Increasingly during that century the boundaries of their

5. Yasu Kawashima, "Legal Origins of the Indian Reservation in Colonial Massachusetts," *American Journal of Legal History*, XIII (1969), 42–56; Yasu Kawashima, "Jurisdiction of the Colonial Courts over the Indians in Massachusetts, 1689–1763," *New England Quarterly*, XLII (1969), 532–550.

6. Joab L. Blackmon, Jr., "Judge Samuel Sewall's Efforts in Behalf of the First Americans," *Ethnohistory*, XVI (1969), 165–176.

territories were more closely defined and confirmed in treaties such as that of Fort Stanwix with the Iroquois in 1768 and that of Augusta in 1763 with the southeastern nations. The boundaries set forth in those treaties cannot be considered to describe "reservations" in the later sense since they were the result of a process of negotiation between sovereign nations of roughly equal power. Nevertheless, such treaties and subsequent ones, by ceding to the whites, for a consideration, surplus lands while defining, and hopefully sanctifying, the essential homelands retained by the nations involved, did begin the process of shaping the size and character of the "reservations" to which these powerful Indian nations would later be restricted.

The confinement of an Indian nation to a reservation did not necessarily extinguish its nationhood even after its effective power was gone. Though by 1763 the Catawba Indians of South Carolina numbered only a few hundred fighting men, and were bound by ties of interest and fear to the English colony of South Carolina, they were still regarded as an independent nation by the South Carolinians. As a contemporary observer put it,

. . . certain it is that they are not subject to our Laws; that they have no Magistrates appointed over them by our Kings; that they have no Representatives in our Assemblies; that their own Consent is necessary to engage them in War on our Side; and that they have the Power of Life and Death, Peace and War, in their own Councils, without being accountable to us; . . .[7]

Yet the fate of the Catawbas was bound intimately to the English. Increasingly surrounded by English settlers, they complained to the South Carolina authorities of such encroachment and lack of sufficient hunting territory, and asked at the great Indian congress held in Augusta, Georgia, in November, 1763, that a reservation of thirty square miles be confirmed to them. They were granted a reservation of fifteen square miles and promised their former hunting rights outside that area.[8]

Though the Catawbas contributed warriors to help the colonists during the American Revolution, their effective power was then

7. Dr. George Milligen, quoted in Charles M. Hudson, *The Catawba Nation* (Athens, Ga., 1970) , p. 50.
8. Hudson, pp. 50–51; Robert L. Meriwether, *The Expansion of South Carolina, 1729–1765* (Kingsport, Tenn., 1940) , p. 245.

drawing to a close. By the end of the century, scarcely one hundred Catawba Indians remained, but they continued to reside on their then fifteen-square-mile reservation and to be denominated a nation. Indeed, the white people in the area of the reservation, near Rock Hill, South Carolina, still refer to the remaining Catawbas (631 in number in 1960) as the "nation."[9]

One can jump too readily to the belief that lacking the full panoply of power of a European-style nation, the designation of the Catawbas as a nation, even in the late eighteenth century, was a misnomer. But, in fact, the independence maintained by the Indians in their internal affairs throughout most of their existence suggests rather the model of small dependent nations in the international community who concede their independence in foreign affairs to a neighboring power in return for a guarantee of internal autonomy and "protection" from other outside powers. "Nations" like the Catawbas reflected the reality defined by Chief Justice Marshall in the Cherokee cases when he coined the phrase "domestic dependent nations." The Catawba and many other Indian nations went from complete independence to limited dependence without losing their basic integrity as distinct nations.

The reservation system in its final evolution represented a total reversal of roles for white and Indian. Political authority was withdrawn from the native leaders and assumed by the representatives of the United States. Dependence upon a subsistence system controlled by the Indian was replaced by dependence upon one controlled by the white man. Freedom to carry on intertribal warfare, tribal ceremonies, and traditional law was increasingly denied or restricted by the new authority. The shock of this change can be appreciated more fully by recalling the plane of physical and psychological equality upon which Indian and white man had formerly met. The more powerful Indian nations, even when occasionally defeated by the European settlers, had tended to maintain their pride, their customs, and their honor during the colonial period. Their reaction to defeat was less that of despair than of a resolution to avenge the insult.

The removal of hunting and warfare from the list of approved activities of the Indian male was enough of a blow. But for the

9. Hudson, *op. cit.*, p. 51.

government to substitute its own authority in what few significant male pursuits were left was a blow from which few Indian groups could recover. When decisions about subsistence activities, law and order, and education began to be made by Indian agents rather than by Indian leaders themselves, the loss of hope was complete. The whole structure of kinship relations by which unanimous group decisions were arrived at was short-circuited. Instant factionalism was substituted for laboriously achieved unanimity. Those who dealt with the real authorities—the representatives of the United States government—were caught between the expectations of their own people and the demands of the white agents. "Community paralysis" was often the outcome of this loss of tribal autonomy.[10]

Commissioner of Indian Affairs T. J. Morgan, in his annual report for 1892, after outlining the history of the evolution of the Indian agent, summed up the situation:

The Indian agent, as shown by the foregoing, now has almost absolute power in the Indian country, and so far as the people over whom he rules are concerned, he has none to contest his power. Appointed at first in the capacity of a commercial agent or consul of the United States in the country of an alien people, the Indian agent, under laws enacted and regulations promulgated in pursuance thereof, has developed into an officer with power to direct the affairs of the Indians and to transact their business in all details and in all relations. This is a curious chapter in our history. There is a striking contrast between "ministers plenipotentiary," appointed by the United States to treat with powerful Indian nations, and an army officer, with troops at his command, installed over a tribe of Indians to maintain among them an absolute military despotism. Yet our policy of dealing with them has swung from one of these extremes to the other in a strange vacillating way. Indeed, at present, the agent among the Five Civilized Tribes performs rather the functions of a consul in a foreign nation than those of an agent, while the Commission who have recently negotiated with the Cherokees for the cession of the Outlet,

10. Frederick O. Gearing, *The Face of the Fox* (Chicago, 1970), pp. 103–104. Factionalism among the Seneca Indians is discussed in Anthony F. C. Wallace, *The Death and Rebirth of the Seneca* (New York, 1970), p. 296; in Robert F. Berkhofer, Jr., "Seneca Faith and Factionalism," *Ethnohistory*, XII (1965), 101; and in William N. Fenton, "Toward the Gradual Civilization of the Indian Natives: The Missionary and Linguistic Work of Asher Wright (1803–1875) among the Senecas of Western New York," American Philosophical Society, *Proceedings*, C (1956), 573.

commonly called the "Strip," have really treated with them as with an independent nation and have performed the functions of, in one sense, ministers plenipotentiary. On the other hand, the absolute military rule finds its illustration in the presently prevailing conditions at San Carlos and in a modified way at Pine Ridge.[11]

The character of Indian agents became the subject of bitter political debate. Bishop Henry B. Whipple of Minnesota complained to President Lincoln in 1862 that Indian agents were selected "without any reference to their fitness for the place" and largely as a reward for party work. The agent then appointed his subordinates from similar motives. Whipple noted:

They are often men without any fitness, sometimes a disgrace to a Christian nation; whiskey sellers, barroom loungers, debauchees, selected to guide a heathen people. Then follow all the evils of bad example, of inefficiency, and of dishonesty. The school a sham; the supplies wasted; the improvement fund squandered by negligence, or curtailed by fraudulent contracts. The Indian bewildered, conscious of wrong, but helpless, has no refuge but to sink into depths of brutishness never known to his fathers.

Not that the fact was unknown in Washington. Secretary Edward M. Stanton in 1864 remarked to General Henry Halleck:

What does Bishop Whipple want? If he has come here to tell us of the corruption of our Indian system, and the dishonesty of Indian agents, tell him that we know it. But the Government never reforms an evil until the people demand it. Tell him that when he reaches the heart of the American people, the Indians will be saved.[12]

The report of Bishop Whipple about the causes of the Minnesota Sioux uprising in August, 1862, and the reforms in the Indian Department necessary to correct it, reportedly shook up President Abraham Lincoln, who told a friend that Whipple's account of the "rascality of this Indian business" had made him feel it "down to my boots." "If we get through this war, and I live," Lincoln added, "this Indian system shall be reformed."[13]

11. *Annual Report of the Commissioner of Indian Affairs for 1892*, p. 24.
12. Quoted in Laurence F. Schmeckebier, *The Office of Indian Affairs: Its History, Activities and Organization* (Baltimore, 1927), p. 47.
13. Quoted in Robert Winston Mardock, *The Reformers and the American Indian* (Columbia, Mo., 1971), p. 12.

The "model" of the late-nineteenth-century Indian agent—condescending, self-righteous, culturally blind—may well be Nathan C. Meeker, who became agent to the Ute Indians at the White River agency in Colorado in 1878. Meeker, an erstwhile poet, novelist, newspaper correspondent, and organizer of cooperative agrarian colonies, was determined to uplift the Utes, wean them from their savage concerns with hunting and wandering, and make farmers out of them. In a series of unilateral actions, he attempted to plow up their pasturelands, reduce their herds of ponies, develop irrigation ditches, and introduce traditional white subsistence patterns among them. Meeker contemptuously and wrongly asserted that the Utes did not own their reservation; rather, he asserted, the government did, and if they did not do his bidding, he would call in the troops and they would lose their land. Meeker's views were published in Colorado newspapers and he soon had strong allies among local political leaders who looked longingly on the Utes' valuable land. "The Utes Must Go" soon became a cry that foreshadowed the tragedy that eventually ensued. As a result of a series of cross-cultural misunderstandings and hurt pride, Meeker in 1879 called in troops; the Utes assumed that war was being planned against them with the purpose of removing them to the Indian Territory, and bloodshed occurred. Meeker was one of the victims. The ferocious local politicians urged extermination or removal of the Utes. Most of the Utes were removed to a smaller reservation in Utah. Colorado was swept virtually clean of red men.[14]

The confinement of reservation life produced extreme forms of behavior change among Indians. Sometimes the changes were "transformative" in character—that is, they sought to change the objective *conditions* under which the Indians were forced to live. Sometimes they were "redemptive"—that is, they sought to change the individual Indian to enable him better to accommodate himself to the conditions within which he was required to live. The phenomenon known as the Ghost Dance religion is an example of a transformative movement induced by the reservation system.

14. Dee Brown, *Bury My Heart at Wounded Knee: An Indian History of the American West* (New York, 1970), pp. 367–389. Brown may have overemphasized the narrow-mindedness of Meeker. See, for example, Meeker's letter of May 28, 1878, to Henry M. Teller, Denver Public Library, Teller Papers, #433, predicting an outbreak if he is forced to implement orders from the Department of the Interior to issue no rations to any Indian unless he works.

LOCATION OF CONTEMPORARY INDIAN POPULATION
Source: THE NEW INDIANS by Stan Steiner

Peyotism and the form of the Sun Dance religion that developed on reservations late in the nineteenth century are examples of redemptive movements.

Formulated by a Paiute prophet in the 1870s, in a desolate region of Nevada, the Ghost Dance religion burst into the consciousness of white Americans in 1890, when its doctrines, taught by the later Paiute prophet named Wovoka, were carried throughout many areas of the West by delegates from various tribes. The doctrine held that the Indian dead would be resurrected, the white man would disappear as the result of various natural calamities, and a life free from death, disease, and misery would ensue. The disappearance of the white man was not envisaged by Wovoka or by most of his followers as the consequence of Indian arms. Indeed, his injunction to the warlike Indians to give up fighting and to live in peace with all men, doing justice to all, was a profoundly revolutionary doctrine to most of the Indian tribesmen. Nor was the movement anti-white in other ways. Although looking forward to a return to the life style existing prior to the arrival of the white man and prescribing a return to aboriginal habits, including the readoption of native dress whenever possible, it did not involve a wholesale rejection of white material culture. Rather it showed an unconcern with it.[15]

The revolutionary character of the message was well put by James Mooney, an anthropologist from the Smithsonian's Bureau of Ethnology, who studied the movement in the early 1890s. Mooney noted, "Only those who have known the deadly hatred that once animated Ute, Cheyenne, and Pawnee, one toward another, and are able to contrast it with their present spirit of mutual brotherly love, can know what the Ghost-dance religion has accomplished in bringing the savage into civilization." Mooney asserted, "It is such a revolution as comes but once in the life of a race."[16]

The ceremonial expression of the new belief took the characteristic Indian form of a dance, which normally was performed for four

15. James Mooney, *The Ghost-Dance Religion and the Sioux Outbreak of 1890*, abridged, with intro. by Anthony F. C. Wallace (Chicago, 1965). Mooney's report was originally published as Part 2 of the Fourteenth Annual Report of the Bureau of American Ethnology to the Secretary of the Smithsonian Institution, 1892–1893 (Washington, 1896).

16. *Ibid.*, p. 25.

successive nights at periodic intervals. The prophet Wovoka promised to communicate to believers the messages he expected to receive from time to time from God. Eventually, at an uncertain date, the earth would tremble and natural catastrophes would swallow up the white race, leaving believers in the messiah's message in their primitive Eden, which would be shared with the resurrected dead of the Indian race. The manifestations of the dance itself, Mooney observed, "with its scenes of intense excitement, spasmodic action, and physical exhaustion even to unconsciousness, . . . have always accompanied religious upheavals among primitive peoples, and are not entirely unknown among ourselves." Mooney went on to observe, "In a country which produced magnetic healers, shakers, trance mediums, and the like, all these things may very easily be paralleled without going far from home." Indeed, the Indian interpretation of the cause of their past calamities was reminiscent of Puritan explanations of the calamities visited upon New England in the time of King Philip's War. The Great Spirit, the Sioux believers were told, had sent the white race to punish them for their sins, but their sins were now expiated and they would be delivered from their bondage.[17]

As the doctrine was interpreted by the fierce and powerful Sioux Indians it became tinged with an activist, resistant philosophy uncharacteristic of the passive, resigned character given it in the Great Basin by Wovoka. Still, the tragedy of the Sioux outbreak of 1890 might never have happened had not inexperience and peremptory white administrative action coincided with a sad history of broken promises, the disappearance of the buffalo and deer, short rations, and agricultural failures. The intensity of belief in the hoped-for millennium was exemplified, among the Sioux and certain other Plains tribes, in the belief that the "ghost shirts," made of cloth but ornamented in the Indian fashion, which were worn during the dance, were invulnerable to the white man's bullets. There is uncertainty as to where and why this belief arose, but Mooney attributed it to non-Indian, possibly Mormon sources, with whom many Indians had close ties. The Mormon "endowment robe," worn when one was initiated into the Mormon faith, was, Mooney reported, believed by some Mormons to render the wearer

17. *Ibid.*

invulnerable. The ghost shirt was not a necessary item of the dance as taught by Wovoka, who saw it as a dance of peace and not a dance of war requiring protective devices or "medicine."[18]

The attempt by Indian agents to prohibit the Sioux from engaging in the Ghost Dance was, in several cases, unsuccessful and led to a call for troops by the inexperienced agent—D. F. Royer—at the Pine Ridge reservation. The arrival of the troops and the attempt to arrest Sitting Bull, the Sioux medicine man, led to disaster. Neither Commissioner of Indian Affairs T. J. Morgan nor anthropologist Mooney believed that the "messiah craze" was the cause of the Sioux outbreak of 1890. Numerous sufficient other causes existed. Indeed, Mooney asserted that had a strong agent been in charge at the Pine Ridge reservation, "there would have been no outbreak, in spite of broken promises and starvation, and the Indians could have been controlled until Congress had afforded relief." As it was, Sitting Bull was shot in the melee that occurred when Indian police were sent to arrest him, and bands of Sioux left their reservations. The troops gradually rounded up the "hostiles." The culmination of the mismanaged affair was the battle, or massacre, at Wounded Knee, twenty miles northeast of the Pine Ridge agency, on December 29, 1890, when about two hundred Indian men, women, and children, camped under the control of the Seventh Cavalry, were mowed down by their captors when resistance occurred during the process of disarming the Indians. Nearly thirty soldiers were killed in the fracas.[19]

Quannah Parker, the last of the great Comanche chiefs, who was a peyote cultist at the time of the Ghost Dance phenomenon in the 1880s and 1890s, opposed the latter movement and helped prevent its spread in Oklahoma. Parker helped establish the peyote religion on a legal basis in Oklahoma, testifying before the Oklahoma state legislature in 1908 in a successful effort to effect the repeal of the state's anti-peyote law of 1899. Although friendly to Christianity and, as were the missionaries, strongly opposed to drinking, Parker distinguished between the two religions with the following percep-

18. *Ibid.*, pp. 30, 34.

19. *Ibid.*, pp. 73, 114–120. An account of Wounded Knee as a "tragic accident of war that neither side intended" and "for which neither side as a whole may be properly condemned" is given in Robert M. Utley, *The Last Days of the Sioux Nation* (New Haven, Conn., 1963, reprinted 1973), pp. 200–230.

tive comment: "The white man goes into his church house and talks *about* Jesus, but the Indian goes into his tipi and talks *to* Jesus."[20]

The peyote cult eventually adapted itself to an institutional church format—the Native American Church—primarily for defensive reasons. By so doing, its followers found it easier to combat the attacks of organized Christian churches, who regarded the cult as a rival, and of the Indian Bureau, which looked upon it as an impediment to the Indian's adoption of the white man's way. With an organizational structure, the peyote worshipers could more easily claim the protection of the constitutional guarantees of religious freedom and more effectively defend themselves in court cases and administrative proceedings directed against them.[21]

"The peyote cult," a leading scholar of the subject has asserted, "is the most popular, and one of the most durable of the religious movements created by American Indian groups suffering from the effects of domination by American society." The modern cult, in contradistinction to the centuries-old use of the cactus in Mexico, spread from Oklahoma, where it originated in the late nineteenth century and by the 1930s, despite the opposition of the majority of the tribe as well as of the Indian Service and of missionaries and traders, had established itself in the Navajo country. By 1951, one out of seven Navajo families were members. The spread of the cult, which uses the peyote cactus as the focus of "worship," requires explanation, since it challenges both traditional Indian and traditional white values.[22]

A popular explanation of the success of the cult is its alleged narcotic effect on the user, who eats the "buttons" of the cactus. This theory is rejected by most scholars because neither a dependence nor an addiction to the peyote can be clearly demonstrated among users. On the contrary, use is irregular and difficult and often attended with discomfort. Indeed, the purging effect of peyote use is often related to the presence of sin and the need to purge that sin. Tolerance to peyote is sometimes seen as marking the successful purging of one's sins.

20. Quoted in Hazel W. Hertzberg, *The Search for an American Indian Identity: Modern Pan-Indian Movements* (Syracuse, N.Y., 1971), pp. 242–243.

21. *Ibid.,* p. 240.

22. David F. Aberle with field assistance by Harvey C. Moore, *The Peyote Religion among the Navaho,* Viking Fund Publications in Anthropology, No. 42 (New York, 1966), p. 3.

Nevertheless, it is true that the peyote causes a change in the user. Sometimes this is assumed to be a vision, but many peyote users have never experienced such an effect. Rather, the most general effect seems to be a heightened consciousness of the self in relation to its surroundings, or, as Aberle expressed it, "a feeling of the *personal significance* of external and internal stimuli."[23] Undoubtedly the mescaline and other alkaloids present in the cactus help to induce this state, which may be different for different individuals, but seems to involve a common element of enhanced perception of reality. It would not be unfair to compare the use of peyote in the all-night ceremony—the participants eating peyote, praying, singing, drumming, and partaking in acts of communion—to the use of prayer, fasting, incense, wine and bread, music, and art in Christian churches to aid in the perception of the divine reality.

One authority, Weston La Barre, in considering the cult in the light of the recent psychedelic experience, has reaffirmed his conviction that "there is no grave danger or evil in the Indian use of natural pan-peyotl in religious ceremonies." "The alkaloids in the whole plant," La Barre has asserted, "are not synergistic but antagonistic; in the strict sense the alkaloids are only mildly toxic and have little or no untoward effect in the amounts used; the amount of mescaline is small and barely minimal pharmacodynamically; and peyote, I am certain, is in no sense addictive." La Barre, while upholding Indian use of peyote, condemns Caucasoid Americans who claim to follow the peyote "religion"—using mescaline as a "sacrament"—as followers of a "bogus cult" whose "hypocrisy" is patent. In fact, La Barre points out, Indian and white users of the substance are in a cognitive sense "diametrically opposed": the Indian seeking in peyote "the supernatural visionary experience" while whites are often seeking "assiduously to rid experience of idiosyncratic subjective elements."[24]

To the Indian the peyote is a "power," the peyotist conceiving of power as "an immaterial and invisible supernatural force, which produces characteristic effects in things influenced by it, and can be transferred from one thing to another under the proper ritual conditions."[25] Spirits are the immaterial personifications of power,

23. *Ibid.*, p. 6.
24. Weston La Barre, *The Peyote Cult*, enlarged ed., with new preface by the author (New York, 1969), Preface, xiii–xv.
25. J. S. Slotkin, *The Peyote Religion* (Glencoe, Ill., 1956), quoted in Aberle, *op. cit.*, p. 12.

and include both white and Indian spirits representative of the blend of Christian and native values in the peyote cult. White spirits include the Trinity, devils, and angels. Indian spirits include Waterbird, Peyote, and other traditional spirits deriving from tribal beliefs. The Waterbird is sometimes seen as Thunderbird, the bringer of rain, and sometimes, with the dove, as a symbol of the Holy Spirit or peace. Peyote is seen as a compassionate being, with the sympathetic aspects of Jesus in Christian thought. God, the Great Spirit, made the peyote cactus and put power in it to help the Indian. By eating it, as with the sacramental bread and wine of Christianity, the believer absorbs some of that power.[26]

It will be noted that the relationship of power between God and man in the peyote cult is an individual relationship, though incorporated within the larger community of believers in the cult. Similarly, the peyote ethical code, called the "Peyote Road," is oriented to individual conduct: members should be honest, truthful, and friendly to one another; they should preserve family bonds inviolate; they should show self-reliance in earning their own living; and they should avoid alcohol. The peyote cult, in other words, is a religion of accommodation—it does not, as Aberle points out, "attempt to alter white-Indian relationships by force or supernatural power. . . ." Other nativistic religions, such as the Ghost Dance religion, did attempt to change the Indian's situation. "Peyotism supplies a goal of internal peace and harmony, rather than competition or conflict, and provides a tight reference group of other peyotists, within which approval and esteem can be sought."[27]

Because of its individualism—even though conceived within the framework of the family and one's fellow cultists—the peyote religion is often perceived by those Indians who remain fixed to communal values as a threat to the larger Indian community. Anti-peyote ordinances were passed by a number of Indian tribes, including the White Mountain Apaches, Taos Indians, and the Navajos. The values still surviving in Indian communal societies—in which the individual Indian is under less pressure to separate his economic fate from that of his fellow tribesmen—tend to be at war with the values of the peyotists, who have seemingly accommodated themselves to white-induced individualistic landholding and laboring values. This distinction between the communal and individual

26. Aberle, *op. cit.*, p. 13.
27. *Ibid.*, pp. 14–15.

spirit is expressed in many ways. In the traditional Navajo religion, for example, supernatural power is immanent, not transcendent as in peyotism. The traditional Indian is part of nature, not separated from it as the whites are. He is bound in a reciprocal relationship with the supernatural. The peyotist, on the other hand, deals with a God transcending the natural universe. He deals with Him through prayer and his behavior is regulated by means of internalized individual sanctions rather than through overt tribal pressures.[28]

The traditional explanation for the growth of peyotism and other nativistic religions among the Indians is that it is a response to degraded status. Specifically, in the case of the Navajos, Aberle has correlated the growth of peyotism with the reduction of livestock forced upon the Navajos by the United States government in the 1930s and 1940s. Other hypotheses—such as degree of acculturation—proved less compelling than the sudden deprivation (after a long period of increasing well-being from the time of the release of the captured tribe from Fort Sumner in 1868) experienced by the Navajos in the 1930s. Where relative deprivation was greatest, there the trend to peyotism was significant. Peyotism was redemptive to the individual Navajo caught in a situation in which he had no viable alternative. It created in the believer a new inner state which allowed necessary adaptation to the dominant white culture while permitting pride and belief in Indianness, albeit not of the traditional variety.[29]

Another example of a redemptive response to the pressure induced by reservation life was the utilization of a ceremony traditional among some tribes—the Sun Dance—by other tribes for a different purpose. Among the Utes and Shoshonis it was adopted about 1890 when the promise of the Ghost Dance religion proved vain. The most popular of all Plains Indian religious ceremonies in the period prior to white conquest, the Sun Dance was usually performed when an individual vowed to avenge a death or lead a hunt, or to insure a plentiful supply of buffalo. The ceremony lasted three or four days during which the dancers suffered through ritual fasting, thirsting, and mutilations, in a quest for power and success. The original Sun Dance died out on the rest of the Plains about the time the Utes and Fort Hall Shoshonis began to take it

28. *Ibid.*, pp. 18, 178, 195, 202.
29. *Ibid.*, pp. 15, 23, 310.

up in a restructured version. Why? The explanation, as hypothesized by Joseph Jorgensen, is that the spread of the Sun Dance
occurred when many of the Indians became resigned to their fate.
The Sun Dance, unlike the Ghost Dance, did not seek to reform the
context in which the believer found himself, but to make the
believer able to cope with the life he found himself controlled by. It
did not promise to free the world of whites, but to make men well
and communities happy in a white-dominated world.

In sum, the Utes and Shoshonis reshaped a traditional ceremony
and used it as their virtually sole defense against the deprivation to
which they were subjected by the creation of reservations and the
consequent pressures of white political, social, and economic forces.
As their land and their rights diminished their hope in the efficacy
of the Sun Dance increased.[30]

Adaptation to white cultural pressure was sometimes expressed in
traditional activities engaged in "for show." Among these activities
was "Buffalo Bill's Wild West Exhibition" (he did not like the
word show or circus) in the decade 1883–1893. The Indians who
went with William Frederick Cody—Buffalo Bill as he was called—
to the East and to Europe with his dramatic display of calf-roping,
stage-robbing, straight-shooting Westerners were the heirs of the
Indian chiefs who had been escorted to Europe in the colonial
period to see and to be seen by king and commoner, and of those
headmen who were invited to Washington to see the Great Father
in the earlier years of the new republic. Now the Indians were
reduced to the role of entertainers. They were supported not, as
their predecessors had been, as a diplomatic mission, but as hired
hands. One effect was, of course, to hasten the development of
stereotypes about the Indian (as well as about Westerners) —stereotypes that have never been erased. The image stayed on even after
the "frontier" was no more and the Wild West show a memory.[31]

The Wild West show was discouraged and eventually prohibited
by Commissioner of Indian Affairs T. J. Morgan for the specific
reason that it satisfied the Indian longing for a life that those in

30. Joseph G. Jorgensen, *The Sun Dance Religion: Power for the Powerless*
(Chicago, 1972) , pp. 17, 18, 28.

31. Don Russell, "Cody, Kings, & Coronets," *The American West*, VII, No. 4
(July, 1970), 4–10.

charge of Indian affairs wished to consign to the scrap heap of history. As Morgan wrote in his annual report for 1892:

It tends to create in their minds the idea that what the white man particularly admires is that which really is a mark of their degradation; it tends to foster a roaming spirit; it brings them, almost by necessity, into contact with the low and degraded white man, encourages vice, and begets false ideas of civilized life; it takes them from home, breaks up any habits that may be forming of ordinary industry, and has a tendency to awaken a spirit of restlessness among those that remain behind.[32]

In a similar fashion Commissioner Morgan put a stop to another practice which preserved traditional values—in however abased a form—which white reformers wished to eradicate. That practice was the issuance—on the hoof—of beef cattle due Indians as part of the annuity payments promised in various treaties. The sight of Indians eating raw meat, blood, and intestines after chasing and killing cattle issued to them at agencies was too much for queasy Eastern stomachs. A young female teacher at the Standing Rock agency wrote Herbert Welsh, the Indian reformer, in 1888, suggesting that the Society for the Prevention of Cruelty to Animals be brought in to eliminate the practice. Commissioner of Indian Affairs Morgan issued orders during the summer of 1890 forbidding the practice of "allowing the Indians to chase them [the issued cattle] over the prairie in imitation of the buffalo hunt and to shoot them in the presence of their wives and children, and amidst the howling and yelling of dogs; and then, of allowing the squaws to perform the filthy work of butchering, while the children and the dogs stand about apparently sharing in the sport." "It is needless to say," Morgan asserted, "that this bit of barbarism is a fearful hindrance to the work of civilization." Indian behavior at this time was forced to conform to "civilized" values. The potential value of sustaining a traditional way of life (even so pale an imitation of that life as the chasing of issued cattle in lieu of wild buffalo) could not be allowed.[33]

A form of adaptation to the coercive rule of the white man which proved attractive to many Indians was the assumption of the role of

32. *Annual Report of the Commissioner of Indian Affairs for 1892,* pp. 105–106.
33. Letter of Morgan to Secretary of the Interior, Dec. 8, 1890, and "Instructions to agents in regard to manner of issuing beef," July 21, 1890, in *Annual Report of the Commissioner of Indian Affairs for 1890,* cxliv, cxlvi.

policeman on the reservation. Although substituting a native master for an alien one, the Indian policeman could, as a policeman, play the warrior role otherwise forbidden him. The experiment was an overwhelming success. Captain Pratt, superintendent of the Carlisle Indian School, a well-qualified judge of the value of the Indian police, noted that

I have repeatedly witnessed their loyalty to the Government in the performance of the most arduous and dangerous services. Especially has it been before me during our present conferences with the Sioux. Policemen or soldiers of any other race could not have performed the services that the native policemen have performed without endangering outbreak. Two policemen were sent by the agent 40 miles away and arrested and brought back to the agency Chief John Grass. A full company of soldiers would not have been sufficient for the same service, and in attempting it a miniature war might have resulted.[34]

In the resurgence of Indian nationalism today, there is a tendency to denigrate or ignore the role played by Indian police because of the fact that they served white purposes. Thus Bea Medicine, an Indian anthropologist, in commenting on an author who praised the Indian police, has asserted, "Even today, most Hunkpapa [Sioux] see the descendants of the Indian police as tainted by the very nature of being kin to those 'traitors.' "[35] Medicine's remark may be more a reflection of the emerging Indian perception of the past than it is of the past itself.

Perhaps the most difficult problem confronting the despondent reservation Indian of the nineteenth century was what attitude to take toward the attempt of his new white masters to educate him in the white man's way. The Indian was not insensitive to the importance of acquiring a knowledge of the white man's powerful "medicine" and the literature of Indian-white interaction is filled with plaintive expressions of admiration—concealed and open—on the part of the Indians for the white man's remarkable "gifts." But education was too often presented to the Indian as a value system to

34. Quoted by Commissioner John H. Oberly in *Annual Report of the Commissioner of Indian Affairs for 1888*, xxviii.

35. Review of James McLaughlin, *My Friend the Indian* (Seattle, 1970), in *American Anthropologist*, LXXIV (1972), 172. The best discussion of the subject is William T. Hagan, *Indian Police and Judges: Experiments in Acculturation and Control* (New Haven, Conn., 1966).

be substituted for his traditional one or as an engine to destroy it. The conditions for attending government boarding schools emphasized the fact. One was immersed in a totally different culture: one's clothes, habits, and appearance were changed. Removal of the student from all traditional influences of family and of home was a prerequisite to the acquisition of the white man's learning. Like the presentation of the white man's religion, the presentation of the white man's education was a cleansing process, not an additive one. The Indian was to rid himself of his own forms and values if he wished to acquire the white man's. White administrators carried the process even to the point of attempting to eradicate Indian languages within the confines of the schoolroom. The general rules for Indian boarding schools were quite explicit.

All instruction must be in the English language. Pupils must be compelled to converse with each other in English, and should be properly rebuked or punished for persistent violation of this rule. Every effort should be made to encourage them to abandon their tribal language.[36]

Yet, if the Indian child, and his parents, were prepared to submit to the process of educational rebirth, what could they expect to find? The quality of whites teaching in the Indian schools left much to be desired. General Henry Heth, who had been an inspector in the Indian Service, reported in 1889 that the Indian Bureau has been made "the dumping ground for the sweepings of the political party that is in power." Heth found an abandoned woman in charge of one Indian school and a discharged lunatic in charge of another.[37]

Officially, the government boasted of its generosity in providing education to the Indians while blaming the failure of the system on the perversity of the Indian. Commissioner of Indian Affairs W. A. Jones, in his report for 1901, likened the "child of the wigwam" to "a modern Aladdin who has only to rub the Government lamp to gratify his desires." Yet Jones felt the system had failed because it had not caused the Indians to cease their dependence upon the government. After the expenditure of $240 million over thirty-three years for an Indian population of 180,000 ($45 million of it for

36. Rule 41 of Reservation Boarding Schools, as reported in *Annual Report of the Commissioner of Indian Affairs for 1890,* p. cli.
37. Schmeckebier, *op. cit.,* p. 72.

Indian education) Jones found the Indian still on the reservation, still being fed, his children still being educated by the government, and no nearer to independence than he had been thirty years before. To Jones the record was one of abysmal failure.[38]

Throughout the reservation period, the United States government sought to convert the Indian to white economic practices and values. White farmers were hired to live among the Indians and teach former hunters how to become agriculturalists. Agricultural implements were periodically distributed among annuity goods or directly in an effort to encourage the Indian to settle down on the land in the manner of the white man. Indians were urged to learn the crafts associated with "civilized" life. Too frequently, however, these efforts failed. Yet the faith of the government in the validity of the goals simply led it to modify its tactics in an effort to achieve its ends in other ways. When the carrot did not succeed, the stick was used.

By the end of the nineteenth century, the Bureau of Indian Affairs had introduced a policy by which rations would no longer be issued automatically to able-bodied Indians, and the money thus saved would be used to pay such Indians cash for labor in building roads, reservoirs, and the like. The purpose of the new policy was to teach self-reliance and self-respect and to induce habits of industry by the spur of necessity. It also meant that dealings between the bureau and the tribe would be reduced; now the relationship would be exclusively with the individual. "He would no longer be looked upon simply as one of a dependent community to be dealt with as a whole, but would be considered independently and treated as one capable of developing those qualities which would lift him above the level of a pauper and fit him to become a useful member of society."[39]

Almost simultaneously, Commissioner of Indian Affairs Jones issued a controversial "short-hair" order directing Indian agents "to induce your male Indians to cut their hair, and both sexes to stop painting." Noncompliance with the order was to be made a cause for discharge, if the Indian was an employee of the agency, or for withholding rations and supplies, if not. The commissioner also

38. *Annual Report of the Commissioner of Indian Affairs for 1901*, pp. 2–4.
39. Commissioner W. A. Jones, *Annual Report of the Commissioner of Indian Affairs for 1902*, pp. 7–8.

recommended a "short confinement in the guardhouse at hard labor with shorn locks" to "cure" any returned students of disinclination to obey the order. Indian dances and feasts were also prohibited and the wearing of "citizens' clothing" instead of Indian costume and blanket was to be encouraged.[40]

Neither carrot nor stick, force nor persuasion, served to convert the Indian into a white man. United States reservation policy failed because it sought not merely to prevent the Indian from troubling the white man by keeping him disarmed, isolated, and separate, but because it sought also to perform a grandiose social experiment whose outcome would be a red white man and a Christian heathen. It could not work, at least in so short a time and under such unfavorable conditions. The United States government was not the first or only organization to stub its toe on the hard rock of cultural resistance. Culture never has been, and is not, a force to be overcome by simple military force, congressional legislation, or educational edicts.

40. *Ibid.*, pp. 13–14.

CHAPTER 11

Allotment and the Indian

INITIALLY established as a secure, if diminished, home for the tribe, the reservation soon came to be seen as a school where the individual Indian might be made over in the image of the white man and freed from his tie to the tribe and to the reservation.[1]

The characterization of the reservation as a "nursery, the temporary shelter needful to the Indian in the days of his moral and mental childhood, and before he is fitted for unprotected contact with the world" was made most pointedly by Herbert Welsh, the executive secretary of the Indian Rights Association, in 1892. By this time reformers as well as land-hungry settlers were demanding that reservations be abolished, tribal organizations destroyed, and tribal land allotted in severalty to individual Indians. The reasons were blatant. As Welsh put it:

The Indian and the white man have changed places. We are no longer few in number. The Indian is no longer to be feared. He numbers about 250,000 souls; we 60,000,000. He and his reservations might be likened to islands against which the waters of a restless sea of civilized life are steadily beating.[2]

1. *United States* v. *Clapox* (35 F. 575, D. Ore. 1888) ; Monroe Price, "Lawyers on the Reservation," in *Law and the Social Order, Arizona State Law Journal* (1969) , 161–203, at 202, quoted in Monroe Price, *Native American Law Manual* (California Indian Legal Services, 1970) , multilith, p. 560. See also Monroe E. Price, *Law and the American Indian: Readings, Notes and Cases* (Indianapolis, 1973) , pp. 610–627.
2. Herbert Welsh, *How to Bring the Indian to Citizenship, and Citizenship to the Indian* (Philadelphia, 1892) , pp. 7–8.

By the last decade of the nineteenth century the fate of many tribal Indians had been sealed. Confined on reservations established by their conquerors, their equality gone, their tribal ties were now to be destroyed and their land allotted in severalty. While the destruction of the tribe and the break-up of the reservation would free the individual Indian from the coercion of both institutions, these actions would also deprive him of their protection.

The policy of assimilation of Indians into white society through individual allotment of lands, like the policy of Indian reservations, has roots going back into the colonial period. Amalgamation or assimilation with the white man was often advocated by whites and was normally available to individual Indians who wished to take up the white man's way of life. Yet the early examples that can be cited represented voluntary individual choices during a period when the Indian nations negotiated with, but were not subordinate to, the white colonial governments.

Early treaties of the United States with the Indian nations east of the Mississippi River sometimes provided for allotments of land to individual Indian chiefs, but in general Congress was leery of according fee simple title (that is, absolute title) to Indians in the land transactions that were solemnized in the treaties. Tribal ownership of what white legislators regarded as an Indian possessory or use right in the soil (as distinct from title in fee simple) was considered less of a bar to future change.[3] Secretary of War John C. Calhoun, in a communication to the House of Representatives, December 5, 1818, observed that the neighboring tribes

have, in a great measure, ceased to be an object of terror, and have become that of commiseration. The time seems to have arrived when our policy towards them should undergo an important change. They neither are, in fact, nor ought to be, considered as independent nations. Our views of their interest, and not their own, ought to govern them. By a proper combination of force and persuasion, of punishments and rewards, they ought to be brought within the pales of law and civilization. . . . Our laws and manners ought to supersede their present savage manners and customs. . . . The land ought to be divided among families; and the idea of individual property in the soil carefully inculcated.[4]

3. Wilcomb E. Washburn, *Red Man's Land/White Man's Law: A Study of the Past and Present Status of the American Indian* (New York, 1971), pp. 62–65.
4. *American State Papers . . . Indian Affairs*, 2 vols. (Washington, 1832–1834), II, 181–185, at 183.

Calhoun's was a perceptive vision though it anticipated the future rather than reflected the situation as it then existed. Nevertheless, the Secretary of War clearly foresaw that as Indian power declined the United States would choose to treat the native American in his individual rather than in his collective capacity.

When the eastern tribes were removed west of the Mississippi during the 1830s, those Indians choosing to remain behind were frequently authorized allotments in fee simple, though few took them.

One of the earliest allotment acts, in the modern sense of the term, was that of March 3, 1839, which provided for the allotment of the lands of the Brothertown Indians of Wisconsin by a commission of five of their headmen. Patents in fee simple were to be issued to the individual Indians so allotted. The act provided that upon completion of the process, the Brothertown Indians should be deemed citizens of the United States and subject to its laws and to those of the Territory of Wisconsin. The same policy, with some modifications, was later applied to the Ottawas, Chippewas, Potawatomis, Shawnees, and Wyandots. Commissioner of Indian Affairs T. J. Morgan, in reporting on the "disastrous result" of this policy in his annual report for 1891, noted that "the records show that where their lands were conveyed in fee simple, with no restrictions as to alienation, they soon parted with them without sufficient consideration, and squandered what little they received."[5]

Allotment provisions were frequently included in treaties made with Indian tribes west of the Mississippi during the period of rapid westward expansion. The model for many of the allotment provisions of treaties at this time was Article 6 of the treaty concluded with chiefs of the Omaha tribe of Indians at Washington, March 16, 1854, by George W. Manypenny, Commissioner of Indian Affairs. Article 6 authorized the President, at his discretion, to cause the whole or part of the land reserved to the tribe to be assigned to such Indians "as are willing to avail [themselves] of the privilege, and who will locate on the same as a permanent home." The size of the authorized allotments varied according to the number of individuals in the family unit. A family of at least six persons and not exceeding ten was eligible for one section of land. The President was authorized, after such assignments had been made, to issue a

5. *Annual Report of the Commissioner of Indian Affairs for 1891*, p. 40.

patent providing certain temporary protections against levy, sale, or forfeiture to the person or family living on such lands. But the article also provided for the cancellation of the assignment if the Indian person or family abandoned the tract or failed otherwise to take up the life of an industrious farmer.[6]

One of the treaties using the Omaha article as a model was the Treaty of Hell Gate negotiated by Governor Isaac Stevens of Washington Territory with the Flathead Indians, July 16, 1855. Article 6 provided that the President might cause all or part of the reservation created by the treaty to be surveyed in lots and might assign "the same" to such members or families of the tribe "as are willing to avail themselves of the privilege, . . ." Although the government, fifty years later, by an act of April 23, 1904 (33 Stat. 302) allotted and opened the Flathead reservation, its action, ruled the United States Court of Claims on January 22, 1971 (No. 50233), in awarding damages to the Flathead Indians, was not justified by the words of the treaty since no native consent was sought or received.

In the last quarter of the nineteenth century virtually all white Americans agreed on the validity of assimilation—to be achieved primarily through the break-up of reservations, the destruction of tribal governments, and the individual allotment of lands—as the appropriate goal for Indians in the American union. Virtually no white man advocated the preservation of distinct and separate tribal cultures, although the legal forms in which the Indian-white relationship had earlier been incorporated—in particular the treaty relationship—provided the basis for such a policy. One alternative frequently expressed, though not incorporated into any long-continued governmental policy, was extermination. But this alternative was expressed more often rhetorically than officially, or was carried out by unofficial bodies of citizenry or by individual military commanders acting without authorization. The assumption that the Indians were a dying race, combined with the high cost of killing Indians, further reduced the attractiveness of the extermination alternative.

The difficulty of assimilating the Indians who lived under tribal governments, who could claim the rights accorded by sacred treaties, and who often were the recipients of annuities from the

6. Charles J. Kappler, ed., *Indian Affairs: Laws and Treaties,* Vol. II: *Treaties* (Washington, 1903), 453–456.

government was enormous. Increasingly, officials such as General John Pope, army commander in the frontier West from 1862 to 1886, insisted upon the need to break up the tribal system, invalidate treaties, stop annuities, and coerce the wild tribes under the lash of the military and the rod of the missionaries. Pope's proposals would have provided a more efficient means of assimilating the Indians (in his opinion) than the means chosen by the United States.[7] Yet the goal was always assimilation, whether by coercion, by voluntary conversion, or by default.

Even President Ulysses S. Grant's Commissioner of Indian Affairs, General Ely S. Parker, a Seneca, spoke slightingly of tribal rights:

The Indian tribes of the United States [he asserted] are not sovereign nations, capable of making treaties, as none of them have an organized government of such inherent strength as would secure a faithful obedience of its people in the observance of compacts of this character. They are held to be wards of the government, and the only title the law concedes to them to the lands they occupy or claim is a mere possessory one. But because treaties have been made with them, generally for the extinguishment of their supposed absolute title to land inhabited by them, or over which they roam, they have become falsely impressed with the notion of national independence. It is time that this idea should be dispelled, and the government cease the cruel farce of thus dealing with its helpless and ignorant wards.[8]

Parker took the hard line of his contemporaries that any concept of Indian independence—culturally or politically—was an illusion and a delusion. As Commissioner of Indian Affairs during the so-called Peace Policy of President Grant, he, like the representatives of religious organizations appointed to act as Indian agents under that policy, saw assimilation (a mixture of Christianization and civilization) as the only valid Indian future. The efforts of the religious bodies were directed primarily to speeding that future and smoothing the path toward it. The experiment—so far as the Quakers were concerned—lasted little more than a decade. The increasing pressure to convert the agencies from missionary posts to patronage jobs and the inevitable bureaucratic conflicts between two agencies with divergent "missions" led the Quakers to withdraw

7. Richard N. Ellis, *General Pope and U.S. Indian Policy* (Albuquerque, N.M., 1970), *passim*.

8. Quoted in Joseph E. Illick, " 'Some of Our Best Indians Are Friends . . .': Quaker Attitudes and Actions Regarding the Western Indians during the Grant Administration," *Western Historical Quarterly*, II (1971), 281–294, at 288.

their responsibility for the management of the Indians in 1879.[9] However, religious bodies continued to exert a strong influence, both at the agency level and at the policy-making level.

Nowhere were Indian pretensions to tribal sovereignty taken more lightly than in the halls of Congress. Senator George Hunt Pendleton of Ohio, during the congressional debate on allotment of Indian lands in 1881, noted the changed conditions from the time when the United States made treaties with the Indians:

Our villages now dot their prairies; our cities are built upon their plains; our miners climb their mountains and seek the recesses of their gulches; our telegraphs and railroads and post offices penetrate their country in every direction; their forests are cleared and their prairies are plowed and their wildernesses are opened up. The Indians cannot fish and hunt. They must either change their mode of life or they must die. That is the alternative presented. There is none other.[10]

Even representatives of Indian rights organizations—for example, J. B. Harrison, author of *The Latest Studies on Indian Reservations* (Philadelphia: Indian Rights Association, 1887) —recommended severe measures against tribal living. Harrison, in reporting on a camp of Sioux at the mouth of Cherry Creek on the Cheyenne River reservation in Dakota, urged that it be broken up in order to prevent harassment of individual Indians attempting to live off the reservation on separate allotments under the encouragement of the Indian agent. Harrison recognized that the tribal Indians might resist, but insisted that the agent coerce the Indians, with the help of the U.S. Army if necessary. If anyone resisted, Harrison recommended, "He should be arrested, put in irons and snatched off the reservation, and sent to some prison where he will have to work." The Cheyenne River reservation, he asserted, was "entirely too large; it should be divided and some of the land sold for settlement by white men, whether the Indians are willing or not." Harrison also believed that no more agreements depending upon the consent of the Indians should be made with them. Moreover, "when the changed conditions of the time plainly require the abrogation of some features of existing treaties, in order to give to the Indians opportunity and security which they cannot now have,

9. *Ibid.*
10. Quoted in S. Lyman Tyler, *Indian Affairs: A Work Paper on Termination: with an Attempt to Show Its Antecedents* (Provo, Utah, 1964) , p. 3.

these features of the treaties should be abrogated." With friends like Harrison, the Indians had no need of enemies.[11]

Harrison's approach illustrates the bewildering inconsistencies of the Gilded Age philanthropist. On the same page on which he expressed the sentiments quoted above, Harrison regretted that Indian life had "too much of the moral element in it" for the Indian to be able long to maintain himself in the "state of war" which constituted the practical experience of American civilization. The Indian, Harrison regretted, was too receptive for his own good to the practical teaching of the New Testament.[12]

Benevolent reform organizations such as the Indian Rights Association of Philadelphia and the Lake Mohonk Conference of Friends of the Indian which, with other similar organizations, had been organized in the 1880s agitated for the passage of severalty legislation. The Indian Rights Association, indeed, claimed credit for the passage of the General Allotment Act of 1887. In one of its publications it asserted:

The law providing for the allotment of lands in severalty to Indians, which was passed last winter, was devised and prepared in accordance and cooperation with the plans and objects of our Association, and its passage was the result, as even the enemies of the measure affirmed, of the efforts of the Association in placing the entire subject in the clear light of facts, and thus convincing members of Congress and their constituents that justice to the Indians and the interest of white people of the country alike demanded the passage of the "Dawes Bill."[13]

The traditional Indians not only had no powerful spokesmen within the white community for their position, but their views were, if asked for, usually misrepresented as favorable to the breakup of tribal government and the allotment of land in severalty. The United States Board of Indian Commissioners, a group of distinguished citizens appointed under an act of April 10, 1869, to function as an independent advisory board on Indian policy, shared the prevailing philosophy. In its twelfth annual report for 1880 (March 11, 1881), in discussing "Allotment of Lands in Severalty," the

11. J. B. Harrison, *The Latest Studies on Indian Reservations* (Philadelphia, 1887), pp. 163–166.

12. *Ibid.*, p. 168.

13. *A Brief Statement of the Objects, Achievements and Needs of the Indian Rights Association* (Philadelphia, 1887), p. 5.

board noted that "year after year [it] has without success urged upon Congress this measure of simple justice to the Indian." The board's report asserted, "The Indians themselves have been most persistent in their request for this legislation, but Congress turns a deaf ear to their cry." In a classic statement of misplaced confidence, the board went on to say: "Every year strengthens the convictions of the members of the Board that no single measure of legislation would give such general satisfaction to the Indian, or be productive of more happy results than the passage of this bill."[14]

The role of the railroads in influencing allotment legislation is the subject of dispute. There is some evidence to show that railroad officials pressed for the breakup of tribal holdings and the dissolution of tribal governments as an aid in obtaining land grants for their companies. Yet the railroads appear to have been just as successful in obtaining land grants from Indian tribal leaders before allotment as from individual Indians after allotment.[15] Often the railroads obtained land as a direct consequence of the treaty process by which cessions were made to the United States. Paul W. Gates has concluded, for example, "A fourth of the area of Kansas, and by all odds the best fourth, passed by the treaty process from Indian ownership to individuals, land-speculating companies, and railroads without becoming a part of the public domain or becoming subject to Congressional control."[16]

Methods of ending tribal life on reservations included some extralegal ones. The rich Klamath reservation was a typical target for such methods. J. B. Harrison, reporting on his visit to the reservation in 1886, noted that the surrounding whites predicted that there would have to be "a little Indian war." The "grass outside was 'alla gittin' used up, and the Indians had plenty that they don't make no use of. The cattle *will* drift on to the reserve. The Indians'll object, but a white man aint a goin' to take no impudence from an Indian.'" The cattlemen, Harrison reported, would

14. U.S. Board of Indian Commissioners, *Annual Report for the Year 1880*, p. 10.

15. Ira G. Clark, *Then Came the Railroads: The Century from Steam to Diesel in the Southwest* (Norman, Okla., 1958), pp. 56–57. Wilcomb E. Washburn, *The Assault on Indian Tribalism: The General Allotment Law (Dawes Act) of 1887* (Philadelphia, 1975), *passim*.

16. Paul Wallace Gates, *Fifty Million Acres: Conflicts over Kansas Land Policy, 1854–1890* (Ithaca, N.Y., 1954), pp. 6–7.

tend to the matter themselves if the soldiers were taken away. Harrison concluded that there was a definite purpose in the minds of many of the whites of the area to "crowd" the Indians more and more until the latter struck a blow in self-defense. Then war would exist in fact, a few Indians would be shot, and the U. S. Army would sweep the rest off the reservation to exile in Florida or some place the whites did not want.[17]

Captain R. H. Pratt, founder of the Carlisle Indian School in 1879 and devoted believer in the capacity and dignity of the American Indian, also was dedicated to rooting out tribalism and destroying the Indian's separate reservation status. One of his former students reported on a typical Saturday night meeting in the Carlisle assembly hall at which Pratt, straight and tall in his Prince Albert coat, shouted questions from the platform such as "How shall we solve the Indian problem?" The students responded in chorus with the slogans Pratt had taught them: "Abolish the Reservation system! Abolish the ration system!"[18] Pratt differed from the humanitarian reformers in that he worked daily with Indians and had greater faith in their ability and their future than did most of his fellow theorists. He disagreed with other white reformers when they seized the opportunity to obtain legislation providing land in severalty and citizenship for the Indians without regard to their educational development. Pratt insisted that education in the white man's ways had to come first. He agreed with the then Secretary of the Interior Henry M. Teller, who said at Carlisle in 1883: "Education, preparation, first; lands in severalty and citizenship afterward."[19]

The sudden shift in the mid-1880s from a policy of gradualism, involving careful education as a necessary preliminary to assimilation, to instant bestowal of citizenship and immediate allotment of reservation lands in severalty was largely the result of the political climate of the period in which humanitarians obtained unexpected influence over political decisions and in which a series of Supreme Court decisions made it evident that Congress must act if the Indian was to obtain citizenship. The court, in its decision in *Elk* v.

17. Harrison, *op. cit.*, pp. 105–106.
18. Report of Howard Gansworth quoted in Everett Arthur Gilcreast, "Richard Henry Pratt and American Indian Policy, 1877–1906: A Study of the Assimilation Movement" (Ph.D. diss., Yale University, 1967), pp. 52–53.
19. Quoted in Gilcreast, p. 195.

Wilkins (112 U.S. 94, 1884), upheld the ruling of a lower court denying John Elk, an Indian voluntarily separated from his tribe and living in a "civilized" fashion, the right to register to vote in Nebraska. The Elk decision, and that of the court in *U.S.* v. *Kagama* two years later, in which the plenary power of Congress to legislate for the Indian tribes was spelled out, spurred reformers to seek quick political remedies for the apparent disabilities suffered by the Indians.

The culmination of this national belief (on the part of the white portion of the American population) that Indian tribal relations must be broken up and Indian reservations destroyed was the General Allotment Act of 1887. Theodore Roosevelt was pungently correct when he called the act, in a later message to Congress, "a mighty pulverizing engine to break up the tribal mass."[20] Under the provisions of the act, those who took their land in severalty became citizens of the United States, subject to all its obligations. "Citizenship, accompanied by allotment of lands," Commissioner of Indian Affairs Morgan pointed out, "necessarily looks toward the entire destruction of the tribal relation; the Indians are to be individualized and dealt with one by one and not en masse; . . ." "The American Indian," in Morgan's phrase, was "to become the Indian American."[21]

While civil service commissioner, a post to which he had been appointed by President Benjamin Harrison in 1889, Roosevelt had journeyed to several reservations in the West. His report on a trip that he took in 1893 reflected the social Darwinian philosophy that underlay the thinking of virtually every white American of the period. In noting that the land at the Yankton agency had been divided in severalty among its Sioux inhabitants and that the balance of the land remaining was about to be thrown open to white settlement, Roosevelt commented: "This will bring the whites and Indians into close contact, and while, of course, in the ensuing struggle and competition many of the Indians will go to the wall, the survivors will come out American citizens." Roosevelt rejected the notion, held by some "Eastern sentimentalists," that the Indians

20. James D. Richardson, ed., *A Compilation of the Messages and Papers of the Presidents*, 20 vols. (New York, 1927), XIV, 6674 (First Annual Message, Dec. 3, 1901).

21. *Annual Report of the Commissioner of Indian Affairs for 1892*, pp. 6–7; *Annual Report of the Commissioner of Indian Affairs for 1890*, p. vi.

were being driven off land they owned. "They did not own the land at all, in the white sense," he asserted; "they merely occupied it as the white buffalo hunters did. . . ."[22]

White cultural superiority was assumed by both friend and foe of the Indian, and by all advocates of the allotment policy. As Commissioner of Indian Affairs Morgan noted in his annual report for 1890: "If there were no other reason for this change, the fact that individual ownership of property is the universal custom among the civilized people of this country would be a sufficient reason for urging the handful of Indians to adopt it."[23]

The General Allotment Act of 1887, supported by reformers and land grabbers alike, constituted a body blow to traditional Indian culture wherever it went into effect. Fortunately, it was not applied to many of the more populous tribes living in the desert country of the Southwest and it is largely those tribes that have found it possible to retain their culture along with their land. At the time of the act, which was known by the name of its sponsor, Senator Henry Dawes of Massachusetts, the Indian land base contained 138 million acres. Between 1877 and 1934, when the process was reversed, about 60 percent of this land passed out of Indian hands. Sixty million acres of Indian land were declared surplus to Indian needs and sold to white men. Of the lands allotted to individual Indians and held in trust for them by the government for twenty-five years, 27 million acres, or two-thirds of the land so allotted to individual Indians, were lost by sale between 1887 and 1934.[24]

One writer has called the act "a landmark in public gullibility." Had the act been successful in its purpose—to assimilate the Indian into American life—the loss of land would not have become an issue. Such a loss was expected by the reformers as part of the cost of the experiment. But the failure of the measure to facilitate assimilation, and its destructive effect on the Indian population generally, led the humanitarians to attempt to cast the blame on uncooperative administrators or greedy Westerners rather than accept responsibility for a conceptually defective act.[25]

22. *Report of Hon. Theodore Roosevelt made to the United States Civil Service Commission upon a Visit to Certain Indian Reservations and Indian Schools in South Dakota, Nebraska, and Kansas* (Philadelphia, 1893), pp. 18–19.

23. *Annual Report of the Commissioner of Indian Affairs for 1890*, p. xxxix.

24. Washburn, *Red Man's Land*, p. 145.

25. Gilcreast, *op. cit.*, pp. 216–223.

A distinguished authority on the subject, William T. Hagan, has asserted that the process of reducing the Indian's land base "probably would have run the same course if the celebrated Dawes Act had never been passed." Both prior to and following the act, the President, by executive order, and the Congress, by legislation, negotiated or authorized agreements which reduced the Indian land base and often allotted land in severalty to Indians. Professor Hagan's point is that the thrust to open up Indian lands by the American people was so great that its chosen method, the break-up of reservations and the allotment of lands to Indians in severalty, was a continuing process, and not a single act to be laid at the door of a humanitarian Massachusetts senator.[26]

The effects of the allotment policy were clearly predicted by the pioneer anthropologist of the day, Lewis H. Morgan. In his study *Houses and House-Life of the American Aborigines,* published in 1881, Morgan took note of the recommendation of Carl Schurz, the Secretary of the Interior, that lands be allotted in severalty to the Indians, with the power of alienation to white men after a period of, say, twenty-five years. Morgan "hoped that this policy will never be adopted by any National Administration, as it is fraught with nothing but mischief to the Indian tribes." The Indian, he noted, would remain for many years "entirely incapable" of dealing with the white man in matters of this sort on a plane of equality. "The result of individual Indian ownership, with power to sell," Morgan predicted, "would unquestionably be, that in a very short time he would divest himself of every foot of land and fall into poverty." Morgan cited the example of the Shawnees in Kansas, who as a result of allotment had, in the 1860s, entirely lost possession of their lands. Morgan urged that, instead of being allotted agricultural lands, the Indians be taught to be herdsmen.[27]

Morgan's views illustrate the fact that virtually the only white Americans out of step with the Indian policy of the times were the practitioners of what was to become the discipline of anthropology. Although not yet formalized in university curricula, close study—utilizing extensive field work—of the American Indian was the aim

26. William T. Hagan, "The Reservation Policy: Too Little and Too Late," a paper prepared for a Conference on Research in the History of Indian-White Relations, National Archives, Washington, D.C., June 15–16, 1972, p. 19.

27. Lewis H. Morgan, *Houses and House-Life of the American Aborigines* (1881; reprinted, Chicago, 1965), pp. 80–81.

of a number of scholars. Morgan was the giant among these early field workers. Other ethnologists were to be found on the staff of the Bureau of American Ethnology (known as the Bureau of Ethnology from its founding on March 3, 1879, until 1894) which brought together the anthropological field work formerly conducted under independent government surveys and placed it under the directorship of John Wesley Powell within the Smithsonian Institution.[28] Not all anthropologists, however, were in agreement. Alice Fletcher, a Smithsonian ethnologist, was one of the most vigorous opponents of tribalism and played an influential role in the agitation carried on by Indian rights organizations and by the Board of Indian Commissioners in the 1880s to force the allotment of land in severalty upon the Indians without tribal consent and without the requirement that two-thirds of the adult males should approve before an entire reservation could be allotted in severalty. Earlier versions of allotment bills, which recognized tribal consent and the holding of some lands in common, were scrapped in part because of Miss Fletcher's strong opposition. It is only slight comfort to note that Miss Fletcher was quite aware of the effect the compulsory assimilation policy would have on customary Indian traditions. Miss Fletcher was simply more concerned with assimilating the Indians than in preserving their cultures.[29]

Among the few nonanthropologists who were skeptical of the prevailing anti-tribal sentiments was Senator Henry M. Teller of Colorado, who characterized an earlier proposed version of the General Allotment Act as "a bill to despoil the Indians of their lands and to make them vagabonds on the face of the earth." Teller predicted that within thirty or forty years after the passage of an allotment act the Indians would have lost their lands and would "curse the hand that was raised professedly in their defense. . . ." If the people working for severalty legislation understood Indian character, Indian laws, Indian morals, and Indian religion, Teller asserted, they would not be clamoring for such legislation at all.[30]

28. Neil M. Judd, *The Bureau of American Ethnology: A Partial History* (Norman, Okla., 1967), pp. 3–6.

29. Henry E. Fritz, "The Board of Indian Commissioners and Ethnocentric Reform, 1878–1893," a paper prepared for a Conference on Research in the History of Indian-White Relations, National Archives, Washington, D.C., June 15–16, 1972.

30. Washburn, *Red Man's Land*, pp. 155–156.

The mechanics of the allotment process were complicated and the philosophy of its administration erratic. In the years following passage of the General Allotment Act both the mechanics and the philosophy of the act underwent rapid and sometimes bewildering change.

On issuance of a patent in fee to allotted lands the government's trusteeship relation to the individual Indian came to an end, except insofar as the individual Indian maintained an interest in undistributed tribal funds and other property. The Indian to whom land had been so allotted was then free to hold or dispose of his property as he saw fit. By the General Allotment Act of 1887 patents in fee were to be issued automatically at the end of twenty-five years from the date of the allotment. By the so-called Burke Act of May 8, 1906 (34 Stat. 182), the trust period was left at twenty-five years, but the Secretary of the Interior was given power to issue a patent in fee "whenever he shall be satisfied that any Indian allottee is competent and capable of managing his or her affairs . . . and thereafter all restrictions as to the sale, incumbrance, or taxation of said land shall be removed." Provision was also made to extend the period of trust beyond twenty-five years in certain cases. The Burke Act did not apply to any Indians in the Indian Territory. The act threw the burden of deciding on the individual competency of each Indian applying for a patent in fee to the Bureau of Indian Affairs. The power thus given became the cause of bitter disputes in succeeding years with charges of excessive laxity and excessive strictness both being hurled at the bureau. Of the Indians who received patents during 1907 and 1908 approximately 60 percent sold their land and squandered the proceeds. Greater strictness was then enforced on the applications and between 1909 and 1912 more than half of the 3,400 applications for fee patents were denied.[31]

In April, 1917, a policy change was announced by the Commissioner of Indian Affairs. "Broadly speaking," the commissioner announced, "a policy of greater liberalism will henceforth prevail in Indian administration to the end that every Indian, as soon as he has been determined to be as competent to transact his own business as the average white man, shall be given full control of his property and have all his lands and moneys turned over to him, after which he will no longer be a ward of the Government." All

31. Laurence F. Schmeckebier, *The Office of Indian Affairs: Its History, Activities and Organization* (Baltimore, 1927), pp. 148–151.

Indians of less than one-half Indian blood were deemed immediately capable of receiving complete control of their property. Reservation superintendents were ordered to compile lists of such individuals for the purpose of facilitating the issuance of patents. Indians of one-half Indian blood or more were to be issued patents if, after careful investigation, they were found competent. Competency commissions were organized to make the necessary determinations of competency on the various reservations. As a result of this change of policy, over 10,000 fee simple patents were issued in the three years following the announcement of the policy, more than had been issued in the ten years from 1906 to 1916. The deleterious effects of the policy soon became evident and in 1921 the practice of issuing patents in fee automatically to Indians of one-half or less Indian blood was discontinued, and formal application and proof of competency were once more required.[32]

The effect of the new ruling was to stabilize the issuance of such patents, and a later Commissioner of Indian Affairs blamed the 1917 policy on the propaganda charging the Indian Bureau with being un-American, undemocratic, and tyrannical in applying strict standards in the issuance of such patents. In the reassessment of the policy, the Commissioner of Indian Affairs, in his report for 1921, noted that more than two-thirds of the Indians who had received patents in fee had been "unable or unwilling to cope with the business acumen coupled with the selfishness and greed of the more competent whites, and in many instances have lost every acre they had." The commissioner noted the frequency with which "those of one-half or less Indian blood—often young men who have had excellent educational privileges—secure patents in fee, dispose of their land at a sacrifice, put most of the proceeds in an automobile or some other extravagant investment, and in a few months are 'down and out,' as far as any visible possessions are concerned." The loss of the exemption from taxation of land held in trust by the government for the Indian was rarely fully anticipated or adequately prepared for.[33]

When it became apparent that the Indians were too frequently incapable of cultivating and maintaining the lands they had received in severalty by the General Allotment Act of 1887, legislation

32. *Ibid.*, pp. 152–154.
33. *Ibid.*, pp. 156–157.

to authorize their leasing the lands allotted to them was sought. The General Allotment Act of 1887, in the words of Laurence F. Schmeckebier, "overlooked entirely" the fact that some of the Indian allottees would be physically incapable of utilizing their allotments under the act, even if they were inclined to do so. But, because the United States held the land in trust for the allottee, the latter could not make a valid lease. This defect, if it was a defect, was remedied by an act of February 28, 1891 (26 Stat. 794), which made provisions for leasing allotted lands and tribal lands under regulations prescribed by the Secretary of the Interior. Leasing for agriculture, grazing, and mining purposes was authorized. Under the provisions of this and subsequent acts, enormous amounts of land were leased for such purposes to white men. The pressure for leases was such that the general leasing act of February 25, 1920 (41 Stat. 437) providing for leasing of mineral deposits on land owned by the United States was temporarily ruled applicable to Indian reservations created by executive order (though not by treaty) by Secretary of the Interior Fall on July 9, 1922. As noted in the following chapter, this ruling was overturned on May 12, 1924, by the Attorney General after it aroused humanitarian protests by friends of the Indian.[34]

The leasing of tribal lands had a long history and the extent of the practice influenced the rate at which allotment policies were put into effect. When the question of leasing Indian lands for grazing purposes first arose, Bureau of Indian Affairs officials were confused and uncertain as to what to do. A case study of leasing arrangements on the three-million-acre reservation near Fort Sill, Oklahoma, created by treaty with the Kiowas and Comanches on October 21, 1867, nicely illustrates the problem. Texas cattlemen in the 1870s and 1880s, driving their stock north to Abilene and Dodge City, sometimes by accident and sometimes by design, allowed their cattle to graze on the grass of the reservation. The Indian agent for the reservation attempted at first to keep out the white men's cattle while encouraging the building up of Indian stock. Neither policy worked. When some of the Texas cattlemen and their cooperating

34. *Ibid.*, pp. 84, 178, 180–181. See also D. S. Otis, *The Dawes Act and the Allotment of Indian Lands*, ed. Francis Paul Prucha (Norman, Okla., 1973), pp. 148–152, 185–188; and Washburn, *The Assault on Indian Tribalism*, op. cit., *passim.*

Indian chiefs on the reservation proposed various leasing arrangements, these were rejected at first by the Secretary of the Interior on the grounds that leasing would not produce much revenue and the presence of cattlemen and their herds on the reservation would interfere with the growth of Indian stock raising. After much lobbying and soul searching, leasing arrangements went into operation and continued, with increasing fees, until allotment and the opening of the reservation in the first years of the twentieth century. Between 1885 and 1906 the cattlemen paid $2 million in "grass money" to the Kiowas and Comanches. Their influence in Congress delayed the opening of the reservation for several years. The absence of a cattlemen's lobby, conversely, caused the Cheyennes and Arapahos to be allotted earlier. The disadvantages of leasing probably outweighed the advantages by denying the Indians isolation and the opportunity to strengthen their own economy and culture on the reservation.[35]

Many, but not all, of the Indians of the United States underwent an economic and cultural revolution when the government broke up their reservations, allotted land in severalty to individual tribesmen, and sought to break up tribal authority and tribal relations. Fortunately, some Indian tribes were not allotted and escaped the effects of the policy. Although the roots of allotment policy go back to the earliest years of Indian-white interaction, the climax can be dated by the passage of the General Allotment Act of 1887. Thereafter the American Indian became increasingly an Indian American, although his position in the hierarchy of American society was more often that of the drunk in the gutter than that of self-reliant, God-fearing, landholding farmer. The policy, honestly believed by its supporters to be in the best interest of the Indian, can now be seen to have been in his worst interest. Ignorance of Indian culture, fatuous self-righteousness, and land hunger combined to push the Indian reeling into the twentieth century without any of the economic supports or cultural values that had previously given his life meaning. In a period when "Lo, the poor Indian!" was a virtual byword, many concluded that neither the American Indian nor the Indian American would long survive.

35. William T. Hagan, "Kiowas, Comanches, and Cattlemen, 1867–1906: A Case Study of the Failure of U.S. Reservation Policy," *Pacific Historical Review*, XL (1971) , 333–355.

CHAPTER 12

The Indian in Search of an Identity

T HE contemporary Indian's search for a new identity was highlighted by the occupation of Wounded Knee, South Dakota, in 1973. The incident—a carefully planned, artificially staged, media event—made explicit the gap between existing tribal leaders and new aspirants to Indian leadership on the subject of contemporary federal Indian policy. The site of the incident could not have been more provocatively chosen. The ringing name Wounded Knee evoked memories of a historical tragedy—the massacre of 200 Indians in 1890 by the U.S. Cavalry—an event which had shortly before been recalled to millions of Americans by a runaway best seller, Dee Brown's *Bury My Heart at Wounded Knee*. The site—complete with a steepled white church sitting on a bare ridge—provided a ready-made Hollywood set for the television reporters who flocked to cover the event. The "event"—the "capture" of Wounded Knee, the taking of "hostages" at the trading post, the proclamation of an "independent Sioux nation," and the issuance by its American Indian Organization (AIM) leaders of a demand for a radical change in federal policy—seemed like something out of the romantic past or out of a fantasy future.

Wounded Knee symbolized the emergence of a new and raucous Indian voice, a voice which celebrated separatism instead of integration, political activism instead of a dignified acquiescence, repudiation of white goals and values, and rejection of existing tribal organizations. Wounded Knee, and AIM's earlier trashing of the Bureau of Indian Affairs in Washington in 1972, forced a recon-

THE INDIAN IN SEARCH OF AN IDENTITY 251

sideration of United States policy as restructured by Commissioner
of Indian Affairs John Collier in the 1930s. Can the system of tribal
governments and democratically elected tribal leaders authorized
under the Indian Reorganization Act of 1934 (IRA) survive?

In order to answer this question, one must consider the degree to
which the Indian has changed in the course of the twentieth
century.

In the early years of the twentieth century the tribal ideal—now
celebrated as an indispensable safeguard of Indian culture—was
under attack not only from government administrators and white
reformers, but from many Indian leaders themselves. Their attitude
derived from an acceptance—conscious or unconscious—of the prevailing spirit of individualism. That spirit was so pervasive in the
traditions of western Europe and the United States that even scien-
tists trained in that tradition—to say nothing of Indians subject to
the pressures of white culture—tended to conceive of man as an
individual isolated from his fellow men or from the groups of which
he was a part.[1]

Both Arthur C. Parker, the Seneca who was editor of *The American Indian Magazine*, the quarterly journal of the Society of American Indians (a pan-Indian organization which flourished from 1916
to 1923), and his principal opponent, Carlos Montezuma, a Yavapai
doctor who was instrumental in breaking up the society, saw the
future of the Indian in other than native, tribal terms. Parker
asserted, "The future of the Indians is with the white race, and in a
civilization derived from the old world." He also proclaimed, "The
Sioux is no longer a mere Sioux, or the Ojibway a mere Ojibway,
the Iroquois a mere Iroquois." All were now part of a larger unity,
the "red race." But even pan-Indianism was only a stopping place.
For now, Parker noted, "With a coming race-consciousness the
American Indian seeks to go even further and say, 'I am not a red
man only, I am an American in the truest sense, and a brother man
to all human kind.' "[2]

Carlos Montezuma, while seeking the same goals Parker espoused,

1. Francis L. K. Hsu, "Psychosocial Homeostasis and *Jen:* Conceptual Tools
for Advancing Psychological Anthropology," *American Anthropologist*, LXXIII
(1971), 23–24.
2. Parker's statement in "The Editor's Viewpoint: The Functions of the
Society of American Indians," in the first issue of the journal in 1916, quoted
in Hazel W. Hertzberg, *The Search for an American Indian Identity: Modern
Pan-Indian Movements* (Syracuse, N.Y., 1971), pp. 139–141.

felt that Parker's policy of temporary accommodation to the institutions by which the Indian was dealt with separately from his white brothers in American society was dishonorable. The principal among those institutions was the Bureau of Indian Affairs, which had gradually assumed overwhelming power over Indian tribes and individuals. Although many Indians were by this time citizens under the terms of the Dawes Act, they were still subject to bureau control in their capacity as allottees and beneficiaries of tribal funds. Montezuma broke with the Society of American Indians because he disagreed with its insistence on working within the existing system. He founded, instead, his own journal, *Wassaja*, which he vowed to publish so long as the bureau continued to exist. He advocated the bureau's immediate abolition along with the reservation system, which, he felt, warped Indian development. The Indian, he asserted, should be treated just like anyone else. He should be free, with the *full* privileges of citizenship.[3]

The anti-tribal movement and the assimilationist ideals of the twentieth century were conjoined in the passage of the Indian Citizenship Bill, which was signed into law on June 2, 1924. Under the act all Indians born in the United States were declared to be citizens of the United States, though citizenship did not automatically place Indians on a footing of full legal equality with whites, nor was it universally welcomed by Indians.

While the Indian was achieving a paper political equality, he continued to experience a growing economic inequality. The plight of the Indian stirred the conscience of many whites. White concern was particularly activated when Senator H. O. Bursum of New Mexico introduced a bill in 1921 that would have taken away from the Pueblo Indians large portions of their lands in favor of trespassers. An even greater outcry arose when Secretary of the Interior Albert B. Fall ruled in 1922 that "Executive Order Reservations"— that is, Indian reservations established by executive order rather than by treaty or act of Congress—were "merely public lands temporarily withdrawn by Executive Order" and therefore available for leasing to white oil and gas interests under the General Leasing Act of 1920.

3. Hertzberg, p. 143. See also Wilcomb E. Washburn, "The Society of American Indians," *The Indian Historian*, III (1970), 21–23.

Traditional Indian defense organizations were joined in the fight to preserve the remaining Indian land base by new organizations such as the American Indian Defense Association organized by John Collier—the association's executive secretary—in 1923. The concentrated opposition led to changes in government policy. Fall was replaced as Secretary of the Interior in 1923 by Herbert W. Work. The new secretary invited a group of distinguished Americans to advise the government on the measures it should take in regard to the Indian. The opposition of the members of this Committee of One Hundred—both before and after its appointment—to the "Executive Reservation Order," to the Bursum bill, to orders discouraging certain Indian ceremonies, and to other similar measures, proved instrumental in killing most of them. One by-product of the work of the Committee of One Hundred was a report undertaken at the request of the Secretary of the Interior on the administration of Indian affairs. Issued by the Brookings Institution in 1928 and known as the Meriam Report after Lewis Meriam, the head of the group conducting the study, the report laid the basis for the new directions in Indian policy taken first under President Herbert Hoover and then under President Franklin D. Roosevelt. While upholding integration into the larger white community as the ultimate goal, the Meriam Report pointed out the need for prolonged education to make such integration possible. It also emphasized the economic poverty of most Indian communities and the need to preserve Indian resources if the future prosperity and happiness of Indians were to be assured.[4]

The shock of the Great Depression set the stage for a radical reform of American Indian policy. The plight of the Indian in the 1930s was vividly recorded by agents of the Emergency Relief Administration. Hunger, disease, and social disorganization were endemic. "Something has surely been in error in the allotment of land," commented a South Dakota social worker, overwhelmed by the dismal state of the Indian population in his state.[5]

A radical solution to the "Indian problem" became possible with the appointment of Harold L. Ickes as Secretary of the Interior and

4. Hertzberg, pp. 200–204.

5. Survey of Indian Reservations conducted by South Dakota Emergency Relief Administration, 1935, typescript in Library of Congress, Washington, D.C., Rosebud Agency volume, Part VI, Summary and Recommendations.

John Collier as Commissioner of Indian Affairs early in the administration of Franklin D. Roosevelt. Collier's achievement as
commissioner was not only to end the forced "atomization" of
Indian life, to humanize the Indian administration, and to involve
other agencies in the search for remedies to the problems of Indian
poverty, ignorance, and despair, but above all to resurrect the
"bilateral, contractual relationship between the government and
the tribes (the historical, legal and moral foundation of Govern-
ment-Indian relations)." Collier devised ways in which this bilateral relationship could evolve in modern forms, forms that would
relate the Indian to the "American commonwealth in its fullness,"
not merely to the American government.[6]

Collier's concern that the Indian tribal group survive, both as a
real and as a legal entity, was achieved in the face of a prevalent
attitude that saw the solution to the Indian problem in the destruction of the tribe and the reduction of the individual Indian to just
another member of the dominant society. "Even where a tribal
group is split into factions, where leadership has broken down,
where Indians clamor to distribute the tribal property—even there
deep forces of cohesion persist and can be evoked," wrote Collier.
Citing the record of American legal recognition of the autonomy of
major Indian groups, Collier utilized the past to shore up the shaky
Indian future. The Indian tribe was set to work for modern
community development.[7]

Collier did not profess to be a prophet and to know how long
tribal government might endure. It would vary with the individual
tribe, he believed, but Indians should have "the right of self-
determination" and the United States government should not force
the issue.[8] In response to critics who bemoaned the fact that Collier
was "setting back the clock," D'Arcy McNickle, a Flathead Indian
and one of Collier's associates, boldly proclaimed that the Indian
Reorganization Act was not retrogressive but progressive. "To assert
the right of self-government" for Indian tribes, McNickle insisted,
was to assert "the right of the future." McNickle compared the
tribal authority offered Indians under the act to the rights of a

6. John Collier, "The Genesis and Philosophy of the Indian Reorganization
Act," quoted in S. Lyman Tyler, *Indian Affairs: A Work Paper on Termination: with an Attempt to Show Its Antecedents* (Provo, Utah, 1964), p. 16.
7. Commissioner's Circular No. 3537 (Nov. 15, 1943), in *ibid.*, p. 19.
8. *Ibid.*, p. 20.

board of county commissioners or of a city council to determine how to raise and spend funds for local governmental purposes.[9] The last eight years of Collier's administration (until his resignation in 1945) saw a continuing battle between the commissioner and the House and Senate Indian committees. Bills to abolish the IRA or the IRA in specific localities were introduced. But the act held.[10]

Collier's faith in the persistence and resilience of Indian tribal ties was at least partially justified. In his annual report for 1936, he noted, "Few anthropologists or students of Hopi life were ready to believe that the Hopi Indians in Arizona would ever agree to come together." There were nine independent Hopi villages, speaking two unrelated languages, with various factions diverging in their attitudes toward acceptance of white culture and other problems. "Nevertheless," Collier noted, "what seemed to be the impossible was accomplished." Fifty percent of the eligible voters came to the polls in October, 1936, and 80 percent voted to accept the constitution authorized under the IRA.[11]

Indian opposition to Collier's attempt to recapture the communal heritage of the American Indian must not, however, be minimized. Indians played key roles in the attacks on the program and were not always deluded or corrupted in their opposition. Individualism, the profit motive, and disinclination to share the fruits of one's successful labors with one's unsuccessful fellow tribesmen were powerful motives among those Indians who forced major changes in Collier's draft bill for an Indian Reorganization Act and who later refused to incorporate under the act as eventually passed. Most bitterly opposed of the early provisions of the bill was that providing for the return of private allotments to a tribal landholding pool. When Collier traveled around the country in 1934 to explain the bill, he met frequent and bitter opposition. Particularly strong resistance occurred in Oklahoma, where those individuals possessing valuable oil and mineral rights were loath to lose their privileged positions. Collier, whose inspiration for a reform of Indian affairs derived from his experience with the Pueblo Indians and their still functioning communal societies, and who maintained a secondary pur-

9. D'Arcy McNickle, *They Came Here First: The Epic of the American Indian* (Philadelphia, 1949), pp. 298–299, quoted in *ibid.*, p. 17.

10. *Ibid.*, pp. 22–23.

11. *Annual Report of the Commissioner of Indian Affairs for 1937*, p. 201.

pose of attempting to redirect white America's individualistic ethos toward communal values, reacted bitterly to the opposition of the already allotted and increasingly individualistically minded Indians of Oklahoma and the Plains.[12]

Even the Quapaw Indians of Oklahoma, a majority of whom were landless in 1934 and who would have been in a position, under incorporation, to exercise greater control over the assets of the tribe at the expense of the tribal minority who were successful, maintained an unceasing opposition to the early Collier drafts and refused to accept incorporation under the act as passed. Indeed, a majority of all American Indians repudiated, even in its final attenuated form in the Indian Reorganization Act of 1934, John Collier's ideas.[13]

How strong the pull of white values was is dramatically illustrated in the career of J. C. Morgan, a Navajo, born in 1879, who graduated from Hampton Institute in Virginia in 1900 and returned to his people determined to lead them out of their traditional ways. Morgan spent a number of years teaching in government schools, working as a financial clerk and interpreter, running a trading post, and working with missionary groups as a carpenter, teacher, and translator. In 1918 he formed the Navajo Progressive League, an organization of returned students, dedicated to improving education and sanitation on the Navajo reservation. In 1925 Morgan became assistant to a Christian Reformed minister on the reservation and in succeeding years became more and more prominent in church work. Morgan also became an active member of the Returned Students League, established in 1932, an organization dedicated to assimilation. Such was the background of the leader of the Navajo opposition to John Collier's Indian policies. Collier's antipathy to boarding schools was challenged by Morgan as a slap in the face of Navajo boys and girls. "If it was not for boarding schools," Morgan asserted at the Fort Wingate Tribal Council meeting in 1933 at which Collier outlined his plans to the

12. Kenneth R. Philp, "The Failure to Create a Red Atlantis: John Collier and the Controversy Over the Wheeler-Howard Bill of 1934," a paper prepared for a Conference on Research in the History of Indian-White Relations, National Archives, Washington, D.C., June 15–16, 1972.

13. W. David Baird, comment on session on "Recent Research on Indian Reservation Policy" at a Conference on Research in the History of Indian-White Relations, National Archives, Washington, D.C., June 15–16, 1972.

Navajos, "we would not be here today." Morgan similarly attacked the Indian Reorganization Act, as it was finally enacted, as a step backward. He bitterly accused Collier of trying to keep the Indians unchanged to serve as a human zoo for the amusement of the tourists. Morgan, as a progressive leader, feared that retention and support of the tribal structure would throw political advantage to the traditionalists, who would use their power to destroy the progress toward assimilation achieved by persons committed to bringing the Indians into the larger white world.[14]

By dint of active campaigning on the part of Morgan and others the Navajos in 1935 rejected the Indian Reorganization Act by a vote of 8,197 to 7,679, thus preventing its application to the Navajo reservation. The forces hostile to Collier were aided by the confusion in the popular mind between the Indian Reorganization legislation and Collier's policy of forced reduction of the excessive Navajo sheep and goat herds that were creating an ecological crisis on the reservation. Moreover, the Navajos retained an inherited suspicion that anything the government wanted was liable to be against their best interests. Nevertheless, the "antis" owed much of their strength to the anti-tribal, assimilationist values championed by individuals like Morgan. Morgan reached the peak of power in 1938 when he was elected tribal chairman. That a Navajo who believed that Indians should live among whites, pay taxes, and assume the full responsibilities of citizenship could be elected tribal chairman is a testimony to the potency of the philosophy that he championed. That Morgan lost much of his popularity while tribal chairman does not invalidate this assumption. Incumbent tribal chairmen, particularly on the Navajo reservation, have tended gradually to lose the popularity that gained them election, possibly because of their too close identity with the federal government, possibly because of the workings of envy and fear on the part of their fellow tribesmen. Thus Morgan, though he forced the government to modify its position toward the Navajos, in the long run afforded ammunition to his traditionalist rival Chee Dodge, who defeated him for the chairmanship of the tribe in 1942.[15]

The evidence of the strength of "white" values among Indians of

14. Donald L. Parman, "J. C. Morgan: Navajo Apostle of Assimilation," *Prologue: The Journal of the National Archives,* IV (1972), 83–98.
15. *Ibid.*

the 1920s and 1930s raises the question of whether continuing acculturation means the eventual loss of Indian identity. In fact, it is possible for Indian individuals—to say nothing of Indian tribal groups—to share and retain the values of both societies. The anthropologist Malcolm McFee, in referring to the phenomenon in Blackfoot culture, has spoken of such Indians as 150 percent men: they combine traits of both races to a total greater than the 100 percent attributable to each group. The present Blackfoot reservation, McFee has noted, provides a bicultural community in which both white-oriented people and Indian-oriented people can live and play roles in either—or both—societies. The Indian-oriented group places a high value on generosity, even to the point of self-impoverishment. Attendance at Indian dances, Indian encampments, and other traditional occupations is emphasized, as is the use of the Blackfoot language at home and in conversation with friends. The white-oriented group, on the other hand, is more dedicated to a goal of economic achievement. This group is more independent, acquisitive, and hard-working than the traditional group, and it guards its surplus against the traditional claims made on the generosity of the Indian-oriented group. Each group is stratified with top status going to those who most clearly fulfill the image of ideal behavior in the group. Yet there is a crossing of the line between the two groups in numerous ways. A Blackfoot is not necessarily governed by white values or by Indian values. He can, in some measure, be governed by both.[16]

Although many Indians have retained some traditional values while acquiring additional "white" values, there is no gainsaying the fact that American Indians have increasingly abandoned their traditional material culture, traditional subsistence activities, and even their language and ceremonies. The change of life styles of the Hupa Indians of the Hoopa Valley reservation in northern California in the pre- and post-World War II periods provides an example of this cultural shift. Most of the sixty-three Hupa veterans of World War II returned to the reservation expecting to pick up where they had left off, hunting and fishing the year round, living on the reservation free from the worry of taxes on their land, taking odd jobs as the occasion arose, and sometimes farming. This life

16. Malcolm McFee, "The 150% Man, a Product of Blackfeet Acculturation," *American Anthropologist*, LXX (1968), 1096–1107.

style, which had close links with the traditional pattern of Hupa life, was gradually and subtly altered in the postwar years. Per capita stumpage fees paid by lumber companies for the privilege of cutting the reservation timber were distributed to the individual members of the tribe. New businesses—a gas station, restaurant, general store, and garage—appeared. A new affluence, reflected in a great increase in the number of automobiles on the reservation, emerged. With the arrival of power lines in 1950, further evidence of white material culture was seen on the reservation; television, refrigerators, washers and dryers, became common possessions of Indian homeowners. By 1960 telephone wires were strung through the valley and new service industries sprang up: a barber shop, a beauty shop, a TV repair service, a laundromat, a gift shop, a clothing store, a drive-in, a motel, a trailer park, and a landing strip for small planes. Another restaurant and two more gas stations added to the "American" character of the "Indian" reservation. Hunting and gathering activities, so common in the aboriginal state and persistent in an important form until World War II, declined precipitously throughout these years. Indians increasingly derived their living from the service industries springing up in the valley. Some Hupas owned outright the small businesses; others worked in them. Some Hupas intermarried with whites, who, by the mid-1950s, outnumbered the Hupas.[17]

The effect of this Americanization of the valley was seen not only in the changed character of economic activity, but also in the decline of traditional ceremonies, such as the White Deerskin Dance, a "world-renewal ritual requiring a preliminary payment to all families bereaved by a death during the year and the accumulation and preparation of sufficient foodstuffs to feed all who attended."[18] Formerly held every two years, the ceremony was now held at seven- or eight-year intervals. Basketmaking declined. Fishing was carried on using nylon nets and fiber glass boats. The young people today tend not to know the Hupa language except for a few words; only the old folks speak it as a first language.

From a dependent reliance on an alien agent, the Hupas gradu-

17. John H. Bushnell, "From American Indian to Indian American: The Changing Identity of the Hupa," *American Anthropologist*, LXX (1968), 1108–1116, at 1112.
18. *Ibid.*, 1110.

ally acquired an integrated status in the larger community. The county sheriff replaced the Indian police in maintaining law and order. By virtue of an act of Congress Hupas can now possess and drink liquor although the Hoopa Tribal Council has continued to prohibit the sale of alcohol on the reservation. The reservation itself has been maintained and with it the ancient village sites, burial grounds, and dance field of the Hupa past. The geographic and cultural continuity provided by the existence of the reservation has enabled the Hupas, even while accommodating themselves to white patterns of living, to look back to their native traditions and to attempt to preserve and maintain them. Native dances, basketry, even the use of acorn soup—prepared with the aid of a coffee grinder or blender rather than with a mortar and pestle—reach back to the Hupas' original past. Yet the Hupas are far more American than Indian, notwithstanding the survival of traditional patterns of life. That these patterns of life are cherished consciously by many Hupas does not invalidate the thesis that the Hupas, like the Japanese-Americans or Italian-Americans, are now more closely identified with the larger American culture than with their original native culture.

In contrast to the easy acculturation process evident in tribes like the Hupas, other tribes, particularly the sedentary tribes of the Southwest, cling closely to past traditions. The result, in genetic terms, has been a high degree of inbreeding. The evidence of this inbreeding, in the case of the Hopis, is apparent in the high proportion of albinos in several of the Hopi mesa settlements. Hopis of the First Mesa, who represent a mixing of Hopi and Tewa gene pools (the Tewa Indians of the Rio Grande area in New Mexico arrived about 1700 seeking refuge from the Spanish), have the lowest frequency of the recessive gene for albinism. Hopis of the Second Mesa, who regard themselves as the "most Hopi" of all and who rarely marry non-Hopis, have the highest proportion of inbreeding.[19]

The development of Hopi crafts for sale to outsiders—utilizing both traditional and modern designs—by craftsmen like Charles

19. Charles M. Woolf and Frank C. Dukepoo, "Hopi Indians, Inbreeding, and Albinism," *Science*, CLXIV (1969), 30–37. See also Mischa Titiev, *The Hopi Indians of Old Oraibi: Change and Continuity* (Ann Arbor, Mich., 1972), pp. 326–353.

Loloma; the creation in the 1970s of a Hopi Cultural Center consisting of a motel, restaurant, museum, library, and craft shops; the paving of roads connecting the Hopi villages to the existing network of state and federal roads—have all opened up the Hopi villages to outside scrutiny. Yet the Hopis have been able to keep the outside world at arm's length—keeping some of their villages off limits to whites and allowing visits only under supervision to others—and to maintain their traditional theocratic system of government. Hopi youths are increasingly bothered by the rigidity of the traditional structure, but for the most part accept the existing system because of their commitment to inherited values and because of the continued success of Hopi leaders in dealing with the outside world.

It is not easy to measure the degree to which twentieth-century Indians have, in general, retained or lost their traditional heritage. The acculturation scale provides examples ranging from tribes like the close-knit Hopi, on the one hand, to individual Indians who live in white society and have no visible or overt identification with Indian culture. Perhaps the most significant indicator of cultural stability or cultural disintegration is the ability of a tribal group to retain its native language. The number of Indian languages is declining. The anthropologist Wallace Chafe has estimated that there are forty-five indigenous languages spoken by 1,000 or more speakers in the United States, including Alaska. Of this group, according to William C. Sturtevant of the Smithsonian Institution, eight languages—Cherokee (10,000), Cree (35,000), Creek (8,000), Crow (5,000), Eskimo-Inupik (50,000), Navajo (90,000), Ojibwa (45,000), and Teton-Lakota (15,000)—have a practical orthography, available reading material, considerable Indian literacy, and a technical grammar. The others have less or no reading material and inadequate technical linguistic studies.[20]

The disappearance of Indian tongues should not necessarily be equated to a loss of Indian consciousness. Just as Cornish, Welsh, Scottish, and Irish nationalism can be expressed in the English language, so too can Indian tribal consciousness survive the loss of

20. A. Bruce Gaarder, "Education of American Indian Children," Georgetown University, School of Languages and Linguistics, Monograph Series on Languages and Linguistics, 19th Annual Round Table, *Contrastive Linguistics and Its Pedagogical Implications*, No. 21, ed. James E. Alatis (Washington, 1968), pp. 83–96.

Indian languages. Nevertheless, the existence of Indian languages provides a solid basis for inculcating knowledge of the Indian past in Indian schoolchildren. Instruction in Indian languages allows the Indian child to avoid the choice formerly forced upon him of choosing between a nonliterate, backward Indian world, and a literate, progressive, but alien, white world. By allowing the Indian to be taught by Indians (in 1965 only 1 percent of Indian children in elementary schools had Indian teachers) in his native language, with educational materials emphasizing his own history and culture, the Indian, hopefully, will develop the pride in himself and in his people which was too frequently absent in the past. Experimental schools, such as that at Rough Rock, on the Navajo reservation, have had some success in achieving these objectives.[21]

Another index of cultural change is the Indian's education in the "white man's way." The potential of the Indian for a "white" education has never been doubted by those best able to judge. Benjamin Franklin, Thomas Jefferson, Captain Richard H. Pratt, and Senator Robert F. Kennedy are only a few of those who have expressed their conviction on this point after long study of the evidence. Pratt, head of the famous Carlisle, Pennsylvania, Indian School, insisted that the Indians were as educable as any people in the world. "If I was the Commissioner of Indian Affairs and I had a superintendent of schools who could not see in every little Indian boy a possible President of the United States," Pratt averred in 1916, "I would dismiss him."[22] Senator Kennedy's investigation of Indian education in 1967–1968, under the auspices of a special subcommittee of the Senate Labor and Public Welfare Committee, expressed the same faith and threw the glare of publicity on the continuing inadequacies of Indian education.[23]

The failings of Indian education and the consequent develop-

21. See, for example, Broderick H. Johnson, *Navaho Education at Rough Rock* (Rough Rock, Ariz.: Published by Rough Rock Demonstration School, D.I.N.E., Inc., 1968) ; and Ethelou Yazzie, *Navajo History, Written Under the Direction of The Navajo Curriculum Center, Rough Rock Demonstration School, Chinle, Arizona* (Many Farms, Ariz.: Navajo Community College Press, 1971) .

22. *The American Indian Magazine*, IV (1916) , 246.

23. *Hearings before the Special Subcommittee on Indian Education of the Committee on Labor and Public Welfare, United States Senate, Ninetieth Congress, First and Second Sessions, on the Study of the Education of Indian Children* (Washington, 1969) .

ment of Indian apathy have more often than not had their roots in a white assumption of Indian inferiority and in a white system which ignored Indian cultural patterns. Murray Wax and his collaborators have coined the phrase "Vacuum Ideology" to describe the disposition of white school administrators to conceive of the Indian home and the mind of the Indian child as meager or empty. In their study of education at the Pine Ridge Sioux reservation, they constantly faced the assumption of school administrators that the Indian lacked a coherent pattern of life or viable experiences because he lacked the material attributes of the white man's civilization and did not respond to traditional white values. Sioux children's unfamiliarity with television, jet planes, helicopters, supermarkets, frozen foods, and the like was interpreted in terms of deficiency. The Sioux's familiarity with cows, horses, and streams, on the other hand, was overlooked. Indeed, the Wax group compared the attitude of white administrators of Indian schools to land-hungry white pioneers looking at a landscape filled with Indians and seeing it as empty, awaiting the touch of Western civilization. The ethnocentric blindness displayed by such administrators in the twentieth century suggests the continuing inability of white Americans to understand alien cultures.[24]

While the Indian still finds the white educational system a trial as well as an opportunity (and vice versa), there is a heartening growth in the number of Indians who have made their way through school and through college and, in some cases, gone on to graduate school. While individual Indians have been part of the academic scene since the seventeenth century, never have such large numbers been prepared in universities to make their way in either the white or Indian world. In 1960, 3,441 Indians were enrolled in colleges and universities. The 1970 census revealed that 14,191 Indians were in attendance at institutions of higher education and the number of graduates has continued to increase.[25]

24. Murray L. Wax, Rosalie H. Wax, and Robert V. Dumont, Jr., *Formal Education in an American Indian Community*, Supplement to *Social Problems*, II (1964), 67–71. See also Robert J. Havighurst and Bernice L. Neugarten, *American Indian and White Children: A Sociopsychological Investigation* (Chicago, 1955).

25. U.S. Bureau of the Census, *Census of Population: 1970, Subject Reports, Final Report PC (2)-1F, American Indians* (Washington, 1973), Table 3 (Social Characteristics); *Census of Population: 1960, School Enrollment Report, PC (2)-5A* (Washington, 1964).

Another index of cultural stability and change is the extent to which native religions have been retained and the Christian religion adapted to native needs. The mid-twentieth century has witnessed not only a revival of native religious practices, but a modification and adaptation of the Christian religion as it has developed within Indian communities. The bearers of Christianity in the past tended to come to the Indian in a position of superiority and power: no compromise with native beliefs was necessary. The new Christianity among the Indians augurs well for its continuance as a valid Indian spiritual form. The example of Father Paul Bernhard Steinmetz, S.J., pastor of Our Lady of the Sioux Catholic Church near Pine Ridge, South Dakota, in the period of the 1960s (and of nearby Sacred Heart Church in the 1970s) reflected the new approach. Father Paul, upon his assignment to the area in 1961, obtained an unused church nearby, moved it to the site and remodeled it in accordance with Indian custom and traditions. Decoration, murals, and church furniture were done in the Sioux manner by Sioux. The symbols of the peace pipe, the buffalo, and the thunderbird shared the altar and the walls with the crucified Christ. Father Paul, recognizing the cultural difference between the Indian's speaking from the heart and the missionary's reading from the Bible, emphasized spontaneous prayer. Even the priest's beaded vestment, into which the religious symbols of the Sioux were woven, reflected his respect for the native traditions of his parishioners.

Father Paul's most dramatic adaptation of native tradition was his utilization of the sacred peace pipe, which was central to Sioux religious ceremonies, in the traditional manner: filling it with tobacco, holding it in his right hand, offering it in prayer to the entire universe, and finally touching its bowl to the earth mother. The pipe, Father Paul tells the parishioners, is a foreshadowing of Christ. Christ is the eternal and living Pipe who fulfills and does not destroy the Sioux religion. Just as Christ substituted the Mass for the Jewish Paschal meal and used bread and wine to symbolize His sacrifice, so, Father Paul explains, does the sacred pipe, by being brought into the Christian ceremony, integrate Sioux tradition into Christian and fulfill, not destroy, the Indian spiritual vision.[26] In 1971 Father Paul, under the guidance of Frank Fools Crow, par-

26. Dabney Otis Collins, "A Happening at Oglala," *The American West*, VI, No. 2 (March, 1969) , 15–19.

ticipated in the Oglala Sun Dance, giving the ceremony a Christian dimension.

The revolutionary change in the attitude of white Christianity toward Indian religious life is even more startlingly revealed in the scholarly work of Peter J. Powell, an Anglo-Catholic priest whose book, *Sweet Medicine: The Continuing Role of the Sacred Arrows, the Sun Dance, and the Sacred Buffalo Hat in Northern Cheyenne History,* exemplifies the revolution. Father Powell feels that Plains Indian concepts and ceremonies "can be viewed as prefiguring the Church's life and faith" and that they are "preparations for God's revelation of Himself in human flesh as Jesus Christ." Powell could therefore approach the Cheyennes, whom he regards as the "most completely centered . . . upon the sacred ceremonies" of all the Plains tribes, "able to say to them that I believed their sacred ways to have come from God himself." "I continue to believe, with the Cheyennes," Powell writes, "in the supernatural power that flows from their sacred bundles and sacred ceremonies."[27]

Powell vigorously rejects the castigation of Cheyenne ceremonies as barbarous. He defends the self-torture in which they indulged as an expression of their love of the master of the universe and their desire to make the highest possible sacrifice to the sacred powers. Even the offering of her body to the instructor by the Sacred Woman in the Sun Dance Powell sees as a living prayer for the continuing chastity of all Cheyenne womanhood. Although disturbing some Cheyennes by his close approach to the sacred and supposedly hidden beliefs of the tribe, Powell's work has in fact elevated and dignified Cheyenne religion both in white and Indian eyes.[28]

The continuing strength of religion among contemporary Indians is suggested by the centrality of the religious theme in the work of the leading contemporary Indian writer, Vine Deloria, Jr. In his *God Is Red* (New York, 1973) Deloria analyzes the conflict and congruence of Christianity and native American religions. Though trained in a theological school, and descended from a distinguished Sioux family of scholars, clergymen, and warriors, Deloria rejects institutional Christianity as a corruption of the true spirit of Christ.

27. Peter J. Powell, *Sweet Medicine: The Continuing Role of the Sacred Arrows, the Sun Dance, and the Sacred Buffalo Hat in Northern Cheyenne History,* 2 vols. (Norman, Okla., 1969) , xxiii–xxvi.

28. *Ibid.,* xxx.

Instead, he suggests that Indian religions, with their sense of place as opposed to time, and their belief in a sympathetic involvement in nature rather than a hostile adversary relationship to it, will attract white as well as Indian adherents. Indian religious practices will have to make accommodations to the scientific truths of the twentieth century, Deloria argues, but the Indian view of nature and the supernatural remain valid. Indian religious leaders, like Deloria, have long been uncomfortable about the institutional face of Christianity while sympathetic to the story of Christ. Charles Alexander Eastman (Chiyesa), an acculturated and highly educated Sioux, on the basis of thirty-five years' experience as a Christian, concluded, in 1911, in his book, *The Soul of the Indian: An Interpretation,* that "Christianity and modern civilization are opposed and irreconcilable, and that the spirit of Christianity and of our ancient religion is essentially the same."[29]

A growing sensitivity to Indian cultural needs, including religious needs, has marked the federal government's policy toward the Indians in recent decades. This attitude has given a fillip to Indian political life and caused hope to replace despair and anger to succeed resignation. The turning point in the government's position occurred with the passage of the Indian Claims Commission Act of 1946 which authorized tribal suits against the United States for past misdeeds and faults of the government. Hundreds of cases have been heard and are scheduled to be heard before the Indian Claims Commission and occasionally, on appeal, before the Court of Claims and the Supreme Court. The new government attitude to Indian claims for justice is perhaps most startlingly revealed in the handling of the claim of the Taos Indians of New Mexico to Taos Blue Lake and the area surrounding it. This remote lake and its watershed have always been regarded as a religious site by the Indians. Only with difficulty did the Indians retain access to the area. Though recognized by the Indian Claims Commission in its decision of September 8, 1965 (15 Ind. Cl. Comm. 666) to have had aboriginal Indian title to the lake and its watershed, a title which the Commission further ruled had been wrongfully taken away from the Taos on November 7, 1906, when the lands were incorporated into the newly established Taos Na-

29. Charles Alexander Eastman, *The Soul of the Indian: An Interpretation* (Boston, 1911) , p. 24.

tional Forest (later part of the Carson National Forest), the Indians had in the interval been harassed and exhausted by increasingly peremptory and unsympathetic Forest Service administrators. The sacred land of the Taos was opened to incursions by tourists, lumbering firms, "sportsmen," and others whose use was antithetical to the Indians' secret and reverent worship of the unspoiled natural spirit of the place.[30]

Blue Lake, to the Taos Indians, is the source of all life both literally and figuratively. Feeding the river which provides the water which sustains the Taos people, it is also the retreat of souls after death. It is at once the actual and symbolic guarantee of the continuity of the people. The attempts of the Forest Service in the years when it managed the land to restrain Indian use of the area and to facilitate non-Indian access were particularly jarring to the Indians. As Paul Bernal, secretary of the Tribal Council of the Taos Pueblo Indians, put it in testimony on May 16, 1969, before the Subcommittee on Indian Affairs of the House Interior and Insular Affairs Committee:

In all of its programs the Forest Service proclaims the supremacy of man over nature; we find this viewpoint contrary to the realities of the natural world and to the nature of conservation. Our tradition and our religion require our people to adapt their lives and activities to our natural surroundings so that men and nature mutually support the life common to both. The idea that man must subdue nature and bend its processes to his purposes is repugnant to our people.[31]

The attempt of the Taos tribe to get title to the land and to free itself from the arbitrarily administered special use permits led to the submission of bills in the 90th and 91st Congresses to give the area back to the Indians. The bills were strongly supported by the Department of the Interior but opposed by the Department of Agriculture, which warned against the precedent of giving back the *land* to the Indian rather than a monetary payment.[32] The idea of a money settlement was repellent to the Taos, and in their presentation to the Indian Claims Commission and elsewhere they

30. Memorandum of William C. Schaab, special attorney for the Taos Pueblo, May 4, 1968, printed in *Hearings before the Subcommittee on Indian Affairs of the Committee on Interior and Insular Affairs, 91st Cong., 1st Sess. on H. R. 471 . . . May 15 and 16, 1969* (Washington, 1969), pp. 13, 15.

31. *Ibid.*, pp. 67–68.

32. Letter of Russell E. Train, Under Secretary of the Interior, May 13, 1969, in *ibid.*, pp. 2–6.

always insisted that they wanted the land rather than a monetary substitute. The struggle of the Indians ended happily. As one of the first acts of President Richard Nixon's Indian policy the sacred land of the Taos Pueblo was given back to its original owners.

The return of Taos Blue Lake reflected the new look in Indian affairs in the late 1960s and early 1970s. The policy of "termination"—that is, the forced dissolution of tribal organizations and the break-up of existing tribal assets—which had been put into effect in the 1950s with the termination of the Menominee tribe of Wisconsin, the Klamath tribe of Oregon, and others—was reversed. Both the Congress, which had instituted the policy in the first place, and the executive belatedly recognized the unfortunate consequences of the policy. In a 1970 policy paper, President Nixon declared the Indian policy of the executive branch to be "self-determination without termination." Under the new policy, tribal governments have been given a greater role in administering federal programs relating to their tribes.[33]

In the economic sphere, Indian tribal governments have assumed an increasingly active role in the development of tribal resources. The coal deposits of the Navajo tribe on Black Mesa, for example, are being mined by the Peabody Coal Company. The contract between the company and the tribe (and similar contracts between other extractive industries and western tribes) have been bitterly opposed by factions within the tribes and have led to divisive quarrels among tribal members. Millions of dollars and the character of economic development of the tribes (and often its political leadership) are at stake.

Often industries are drawn to locate plants on or near reservations by the promise of cheap labor, raw materials, underwriting by tribal funds, tax benefits, and the like. Occasionally such ventures prove unprofitable and the industries move out, leaving disruption in their wake. Nevertheless, there has been a slow but steady increase in economic opportunities for reservation residents, and "development," which can be synonymous with exploitation of Indian resources, has become increasingly responsive to Indian needs. While the income of Indians living on reservations is still

33. July 8, 1970. See also Wilcomb E. Washburn, *Red Man's Land/White Man's Law: A Study of the Past and Present Status of the American Indian* (New York, 1971) , pp. 243–244.

about a quarter that of whites, the income of off-reservation Indians has risen to nearly half the white level and now approximates the level of black income. Despite the numbers of Indian families still below the poverty level, the census of 1970 strikingly illustrates the rapidly improving economic condition of the American Indian.[34]

In the eyes of some observers the move to "development" of tribal resources is equivalent to the thrust to "civilization" characteristic of the nineteenth century and, in the eyes of the legal scholar Monroe Price, is equally "chimerical, . . . remote, romantic, and false a goal. . . ." Underlying the development campaign, in Price's view, is the Protestant ethic that fueled the allotment effort. In both, individual hard work by the Indians in a laboring system is visualized as the only valid way of life. Utilization of the increasingly valuable land resources of the Indians to provide a steady or growing income to the Indians without the necessity for work is rarely contemplated.[35]

As the economic stakes of the tribes have risen there have been frequent challenges to existing political leaders. Not the least of these challenges has been by legal aid groups responsible neither to the tribe nor to the Bureau of Indian Affairs. Title II of the Economic Opportunity Act of 1964 authorized the establishment of community action agencies to coordinate programs designed to improve the well-being of individuals within those communities. The term "community" was defined to include Indian reservations. Under the terms of the act legal services programs were set up on reservations: The Navajo DNA program (named after Navajo words meaning "Attorneys who contribute to the economic revitalization of the people") was established in 1967, the first legal services program on an Indian reservation.

The DNA lawyers and others like them on other reservations dealt primarily with cases involving credit arrangements made by Indians with off-reservation automobile dealers, administrative problems concerning welfare rights, and the like. Nevertheless, the

34. U.S. Bureau of the Census, *Census of Population: 1970, Subject Reports, Final Report PC (2)-1F, American Indians* (Washington, 1973), Table 9 (Family Income).

35. Monroe E. Price, "Lawyers on the Reservation: Some Implications for the Legal Profession," *Arizona State Law Journal*, 1969, *Law and the Social Order*, 161–203, at 183n, reprinted in Monroe E. Price, *Law and the American Indian: Readings, Notes and Cases* (Indianapolis, 1973), pp. 610–627.

very size and efficiency of the program upset traditional processes of tribal government. While programs such as that on the Papago reservation were organized to minimize their impact on the tribal authority, that on the Navajo reservation led to a confrontation with the tribal leadership. Although the conflict has been related by some to the personalities of the two leaders—Chairman Raymond Nakai of the Navajo Tribal Council and DNA chief Theodore Mitchell, a white man—it was in essence a struggle between two rival power structures. DNA in 1970 operated in each of the five geographical subdivisions of the Navajo reservation and employed ninety persons, including seventeen attorneys and twenty-eight lay advocates. With a large budget and a record of accomplishment in aiding individual Navajo clients, DNA threatened to eclipse the tribal government. Attempts to bring its operations under council control were successfully resisted. The conflict was symbolized by a classic case, *Dodge* v. *Nakai* (298 F. Supp. 26, D. Ariz., 1969). In this case the authority of Tribal Chairman Nakai to exclude Mitchell from the Navajo reservation was denied by the district court on the grounds that the causes of expulsion did not meet the test of due process required by the Civil Rights Act of 1968. The Civil Rights Act of 1968, with its so-called Indian Bill of Rights, guaranteed to any individual complainant against tribal authority most of the privileges in the Bill of Rights (which until that time could not be enforced against tribal governments). As a result of the decision in *Dodge* v. *Nakai* the Navajo tribe, which by its treaty of 1868 with the United States had been authorized to exclude from the reservation anyone it wished other than properly constituted representatives of the United States, lost this power except when the exclusion did not violate the right of free speech, due process of law, the prohibition against bills of attainder, and other rights guaranteed to all persons—Indian or others—against the actions of tribal governments.

Although Chairman Nakai was defeated for reelection in 1970 by Peter McDonald, who supported, as a candidate, the independent functioning of DNA; and though Theodore Mitchell resigned in the same year, the role of such a powerful independent force on the reservation continued to be disturbing to both the tribal government and the Bureau of Indian Affairs. Although DNA and legal services organizations on Indian reservations generally have expressed their intention of upholding tribal integrity, their activities are more often directed to the defense of individual rights in the context of a non-Indian judicial tradition. Put another way, OEO lawyers do not see their role as upholding tribal customs and procedures as interpreted by existing tribal leaders, councils, and courts. They have a larger vision of individual rights which neither tribal chairmen, off-reservation whites, or the federal government can violate. While their attitude is infused with goodwill and altruism, it is strangely reminiscent of the liberalism that motivated the advocates of severalty legislation of the nineteenth century. Then, tribal practices were to be reformed to make them conform to the dominating concepts of private property, individual initiative, and Anglo-Saxon jurisprudence. Only the concepts have changed. The target is still—consciously or unconsciously—the corporate tribal structure. "Should not the tribal courts be forced to meet white standards of judicial behavior?" ask the reformers. If so, a system which, however artificially revived by a recent generation of white men, reflects many native values and traditions will have to be reformed from top to bottom. Many tribal courts hand down justice without the presence of legally trained advocates or judges. Tribal rulings—as they did in the past—place greater emphasis on compensation, shame, and banishment than on retribution. The native legal tradition has, in the past, been eroded by white refusal to accept Indian values, as demonstrated most clearly by the passage of the Major Crimes Act of March 3, 1885 (23 Stat. 385) by which the law of white society was substituted for Indian law in the case of major criminal acts. A similar erosion of informal or customary legal procedures is liable to take place under the rule of individual rights guaranteed to the Indian under the Civil Rights Act of 1968 and by other statutes and rulings.[36]

Although Monroe Price has asserted that the confrontation between DNA and the Navajo tribe "should be seen as involving not a withering of the strength of the tribe, but a strengthening of the normal political process within the reservation," and though Price sees the possibility that the DNA program can be "a reinforcer of the tribal structure," his hopes rest more on a dedication to individual Indian rights rather than respect for the Navajo tribal structure as it is presently constituted. Significantly, when the OEO

36. Washburn, *Red Man's Land,* pp. 191–193.

approached eight Pueblo tribes to ask if they would like a legal
services program, the Pueblos, after careful consideration, accepted
with the limitation that the OEO-funded lawyers agree not to bring
any action against the tribal organizations.[37]

The implications of the Civil Rights Act of 1968 for tribal
autonomy have caused the growing band of Indian legal scholars
some concern. Vine Deloria, Jr., has called for court cases to challenge the act in the interest of tribal autonomy and has urged
Indian legal scholars to develop "a new legal ideology"—the concept of "Indian common law"—which can be applied in tribal
courts in place of English common law. The burden of developing a
body of Indian common law and of challenging or utilizing the
Indian Civil Rights Act of 1968 rests with the new generation of
Indian legal scholars; the outcome of their efforts is still uncertain.[38]

American Indians have passed through one trial after another—
disease, war, famine, removal, despoliation, and despair—and they
have survived. Since the early twentieth century there has been no
way to go but up. Perhaps the slow movement back to self-respect
and self-sufficiency should be dated from 1917, when for the first
time the Commissioner of Indian Affairs reported that more Indians were being born than were dying. From that time, all statis-
tics, shocking as many have been, have shown gradual improvement
in the education, health, and economic well-being of the Indian. In
the 1930s Indian culture—as exemplified in arts and crafts—and
Indian self-government—as exemplified in tribal structures—were
for the first time encouraged rather than discouraged. During
World War II many Indians left the reservation for the armed
forces; many others migrated to factories engaged in war production. Income rose and the Indian became more intimately involved
with the larger white society and economy.

After fighting off the threat of termination in the immediate
postwar period, Indians began the long hard ascent to the position

37. Price, *op. cit.*, at 179. See also Robert C. Swan, "Indian Legal Services Pro-
grams: The Key to Red Power?" *Arizona Law Review*, XII (1970), 594–626.
See also "The Indian Bill of Rights and the Constitutional Status of Tribal
Governments," *Harvard Law Review*, LXXXII (1969), 1343.

38. Vine Deloria, Jr., "Implications of the 1968 Civil Rights Act in Tribal
Autonomy," *Indian Voices: The First Convocation of American Indian Scholars*
(San Francisco, 1970), pp. 85–104, at pp. 90, 101–102.

they occupy in the 1970s: a position of rapidly improving economic well-being, enormously enhanced access to educational opportunities, strengthened legal protections of inherited tribal and individual rights. These gains have stimulated, as well as been encouraged by, the development of a pan-Indian consciousness and a more activist mentality on the part of Indian leaders. Demands for protection of Indian water rights, preservation of the Indian land base, and expansion of tribal autonomy, have increasingly been heard. Organizations such as the National Congress of American Indians, established in the 1940s, have been increasingly eclipsed by more activist organizations, such as the American Indian Movement founded in the 1960s.

Yet the answer to the question posed at the beginning of this chapter—can the structure inherited from the 1930s survive the assaults of the radicals of the 1970s?—is still in doubt. But it seems likely that the AIM vision of an Indian future will not be translated into reality. First of all, AIM does not represent a majority viewpoint among Indians. Second, the earlier traditions evoked by AIM (including those of nonelected hereditary or traditional leaders) are no longer sufficiently viable to overcome the later tradition of democratically elected tribal leaders authorized under the Indian Reorganization Act. Finally, the dominant white majority, upon whose goodwill any major change in Indian policy is ultimately dependent, does not stand behind the radical outlook presented by AIM.

The rapidity with which cultural traditions change often surprises ideologues and idealists. John Collier discovered this when he attempted to persuade Indians to return their allotted lands to a communal land pool controlled by the tribe. In a similar way it is doubtful that tribal members, authorized to elect their tribal chairmen by majority vote, will readily accept hereditary or traditional chiefs designated by a process which obtains consent less by positive agreement than by the absence of overt opposition. Both systems are historically valid expressions of conditions that existed at different times. The conditions for a return to hereditary or traditional chiefs seem incapable of realization at the present moment except in a few places.

AIM leaders at Wounded Knee proved unable to relate their demands to the context of American political realities, thereby letting slip an opportunity to promote Indian advancement. In their assault on elected tribal leaders like Richard Wilson of the Oglala Sioux, and by their demand that such leaders be summarily removed and the elective system abolished, AIM leaders threatened one of the major props of Indian autonomy and self-government. AIM's vision of an Indian past that could be re-created *de novo* reminds one of the vision of the Ghost Dancers of the 1890s who looked for the miraculous disappearance of the white man and a resurrection of the Indian dead. Even AIM's cavalier assumption that its members could not be hurt by the white man, no matter how violently they acted in destroying the symbols of his authority, smacks of the belief of the Ghost Dance followers among the Sioux in the 1890s that their Ghost Dance shirts were invulnerable to the white man's bullets. Fortunately the outcome of the 1973 Ghost Dance "uprising" was not a repetition of the 1890 massacre at Wounded Knee. Nevertheless, bitterness and divisiveness have been its consequences.

The American nation and the American spirit can encompass and absorb such extreme manifestations of dissent and alienation as exemplified by AIM partly because of the continuing work of less spectacular organizations. National Indian legal aid organizations, increasingly Indian led, have quietly gone about entering lawsuits against federal and local governments in behalf of Indian land and water rights. In the Pyramid Lake, Nevada, water use case argued in 1972 and 1973, the federal government, and the states of Nevada and California, were forced to alter their past practices and future plans in regard to the use of the waters of Pyramid Lake. Beneficiaries were the Paiute Indians living on the reservation bordering on the lake, whose livelihood had been threatened by the constantly decreasing level of the lake.

Despite the turmoil caused by the activist Indian leadership, including the trashing of the Bureau of Indian Affairs in Washington, the United States government has continued to seek to obtain maximum Indian input into plans for the reform of Indian administration. If the larger American public continues to view Indian aspirations sympathetically and not as a threat to its own rights, it is conceivable that the Indian will be able to retain his special status within the American nation and convert its former deficiencies into future advantages. No other group within the borders of the United States is able legitimately to lay claim to a permanently secure tax-exempt land base, to autonomous tribal governments tied to the larger body politic by mutually negotiated agreements which continue to be respected and enforced by the now dominant partner, and to a way of life the preservation of which is now supported, as well as encouraged, by the non-Indian majority. On the other hand, the Indian of today, though he can now once again claim his tribal heritage, is free also to abandon it and to live as an individual within the larger society of whites and Indians outside the protected reservations. The new multiracial society of the United States is more than ever open to individual Indians who may wish to find their way in that society even while retaining as much as they can, or as they desire, of traditional customs or values. The Indian provides a unique element in the American nation: at once a part and not a part of American society. Yet that society is enriched by the Indian presence. From the conflicts, crises, and tragedy of the past relationship of white man and red has arisen a new union in which both the first Americans and the later arrivals can coexist, neither seeking the destruction or absorption of the other.

Bibliographical Essay

Bibliographies

Two recent studies of writings in American Indian history are Wilcomb E. Washburn, "The Writing of American Indian History: A Status Report," *Pacific Historical Review*, XL (1971), 261–281; and William T. Hagan, *The Indian in American History*, American Historical Association, Pamphlet No. 240 (Washington, D.C., 1971). A revision of the *Pacific Historical Review* article, along with other articles in the Indian history issue in which it appeared, is reprinted in Wilcomb E. Washburn *et al.*, *The American Indian* (Santa Barbara, Calif., 1974). An earlier bibliography presently in the process of revision, but still useful, is *American Indian and White Relations to 1830: Needs and Opportunities for Study*, an Essay by William N. Fenton and a Bibliography by L. H. Butterfield, Wilcomb E. Washburn, and William N. Fenton (Chapel Hill, N.C., 1957). George Peter Murdock, *Ethnographic Bibliography of North America*, 3d ed. (New Haven, Conn., 1960) is an indispensable guide to the anthropological literature.

Reference Works

A valuable reference work, *The Indian Tribes of North America* by John R. Swanton, Smithsonian Institution, Bureau of America Ethnology, Bulletin 145 (Washington, D.C., 1952, reprinted 1969), gives a brief account of the location, connections with other tribes, history and population of the tribal groups of North America. Tribes are discussed under the heading of the present states of the union. The *Handbook of*

American Indians North of Mexico, edited by Frederick Webb Hodge, Smithsonian Institution, Bureau of American Ethnology, Bulletin 30, 2 vols. (Washington, D.C., 1907–1910), provides an alphabetized guide to Indian-related matters. It is currently in the process of revision, under the general editorship of William C. Sturtevant of the Smithsonian Institution, in approximately twenty volumes with an expected publication date of 1976.

Alfred L. Kroeber's *Cultural and Natural Areas of Native North America* (Berkeley, Calif., 1939, rev. ed., 1947) and John Wesley Powell's *Indian Linguistic Families of America North of Mexico,* Smithsonian Institution, Bureau of American Ethnology, 7th Annual Report, 1885–1886 (Washington, D.C., 1891), underlie all subsequent divisions of the American Indian into linguistic and cultural areas. C. F. Voegelin and F. M. Voegelin, *Map of North American Indian Languages,* American Ethnological Society, Publication 20 (rev. ed., Menasha, Wis., 1966), provides a linguistic breakdown. Harold E. Driver and William C. Massey, "Comparative Studies of North American Indians," American Philosophical Society, *Transactions,* new ser., XLVII, pt. 2 (1957), 172–174, and Harold E. Driver, and others, *Indian Tribes of North America,* International Journal of American Linguistics, Mem. 9 (Baltimore, Md., 1953), provide cultural and tribal area divisions. Tribal, cultural, and linguistic divisions are brought up to date by Willam C. Sturtevant and incorporated in the maps published in U.S. Department of the Interior, Geological Survey, *The National Atlas of the United States of America* (Washington, D.C., 1970), pp. 129–132.

Journals

The *American Anthropologist,* the official journal of the American Anthropological Association, carries important articles on the American Indian though its coverage is world wide. Similarly, *Current Anthropology,* A World Journal of the Sciences of Man, published by the University of Chicago Press, carries on a vigorous exchange between its authors and commentators throughout the world whose responses to the articles enliven the journal. *Ethnohistory,* the journal of the American Society for Ethnohistory, begun in the 1950s as a journal devoted to ethnohistorical research on the American Indian, has now extended its coverage throughout the world. Its principal focus is still on the American Indian, however. Numerous specialized periodicals provide coverage for specific geographical areas of the country and for specialties such as archaeology and linguistics.

Two Indian-run journals of interest include *The American Indian Magazine*, published by the short-lived Society of American Indians from 1914–1923, and the currently flourishing *The Indian Historian*, published by the American Indian Historical Society. Both journals have contributed to the creation and presentation of an Indian point of view on the subject of Indian-white relations.

General Works (by Anthropologists)

Perhaps the most comprehensive and well balanced account of the various North American Indian cultures is Harold E. Driver, *Indians of North America*, 2d. ed., rev. (Chicago, 1970). The Driver work has superseded older works such as Clark Wissler's *Indians of the United States*, first published in 1940, and recently reprinted in a revised edition prepared by Lucy Wales Kluckhohn. Ruth M. Underhill's *Red Man's America: A History of Indians in the United States*, rev. ed. (Chicago, 1971) tends to be more in the Wissler tradition, with heavy emphasis on material culture, than in the Driver tradition. Driver's revised edition includes several historical chapters in keeping with the trend in anthropology to a more careful consideration of the historical dimension of American Indian cultures. Edward H. Spicer's *A Short History of the Indians of the United States* (New York, 1969) is an example of this new emphasis on the historical approach. Wendell H. Oswalt's *This Land Was Theirs: A Study of the North American Indian* (New York, 1966) is also able to deal in depth with the historical record by isolating particular tribes in each of the major culture areas and carrying their story through the contact period.

Many anthropological approaches to Indian history are collaborative in nature. Outstanding among this genre is *North American Indians in Historical Perspective*, edited by Eleanor Burke Leacock and Nancy Oestreich Lurie (New York, 1971), which includes contributions on major culture areas, or major peoples of particular culture areas, by leading anthropologists. *The Native Americans* by Robert F. Spencer, Jesse D. Jennings, and a number of other specialists (New York, 1965) is an excellent college textbook with strong emphasis on the prehistory of the Americas.

The best guide to the prehistory of North America is Gordon R. Willey, *An Introduction to American Archaeology*, Vol. 1: *North and Middle America* (Englewood Cliffs, N.J., 1966).

The predecessor to the present volume in the original American Nation series was by an anthropologist, Livingston Farrand, and entitled *Basis of American History, 1500–1900* (New York, 1904). The volume is completely out of date.

General Works (by Historians)

Historians who have attempted to chronicle the history of North American Indians include Alvin M. Josephy, Jr., whose *The Indian Heritage of America* (New York, 1968) is perhaps the most comprehensive of all. Angie Debo's *A History of the Indians of the United States* (Norman, Okla., 1970) is a hurriedly compiled summary which retains the strong emphasis Debo has always accorded to the Oklahoma Indians about whom she has written numerous books.

Briefer treatments include William T. Hagan, *American Indians* (Chicago, 1961), and D'Arcy McNickle, *They Came Here First: The Epic of the American Indian* (Philadelphia, 1949). More popular treatments include William Brandon, author of the narrative for *The American Heritage Book of Indians* (New York, 1961), by the editors of *American Heritage,* under the general editorship of Alvin M. Josephy, Jr.; and Peter Farb, *Man's Rise to Civilization as Shown by the Indians of North America from Primeval Times to the Coming of the Industrial State* (New York, 1968). Brandon has more recently published a massive, 553-page history entitled *The Last Americans: The Indian in American Culture* (New York, 1974).

Tribal Ethnographies and Histories

The literature concerning individual tribes is vast. Guides to that literature are available in the general accounts alluded to earlier. Both anthropologists and historians have contributed to the literature on the subject. Among the anthropologists most sensitive to, and conversant with, historical materials is Anthony F. C. Wallace, whose *Death and Rebirth of the Seneca* (New York, 1970) is a brilliant blending of history, anthropology, and psychiatry. Wallace is a leading exponent of the personality and culture school of American anthropology, as is evident in his *King of the Delawares: Teedyuscung, 1700–1763* (Philadelphia, 1949) and in his *The Modal Personality Structure of the Tuscarora Indians, as Revealed by the Rorschach Tests,* Bureau of American Ethnology, Bulletin 150 (Washington, D.C., 1952).

The vast extent of research on the Iroquois, to which Wallace has made signal contributions, is apparent in Paul L. Weinman, *A Bibliography of the Iroquoian Literature Partially Annotated,* Bulletin 411, New York State Museum and Science Service (Albany, 1969). Fundamental is the work of the pioneer American ethnologist, Lewis Henry Morgan, whose *League of the Ho-De-No-Sau-Nee or Iroquois* was published in New York in 1851. William N. Fenton, the leading Iroquoianist of today, has edited Morgan's classic work (New York, 1962), as well as the Iroquois studies of the Seneca ethnologist Arthur C. Parker, under the title *Parker on the Iroquois* (Syracuse, N.Y., 1968). Among Fenton's numerous studies are two symposia: *Symposium on Local Diversity in Iroquois Culture,* edited by Fenton, Smithsonian Institution, Bureau of American Ethnology, Bulletin 149 (Washington, D.C., 1951), and *Symposium on Cherokee and Iroquois Culture,* edited by Fenton and John Gulick, Smithsonian Institution Bureau of American Ethnology, Bulletin 180 (Washington, D.C., 1961).

Two important historical studies dealing with the Indians of New York are Allen W. Trelease, *Indian Affairs in Colonial New York: The Seventeenth Century* (Ithaca, N.Y., 1960), and Barbara Graymont, *The Iroquois in the American Revolution* (Syracuse, N.Y., 1972). Georgiana C. Nammack, *Fraud, Politics, and the Dispossession of the Indians: The Iroquois Land Frontier in the Colonial Period* (Norman, Okla., 1969), documents one aspect of Indian-white relations in the area.

An anthropologist who is equally at home with history or ethnology is John C. Ewers, whose *The Blackfeet: Raiders on the Northwestern Plains* (Norman, Okla., 1958) reflects his lifelong study, in the field and in the library, of the Plains Indians. Ewers has also contributed a series of brief but significant studies of painters of the American Indian. Among these studies are Ewers's "George Catlin, Painter of Indians and the West" from the Smithsonian Institution, *Annual Report for 1955,* pp. 483–528 (Washington, D.C., 1956), and his "Early White Influence upon Plains Indian Painting: George Catlin and Carl Bodmer among the Mandan, 1832–34," Smithsonian Institution, *Miscellaneous Collections,* Volume 134, Number 7 (Washington, D.C., 1957). All students of the character and appearance of the Plains Indians are dependent upon George Catlin's *Letters and Notes on the Manners, Customs, and Condition of the North American Indians,* 2 vols. (New York, 1841), as they are upon Thomas L. McKenney and James Hall, *History of the Indian Tribes of North America,* 3 vols. (Philadelphia, 1836–1844).

A leading authority on the Indians of Northeastern Canada is anthropologist Bruce G. Trigger, who has produced a series of sophisticated studies—both books and articles—which are thoroughly informed by knowledge of the historical record and by an understanding of traditional anthropological methods. Among these works is *The Huron: Farmers of the North* (New York, 1969).

An anthropologist specializing in the Southwestern area of the United States who has successfully incorporated historical data into his analysis is Edward H. Spicer. Spicer demonstrates this ability in his *Cycles of Conquest: The Impact of Spain, Mexico, and the United States on the Indians of the Southwest, 1533–1960* (Tucson, 1962, reprinted 1970).

Tribal histories by historians are numerous. A leading practitioner in the field is Arrell M. Gibson, whose books include the comprehensive studies *The Chickasaws* (Norman, Okla., 1971) and *The Kickapoos: Lords of the Middle Border* (Norman, Okla., 1963). William T. Hagan published a study of *The Sac and Fox Indians* (Norman, Okla., 1958). Two important historical studies of the Sioux are James C. Olson, *Red Cloud and the Sioux Problem* (Lincoln, Neb., 1965), and Roy W. Meyer, *History of the Santee Sioux: United States Indian Policy on Trial* (Lincoln, Neb., 1967). Alvin M. Josephy, Jr., has provided massive documentation in his *The Nez Perce Indians and the Opening of the Northwest* (New Haven, Conn., 1965). Grant Foreman and Angie Debo have produced a number of studies relating to the Five Civilized Tribes of Oklahoma, all published by the University of Oklahoma Press. Many tribal studies have been included in the separate volumes of *The Civilization of the American Indian Series* published by the University of Oklahoma Press.

Important works dealing with the Indians of the Southeast in the colonial period include John R. Alden, *John Stuart and the Southern Colonial Frontier, A Study of Indian Relations, War, Trade, and Land Problems in the Southern Wilderness* (Ann Arbor, Mich., 1944); Robert L. Meriwether, *The Expansion of South Carolina, 1729–1765* (Kingsport, Tenn., 1940); and John R. Swanton, *The Indians of the Southeastern United States,* Smithsonian Institution, Bureau of American Ethnology, Bulletin 137 (Washington, 1946). Basic both as a source and as an interpretation is James Adair's *History of the American Indians; particularly Those Nations adjoining to the Mississippi, East and West Florida, Georgia, South and North Carolina, and Virginia* (London, 1775, reprinted by Johnson Reprint Corporation, New York, 1968). Another important source is *Indians of the Southern Colonial Frontier: The Edmond Atkin Report and Plan of 1755,* ed. Wilbur R. Jacobs (Columbia, S.C., 1954). Similarly, William Gerard De Brahm's *Report of the General Survey in the Southern District of North America,* ed. Louis De Vorsey, Jr. (Columbia, S.C., 1971) provides important background on the Indians of the area. David H. Corkran has produced two detailed studies, *The Creek Frontier, 1540–1783* (Norman, Okla., 1967) and *The Cherokee Frontier: Conflict and Survival, 1740–62* (Norman, Okla., 1962). James H. O'Donnell, III, carries the story further along with his *Southern Indians in the American Revolution* (Knoxville, Tenn., 1973). Arthur H. DeRosier, Jr., in *The Removal of the Choctaw Indians* (Knoxville, Tenn., 1970), has contributed a valuable study of the removal of one of the Five Civilized Tribes.

The relations between Indians and whites in New England have always caused controversy, from the time of the first historians of the seventeenth century to the present day. Observers of the New England scene have usually been tinged with moral conviction, either in defense of the Puritans or of the Indians. Alden T. V,aughan's *New England Frontier: Puritans and Indians, 1620–1675* (Boston, 1965) upholds Puritan justice against its detractors. Vaughan's views have been vigorously challenged by Francis Jennings in articles such as his "Virgin Land and Savage People," *American Quarterly,* XXIII (1971), 519–541, and in a forthcoming book. The story of King Philip's War continues to fascinate historians of seventeenth-century New England. Although Douglas Edward Leach published a comprehensive study in his *Flintlock and Tomahawk: New England in King Philip's War* (New York, 1958), the causes of the war—and particularly whether it was a pre-planned conspiracy of the Indians or not—are still in doubt. The evidence on this subject, as on other aspects of Plymouth's history, has recently been considered by George D. Langdon, Jr., in *Pilgrim Colony: A History of New Plymouth, 1620–1691* (New Haven, 1966).

From the time of Franz Boas, anthropologists have been fascinated by the Northwest Coast Indians and have produced a vast amount of literature on the natives of the region. Historians have been somewhat slower in the field. Perhaps the most successful historical entry in the field in recent years has been Warren L. Cook, whose *Flood Tide of Empire: Spain and the Pacific Northwest, 1543–1819* (New Haven, 1973) is at once comprehensive and sophisticated in its handling of the tangled web of relationships between white man and red in the area.

Two authoritative students of California Indian history are Robert F. Heizer and Sherburne F. Cook. Both singly and in conjunction they have produced a kaleidoscopic array of publications on all aspects of California Indian life. Cook's special studies on California's Indian population and some of Heizer's work on the archaeology, ethnology, and history of the area are listed in the bibliography of *The California Indians: A Source Book,* comp. and ed. R. F. Heizer and M. A. Whipple, 2d ed. (Berkeley, 1971).

The massive journal literature on the American Indian must be pursued in the traditional historical and anthropological periodicals. Occasionally the journal literature is collected in book form. Wilbur R. Jacobs's *Dispossessing the American Indian: Indians and Whites on the Colonial Frontier* (New York, 1972) contains many penetrating essays on the relationship between Indian and white, particularly in the eighteenth century. Jacobs is also the author of an important study, *Wilderness Politics and Indian Gifts: The Northern Colonial Frontier, 1748–1763* (Lincoln, Neb., 1966).

Specialized Anthropological Works

The historian of the American Indian is increasingly dependent upon anthropological studies of specialized aspects of Indian life for a full understanding of Indian history. Phenomena such as the Ghost Dance religion, the peyote cult, and the Sun Dance religion have traditionally been the concern of anthropologists but their studies help the historian understand the springs of Indian action in his dealings with the white man. James Mooney, the Smithsonian ethnologist, was able to study the Ghost Dance religion in the field to produce his *The Ghost-Dance Religion and the Sioux Outbreak of 1890,* abridged, with intro. by Anthony F. C. Wallace (Chicago, 1965). Similarly, David F. Aberle and Weston La Barre were able to study the peyote cult in the field, but also relied on library research. Aberle, with field assistance by Harvey C. Moore, published *The Peyote Religion among the Navaho* (New York, 1966), and La Barre published *The Peyote Cult,* enlarged edition, with new preface by the author (New York, 1969). Increasingly, anthropologists have delved deeper into the historical record even while continuing to avail themselves of intensive field work and interviews with native informants who may be available. A provocative study of the Sun Dance religion, showing how it was shaped by the pressures induced by reservation life, Joseph G. Jorgensen's *The Sun Dance Religion: Power for the Powerless* (Chicago, 1972) illustrates the trend.

Governmental Policy

The governmental aspects of Indian-white relations have been dealt with by a number of authors. For an overall survey see Wilcomb E. Washburn, *Red Man's Land/White Man's Law: A Study of the Past and Present Status of the American Indian* (New York, 1971). For more detailed treatment of specific periods, see Jack M. Sosin, *Whitehall and the Wilderness: The Middle West in British Colonial Policy, 1760–1775* (Lincoln, Neb., 1961); Walter H. Mohr, *Federal Indian Relations, 1774–1778* (Philadelphia, 1933); Reginald Horsman, *Expansion and American Indian Policy, 1783–1812* (East Lansing, Mich., 1967); George Dewey Harmon, *Sixty Years of Indian Affairs: Political, Economic, and Diplomatic, 1789–1850* (Chapel Hill, N.C., 1941); Francis Paul Prucha, *American Indian Policy in the Formative Years: The Indian Trade and Intercourse Acts, 1790–1834* (Cambridge, Mass., 1962); and Alban W. Hoopes, *Indian Affairs and Their Administration: With Special Reference to the Far West, 1849–1860* (Philadelphia, Pa., 1932).

Government policy in the post-Civil War period is currently under close study by a number of students, including Paul Prucha and Henry E. Fritz. Fritz dealt with the period in his first book, *The Movement for Indian Assimilation, 1860–1890* (Philadelphia, 1963). An earlier study, still useful though some of its conclusions have been challenged or modified, is Loring Benson Priest, *Uncle Sam's Stepchildren: The Reformation of United States Indian Policy, 1865–1887* (New Brunswick, N.J., 1942). Another earlier work, based on a detailed consideration of the primary sources, is

Jay P. Kinney, *A Continent Lost—A Civilization Won: Indian Land Tenure in America* (Baltimore, Md., 1937). Basic to an understanding of the period are the publications of the Indian Rights Association of Philadelphia. Founded in 1882, the association continues its work of lobbying on Indian policy in ways it judges effective. Its annual reports, special publications, and newsletter contain significant amounts of original material.

Basic also to an understanding of the period are the annual reports of the Board of Indian Commissioners, a civilian body set up by an act of April 10, 1869, to give independent advice on Indian policy to the executive branch.

The *Annual Reports of the Commissioner of Indian Affairs* provide a gold mine of material, particularly in the last half of the nineteenth century and the early years of the twentieth, when they included vast appendices of original material submitted from the field. The commissioners of the period also held strong views on their responsibilities and often expressed those views vigorously and at length. Later in the twentieth century the reports of the commissioner were subordinated more and more to those of his superior, the Secretary of the Interior, and the reports from agents in the field were omitted. Former commissioners occasionally published separate volumes; one was George Manypenny, whose *Our Indian Wards* (Cincinnati, 1880) provides an insight into reservation policy.

The functioning of the Bureau of Indian Affairs was dealt with comprehensively by Laurence F. Schmeckebier, *The Office of Indian Affairs: Its History, Activities and Organization* (Baltimore, Md., 1927). Schmeckebier's study was closely followed by another one commissioned by the Secretary of the Interior and published by the Brookings Institution under the authorship of the chairman of the study commission, Lewis Meriam, with the title *The Problem of Indian Administration* (Baltimore, Md., 1928).

The specialized literature bearing on the Indian and the law is assembled in Monroe E. Price, *Law and the American Indian: Readings, Notes and Cases* (Indianapolis, 1973). *The American Indian and the United States: A Documentary History*, 4 vols., ed. Wilcomb E. Washburn (New York, 1973), brings together acts and treaties, court decisions, congressional debates, and reports of Commissioners of Indian Affairs in order to document the evolution of the relationship between the United States government and the American Indian.

Literary Works

Creative writers have frequently attempted to assess the impact of the red man on the soul as well as on the mind and body of the white man. Many of America's greatest writers—for example, James Fenimore Cooper,

Ernest Hemingway, and William Faulkner—have woven the Indian into the work they have produced. Excerpts from some this literature are incorporated in *The Indian and the White Man,* ed. Wilcomb E. Washburn (New York, 1964).

The impact of the Indian in American intellectual life has exercised many literary scholars. Henry Nash Smith gave impetus to the study of the Indian as he affected the American mind in his *Virgin Land: The American West as Symbol and Myth* (Cambridge, Mass., 1950). Three years later Roy Harvey Pearce published his *The Savages of America: A Study of the Indian and the Idea of Civilization* (Baltimore, 1953), which more fully considered the Indian along with the land as the object of the so-called civilizational process.

Leslie A. Fiedler's *The Return of the Vanishing American* (New York, 1968) echoes the earlier fascination of D. H. Lawrence at the ability of the Indian to haunt the consciousness of the white American and to become part of him in spirit. More recently Bernard Sheehan, in "Indian-White Relations in Early America: A Review Essay," and "Paradise and the Noble Savage in Jeffersonian Thought," *William and Mary Quarterly,* XXVI (1969), 267–286, 327–359, has attempted to demythologize and deromanticize the Indian and to correct what he regards as the erroneous views of those who presently see the Indian through tinted and tainted glasses. In his *Seeds of Extinction: Jeffersonian Philanthropy and the American Indian* (Chapel Hill, N.C., 1973), he has analyzed the thought of the "Jeffersonian generation" from the same perspective.

Perhaps the most brilliant study of the literature dealing with the American Indian is Richard Slotkin's *Regeneration through Violence: The Mythology of the American Frontier, 1600–1860* (Middletown, Conn., 1973). Comprehensive in scope, subtle in approach, it is intellectual and literary history at its best. Although dealing with the Indian as only one aspect of the frontier context in which European life developed in America, it provides an indispensable basis for the historian anxious to understand the motivations and assumptions of the white man in the period covered.

Contemporary Indian

The upsurge in concern and interest in the contemporary Indian that developed in the late 1960s and early 1970s resulted in a number of studies of his political rights and legal status. *The Indian: America's Unfinished Business, Report of the Commission on the Rights, Liberties, and Responsibilities of the American Indian,* compiled by William A. Brophy and Sophie D. Aberle (Norman, Okla., 1966), is the most comprehensive and unbiased. *Our Brother's Keeper: The Indian in White America,* ed. Edgar S. Cahn (Washington, D.C., 1969) reflects the confusion and special pleading of its authors, a mixed group of white liberals and Indian activists. Harold Cardinal's *The Unjust Society: The Tragedy of Canada's Indians* (Edmonton, Alberta, 1969) is a powerful statement concerning Indians north of the border by an eloquent Canadian Indian. Anthony D. Fisher, in reviewing the Cahn and Cardinal books in the *American Anthropologist*, noted that the two books "indicate that during the past one hundred or so years, anthropologists may have neglected to study the most important variable in historic North American Indian life: the federal government and its local manifestation, the I.A.B. (Indian Affairs Branch, Department of Indian Affairs and Northern Development) or the B.I.A. (Bureau of Indian Affairs, Department of the Interior) ."

A special issue of The Annals of the American Academy of Political and Social Science, Volume 311, entitled *American Indians and American Life,* edited by George E. Simpson and J. Milton Yinger (Philadelphia, 1957) , contains much useful information, as does the special issue on "The Indian Today," published in the *Midcontinent American Studies Journal,* VI (1965) , No. 2.

The role of pan-Indian organizations in the twentieth century has been effectively described in Hazel W. Hertzberg, *The Search for an American Indian Identity: Modern Pan-Indian Movements* (Syracuse, N.Y., 1971) . A sober, quantitative study of the economic and social status of the contemporary Indian is Alan L. Sorkin, *American Indians and Federal Aid,* published by the Brookings Institution (Washington, D.C., 1973) . More recent statistical information is now available in U.S. Bureau of the Census, *Census of Population: 1970, Subject Reports, Final Report PC (2) –1F, American Indians* (Washington, D.C., 1973) .

The Indian point of view has been presented with increasing effectiveness by Indians and by friends of Indians. Stan Steiner's *The New Indians* (New York, 1968) attempted to give voice to the feelings of the increasingly militant "Red Power" movement of the 1960s. Vine Deloria, Jr.'s *Custer Died for Your Sins: An Indian Manifesto* (New York, 1969) was a witty and explosive assault on white attitudes and assumptions about the Indian, which did not spare anthropologists. Deloria, a Standing Rock Sioux, has continued to pummel the establishment with unerring aim and unmerciful power. His *We Talk, You Listen: New Tribes, New Turf* (New York, 1970) expressed his conviction that both Indian and white man should look to the tribal concept in order to find a way out of America's problems. Among Deloria's edited works are *Of Utmost Good Faith* (San Francisco, 1971) , which details "The Case of the American Indian Against the Federal Government of the United States—as documented in treaties, speeches, judicial rulings, congressional bills and hearings from 1830 to the present." Deloria's recent *God Is Red* (New York, 1973) is an expression of his deepest philosophical beliefs. Although couched in his satirical and playful prose, the book perceptively compares Indian spiritual values (particularly those related to place) with white spiritual values (particularly those related to time) and urges greater white movement toward the Indian world view.

Indian histories written by Indians are beginning to appear, in part in response to the support given by governmental and private institutions to the creation of oral history programs among the tribes. One of the first fruits of this effort is *The Zuñis: Self-Portrayals, by the Zuñi People*, trans. Alvina Quam (Albuquerque, 1972). Another example is *To Be an Indian: An Oral History*, eds. Joseph H. Cash and Herbert T. Hoover (New York, 1971), based on interviews conducted by the American Indian Research Project at the University of South Dakota. A third example is Allen P. Slickpoo, Sr., Project Director, and Deward E. Walker, Jr., Technical Advisor, *Noon Nee-Me-Poo (We, the Nez Perces): Culture and History Of The Nez Perces*, Volume I (Lapwai, Idaho, 1973). The publication of such books raises the question of the nature of history and the historian's responsibility to received myths versus his commitment to critical scholarship. From the standpoint of critical scholarship, the tribal works based on oral history presently available must be seen as contributions to history—part of the raw material of history—rather than history itself. Nevertheless, it is not inconceivable that critical history and traditional Indian history can be integrated in the future in the minds of Indian historians—as well as of white historians—to produce a new synthesis.

Index

Reservations, 125, 172, 180, 182, 190,
191, 196, 205, 209–232, 233, 234,
236, 240, 241, 242, 252, 285
Returned Students League (Navajo),
256
Revenge, as principle of Indian justice,
17–20, 136, 138
Robinson, Governor Charles, 199
Robinson, John, 111
Rolfe, John, 113
Rollins, John, 178, 179
Roosevelt, Franklin D., 253, 254
Ross, John, Cherokee chief, 198–200
Rutherford, General Griffith, 152
Roosevelt, Theodore, 242
Royer, D. F., 222

St. Clair, General Arthur, 160, 162
Sand Creek Massacre (1864), 204, 206
Sayenqueraghta, Seneca chief, 149
Schurz, Secretary Carl, 244
Scott, General Winfield, 179
Sergeant, John, 56
Severalty, land in, 239, 242, 271.
See also Allotment and the Indian
Sevier, Lt. Col. John, 154
Sewall, Judge Samuel, 212
Seward, William H., 198
Sex, 22–23, 55, 59–60, 63, 67, 108
Shamans, 52, 54
Sherman, General William T., 205, 208
Sibley, Colonel Henry H., 203
Sioux outbreak of 1890, 221–222
Sitting Bull, Sioux chief, 222
Smith, Captain John, 80, 127
Smithsonian Institution, 245
Society of American Indians, 251, 252
Southeastern United States, 18, 41, 86–
89, 90, 103, 105
Southwestern United States, 5–7, 25–26,
27, 55, 67, 117–119
Spain and the American Revolution,
150–157
Spanish influence on Indian, 7, 41,
43–44, 67, 76, 90–91, 113, 116–119,
143
Stanton, Edward M., 216
Stansbury, Captain Howard, 106
Steinmetz, Father Paul Bernhard, 264
Stevens, Governor Isaac I., 125, 194,
195, 236
Stuart, Secretary Alexander H. H., 192

Stuart, Charles, 107, 150
Stuart, Henry, 151
Stuart, John, 150, 151, 153, 155
Stuyvesant, Governor Peter, 134
Sullivan, General John, 150
Sumner, Colonel Edward V., 184
Sun Dance religion, 220, 226–227, 265,
284

Tabeau, Antoine, 78
Taos Revolt of 1847, 182
Taitt, David, 150
Taylor, Zachary, 178, 191
Tecumseh, Shawnee chief, 163, 164
Teedyuscung, Delaware warrior, 114–
115
Teller, Henry M., 241, 245
"Termination" policy, 268, 272
Texas, 27–28, 116–117, 173–180
Timberlake, Lt. Henry, 71, 98
Totopotomoi, Pamunkey chief, 211
Tracy, Marquis de, 137
Treaty relationship, 97–103, 200, 203,
205, 234–240, 254, 275
Treaties (in chronological order): with
Virginia Indians (1646), 211; with
Southeastern Indians at Augusta
(1763), 213; of Fort Stanwix
(1768), 147–148, 156, 213; of Fort
Stanwix (1784), 100, 158; of Fort
Harmar (1789), 159; of New York,
with Creeks (1791), 161; of
Greeneville (1795), 49–50; of
Edwardsville (1819), 101; of Fort
Harrison with Kickapoos (1819),
101; of Butte des Morts (1827), 92;
with Texas Indians (1837), 173;
of Council Springs (1846), 174–
176; of Guadalupe Hidalgo (1848),
178, 184; with Navajo (1849), 182;
of San Saba (1850), 179; of Fort
Laramie (1851), 192–194; with
Omahas (1854), 235; with Blackfeet (1855), 195; of Hell Gate with
Flatheads (1855), 236; of Fort
Wise, Kansas (1861), 102; with the
Five Civilized Tribes (1861–62),
198–199; with the loyal Creeks
(1863), 200–201; with the Seminoles (1866), 201; with the
Choctaws and Chickasaws (1866),
201